"I have personally worked with Mike and the Strengths appr
years in Microsoft. The belief in people's strengths, and bu
talents to create exceptional business results I personally find inspiring, and has never failed but help me create an environment and teams that have all excelled at delivering incredible outcomes and success, both for the business and for them as individuals. What I love most about working with Mike and building on peoples strengths is the pure positivity and impact it has, and how infectious it is in organisations. I might think that it is for the benefit of my team, but whenever I look back at the results we achieved I can always see the ripple effect that this has on other parts of the business and on the teams that we work closely with, and this creates a wonderfully positive halo on the team, but on the culture too."

Philippa Snare, Chief Marketing Officer, Microsoft Ltd

"My passion is building businesses that are customer focused and deliver success. As a practitioner, I am sometimes wary of management models that look good on paper but do not translate into action. The strengths and super teams approach that we have used with Mike, however, has proved deeply practical. People have taken the ideas on board and developed as both people and professionals. They have used the practical tools in their daily work and have delivered great results."

Alex Miller, CEO at Jam and Partner at Engine

"During the past 15 years I have worked with Mike in several pioneering companies. The strengths and super teams approaches provided practical toolkits that worked. People implemented the ideas successfully to achieve and maintain peak performance."

Jim Brigden, Chief Client and Commercial Officer for iProspect UK

"I have worked with Mike to employ the super teams approach in every business I've run over the last 20 years. And it's worked every time. In fast-paced, entrepreneurial businesses Mike's approach has helped build teams that share a common vision of the company's goals, and a clear appreciation of the contribution every single person will make. Just as importantly, it has equipped employees with an understanding of their individual strengths and value, enabling them to shape their future careers and go on to build successful businesses of their own. I cannot recommend Mike, and his practical, positive approach, highly enough."

Nick Hynes, CEO and Founder, Somo.
Member of the Digital Hall of Fame, 2012

For a complete list of Management Books 2000 titles

visit our web-site on http://www.mb2000.com

The Art of Strengths Coaching

The Complete Guide

Mike Pegg

First published in 2012 by Management Books 2000 Ltd
36 Western Road
Oxford OX1 4LG
United Kingdom
Tel: 0044 (0) 1865 600738
Email: information@mb2000.com
Web: www.mb2000.com

British Library Cataloguing in Publication Data is available

ISBN 9781852526962

Contents

Part 1

The Philosophy and Principles

Part 2

The Practice

Introduction

There are many approaches to encouraging people. This book focuses on the art of strengths coaching. It invites you to take the tools you like and use them to encourage people in your own way.

The strengths approach can be used with individuals, teams and organisations. It always starts by clarifying people's picture of success. This may, of course, mean different things to different people.

Some people may simply aim to be happy. Some may aim to do satisfying work that pays a salary. Some may aim to achieve peak performance. Some may aim to encourage other people.

Some may aim to build a super team that pursues a clear story, strategy and road to success. Some may aim to build a pioneering business that becomes a pacesetter in its chosen field. Some may aim to build a superb organisation that continues to develop its profits, products and people.

Some may aim to regain a sense of control, overcome setbacks and refocus on their life goals. Some may aim to find creative solutions to challenges. Some may aim to leave a positive legacy.

The strengths approach starts by clarifying people's goals. It then provides positive models and practical tools that individuals, teams and organisations can use:

To build on their strengths.

To set specific goals.

To achieve their picture of success.

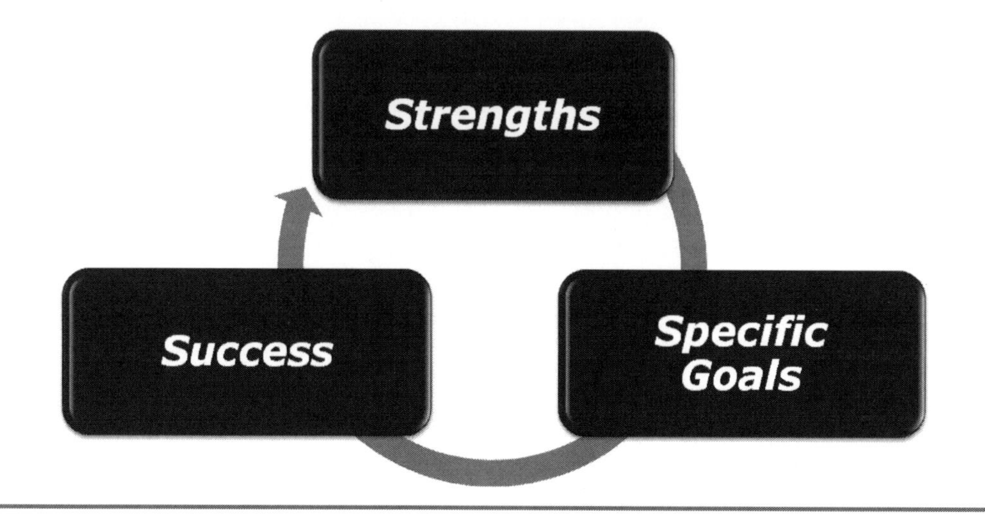

The approach is based on what works. It aims to study what works, simplify what works – hopefully in a profound way – and share what works. One aspect of the approach, for example, is to encourage people, teams and organisations:

To clarify when they have performed brilliantly.

To clarify the principles they followed to perform brilliantly.

To clarify how they can follow these principles – plus add other elements – to perform brilliantly in the future.

People buy success; they don't buy the theory of success. So it is vital to move from the 'concept to the concrete'. People need more than theory. They want practical tools they can use in their daily lives and work.

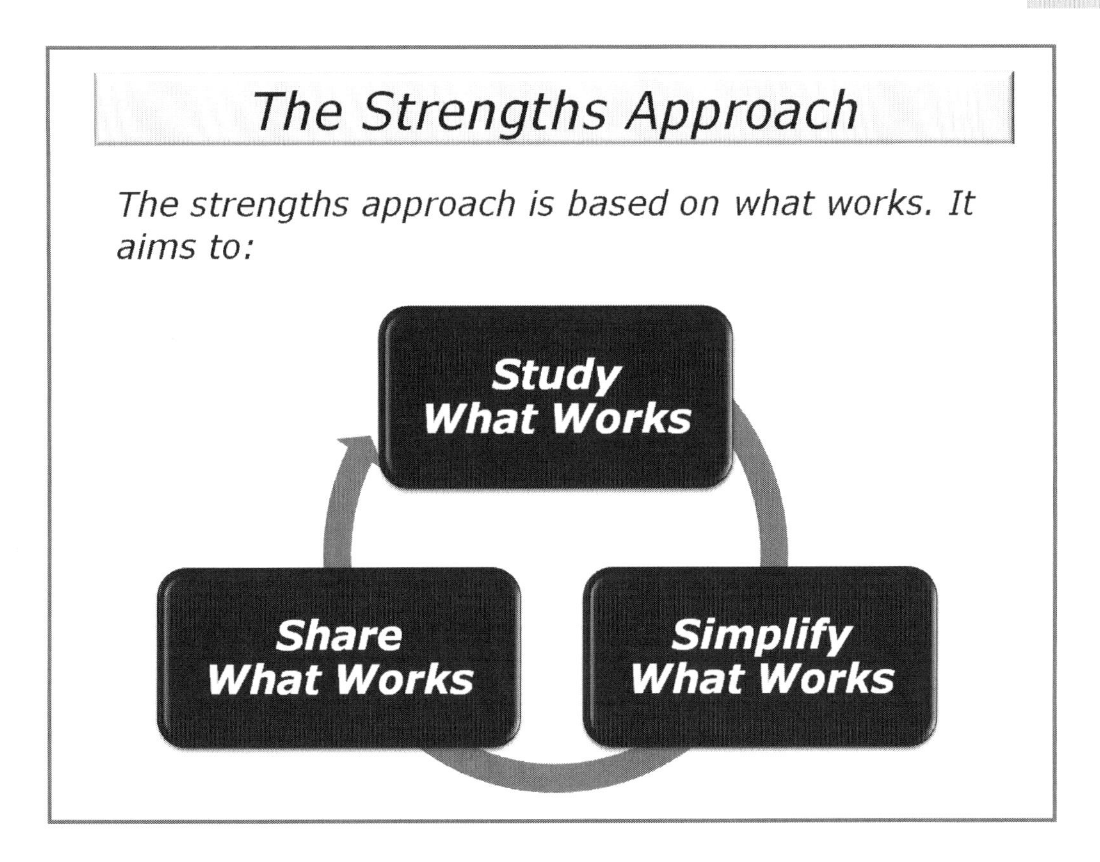

Peak performers are often 'positive realists'. They have a positive attitude, but they also quickly read reality and see patterns. They clarify their strategy, perform superb work and find solutions to challenges. They then do whatever is necessary to achieve their goals.

The strengths way adopts a similar approach. It is positive but realistic. It is based on the following principles.

People can build on their strengths and manage the consequences of their weaknesses

During the past 40 years I have worked with people in many sectors. This has convinced me that people have remarkable strengths. People can learn how to build on these strengths and manage the consequences of their weaknesses.

There are many approaches to discovering what somebody does best. A person can, for example, focus on the deeply satisfying activities in which they do some of the following things.

They deliver As, rather than Bs or Cs. They are in their element – at ease yet able to excel. They have a natural feeling for an activity. They flow, focus and finish. They follow their passion, translate it into a clear purpose and deliver peak performance.

They have the equivalent of a photographic memory. They see the destination quickly. They go 'A, B ______ then leap to ______ Z'. They have a track record of delivering 'Z'.

They see patterns quickly. They have 'personal radar'. They seem to know what will happen before it happens. This seems to give them more time and space than other people. They also have the right repertoire to deal with what happens and deliver the right results.

They have natural self-discipline. They know how to cut through crowdedness – many things happening – and get to the heart of the matter. They know how to manage the grunt work and also deliver the great work.

They make complicated things simple. They are calm during crises. They solve problems by continually focusing on clarity, creativity and concrete results. They are committed to constant improvement.

They follow their successful style of working. They follow their vocation, express it through various vehicles and do valuable work. They focus on what for them will be a stimulating project with stimulating people in a stimulating place. They know their perfect customers and how they can help those customers to succeed.

They always do the basics and then add the brilliance. They score highly on drive, detail and delivery. They may also know how – when appropriate – to be entrepreneurial, build an engine that works and deliver excellence. They have a track record of finishing. They perform superb work, deliver the goods and then add that touch of class.

People can use their strengths to help others to succeed

People can choose how to use their talents. We each make choices every day. Each choice has consequences, of course, with both pluses and minuses.

People can start by choosing their attitude. They can choose to be positive or negative; to be creative or criticise; to count their blessings or count their burdens. They can choose to take responsibility or avoid responsibility.

People can use their strengths to serve themselves or also to serve others. They can do satisfying work that nourishes their soul. If they want to do such work that also earns a salary, however, they may need to be savvy.

How to make a living doing what they love? One approach is to learn from great service givers throughout history. Such people often focus on their:

> ***Strengths:*** *they build on their strengths.*
>
> ***Sponsors:*** *they find sponsors – customers or employers – who will hire them for what they do best.*
>
> ***Success:*** *they help those sponsors to achieve success.*

People can follow these paths in their own way. They can, if they wish, embody the qualities shown by people in what Erik Erikson called The Generative Age. They can pass on their knowledge to help future generations. They can encourage and enable people to achieve ongoing success.

People can employ their strengths as individuals. They can also employ them to make their best contribution to a superb team or organisation.

People can use their strengths to build super teams – and superb organisations – that achieve their picture of success

Many organisations have used the super teams approach to reach their goals. Providing people are serious about implementing it properly, the model works.

Super teams are special. They often start by building on their strengths and clarifying their picture of success. They then translate this into a clear story, strategy and road to success. People know which mountain they are climbing, how they will climb it and when they will reach the summit.

Such teams are based on similarity of spirit and diversity of strengths. They are made up of people who aim to be positive, professional and peak performers. They choose to opt in and make clear contracts about their best contribution towards achieving the goals.

People co-ordinate their strengths to perform superb work and give great service to customers. People encourage each other, overcome setbacks and find creative solutions to challenges. Super teams do whatever is required to achieve the picture of success.

The strengths approach has been used to build superb teams and organisations. Later we will be exploring how you can help people to take these steps in their own ways.

Super Teams

Super teams are special. They often start by building on their strengths and clarifying their picture of success. They then translate this into a clear story, strategy and road to success.

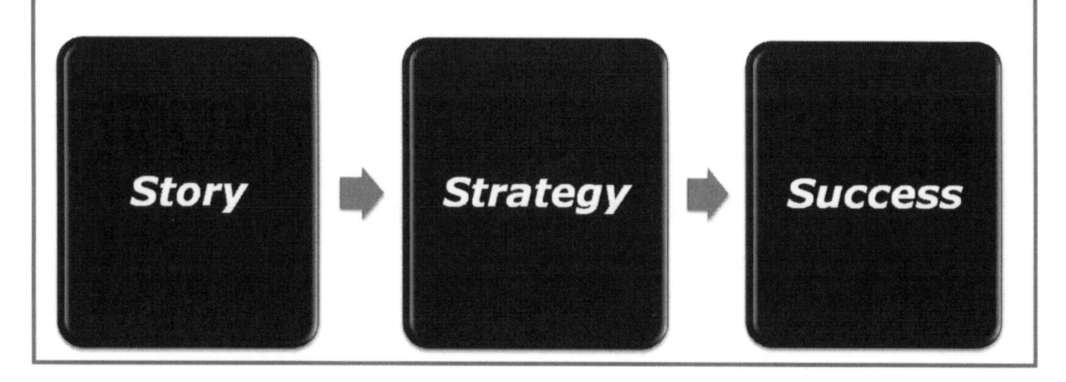

The Book – An Overview

This book aims to provide a compendium of tools you can use to help people, teams and organisations to achieve their goals. Here is an overview of the various sections.

The Art of Strengths Coaching – The Philosophy and Principles

This section provides an introduction to the strengths philosophy. We have already covered some aspects. But we will take a deeper look at the strengths tradition and the principles it follows.

The Art of Strengths Coaching – The Practice

This section goes into depth about how the principles can be translated into practice. We will be focusing on two aspects of making this happen.

The Art of Helping People To Build On Their Strengths

This section provides practical tools that can be used to help people to build on their strengths, set specific goals and achieve ongoing success.

The Art of Helping People To Build Super Teams

This section provides practical tools that can be used to help people to build super teams – and superb organisations – that achieve their picture of success.

This book outlines the philosophy, principles and practice of strengths coaching. There is a lot of material, however, so it is designed so that you can dip in and out as you wish. You can then use the ideas in your own way.

Let's move on to looking at people who have contributed to the strength sapproach over the years.

Part 1

The Philosophy and Principles

Introduction – The Strengths Tradition

Focusing on strengths has become increasingly popular over the past decade, but the tradition goes back many years.

The following pages provide an introduction to some of the philosophers and practitioners who have contributed to the approach. Please skip this section if you prefer to go straight to the practice of coaching.

The strengths philosophy stretches back to educators such as Heinrich Pestalozzi and Friedrich Froebel. So let's begin with these pioneers.

Heinrich Pestalozzi

Johann Heinrich Pestalozzi was a Swiss educator and social reformer who had a profound influence on education.

Living between 1746 and 1827, he created several educational communities and also wrote best-selling books, such as *How Gertrude Teaches Her Children.* His ideas spread across the world, influencing people such as Friedrich Froebel, the inventor of the Kindergarten.

Philosophy

Heinrich – as he was known – believed the purpose of education was to help people to fulfil their potential and reach what he called their 'moral state'. They would then be more able to help others and give their best to the world.

He believed that every child had inner powers – certain unique strengths. Like many great educators, he felt the first step was to engage a person's heart. He felt this was relatively simple, however, providing you followed the child's interests – what they wanted to reach out and learn. The key was to follow their aspirations and help them to master certain skills. He wrote in *Swansong:*

> *"Man is also **driven** by the nature of each of these powers within himself, to use them.*
>
> *"The eye **wants** to see, the ear **wants** to hear, the foot **wants** to walk and the hand **wants** to seize. But in the same way, the heart **wants** to believe and love. The mind **wants** to think.*
>
> *"In every gift of human nature lies an urge to rise from the state of inactivity and lack of dexterity to that of a trained force which, if left untrained, lies within us like a seed of strength and not as strength itself."*

The educator must be a person who embodied love, because children learn from their models. They could then help the child to learn through:

> *The heart – to explore what they want to learn and also develop their moral qualities, such as helping other people.*
>
> *The head – to intellectually understand objects, concepts and experiences.*
>
> *The hand – to learn the craft of doing good work and also develop their physical skills.*

Contribution to the strengths approach

Pestalozzi's ideas can be seen in many elements of the strengths approach. For example:

He encouraged people to develop their inner powers – their unique strengths.

He enabled people to learn through all their senses and develop their hearts, heads and hands. He encouraged people to develop their skills and moral qualities by actually translating these into action.

He encouraged people to develop towards the 'moral state' – a state where they also helped others to fulfil their potential.

Friedrich Froebel

Friedrich Froebel was an educational pioneer who lived from 1782 to 1852. He gave birth to the kindergarten – 'the children's garden'. He believed children needed a place where they could be cherished and helped to flourish. He said:

> *"Children are like tiny flowers; they are varied and need care, but each is beautiful alone and glorious when seen in the community of peers."*

Philosophy

"Man is a creative being," proclaimed Froebel. He believed that each person was many sided. He used the analogy of a crystal. Shining a light on one side may or may not highlight their brilliance. A loving environment was crucial, but children also wanted to learn. How could they be encouraged in this process?

Froebel created what we would now call 'educational materials'. He called these 'Gifts'. They encouraged the child to play, be creative and explore designs that mirrored the unity of the universe.

He believed that each child had their own rhythm. They would learn when they were ready to learn. The educator's role was to provide the stimulation to help them develop.

Play can be a starting point for creativity, but progress does not always come easily. Doing what you love can involve overcoming tough challenges. Froebel wrote:

> *"A child who plays and works thoroughly, with perseverance until physical fatigue forbids will surely be a thorough, determined person, capable of self-sacrifice."*

Contribution to the strengths approach

Froebel's work made an enormous contribution to the strengths philosophy. For example:

He saw each child as a creative being. His approach encouraged thousands of parents and teachers to focus on each child's passions and strengths.

He showed how to create a 'garden for children'. This helped many parents and teachers to provide stimulating sanctuaries where children could pursue their interests.

He carried the torch for nurturing and educating the human soul – rather than stuffing facts into children. His views encouraged parents and teachers to side with their children's potential.

Maria Montessori

Maria was an Italian educational pioneer who lived between 1870 and 1952. Her work has helped many people to find and build on their strengths. This often involves students pursuing the learning process of absorption, adventure and achievement. Explaining her philosophy, Maria wrote:

> *"There is a part of a child's soul that has always been unknown but which must be known. With a spirit of sacrifice and enthusiasm we must go in search, like those who travel to foreign lands and tear up mountains in their search for hidden gold."*

What actually happens in a Montessori environment? Imagine you are visiting a class for the youngest children. You will probably see over 30 children, ranging from two and a half to six years old.

The room has a prepared environment in which children can follow their natural tendency to work.

It will embody the characteristics of beauty, simplicity, order, accessibility and reality. Children will have many enticing materials that are designed to help them explore their world and develop their skills.

The children will be 'working'.

Some will be totally concentrated on their activity; some will be co-operating with others; some will be tidying up after their last activity and moving onto the next. Some may be preparing food. Some may be engaged in other activities.

The children will be given freedom to work, learn and develop.

They will move around within suitable guidelines that enable them to act as part of a social group. They can pursue their own interests – though they must also respect others.

The educator will be watching the children.

They will see when they become enraptured and, when appropriate, encourage and guide them to further exploration on this theme.

The children will continue to develop their skills.

They will repeat an activity until it satisfies an 'inner goal'. They will then move onto the next activity they want to explore.

Philosophy

There was a time – during the early part of the 20th Century – when it seemed Maria's approach would be adopted throughout education. Her ideas made a profound impact, but some fell victim to other philosophies and mass schooling.

During the past half century, however, there has been an appreciation of the Montessori approach and what it can do for children. Certainly there have been critics, but the overwhelming reaction has been positive.

(One contributing factor to the criticism has been that there is no protection of the name. Anybody can set-up a school and call it 'Montessori'.)

Maria became one of the first women in Italy to qualify as a doctor.

Interested in the physical and mental development of children, she began working with children in hospital. This led to meeting children in asylums. The Association Montessori Internationale explains:

> *"She started to e-ducate them: to lead them out of their isolation and deprivation of any stimulus. Maria really became an educator through force of circumstance and her dedication to truly invest in these 'idiot' children.*
>
> *"The children in the asylums started to develop positively beyond anybody's imagination. So Montessori started wondering how well 'normal' children might benefit from the sensory didactic materials. She was part of a group of socially committed young people that had connections. Through these she came into contact with Signor Talamo, who was responsible for the San Lorenzo social housing project.*
>
> *"He asked her to do something with the children of the San Lorenzo tenants. As their parents were away during the day to earn money, they were left to their own devices. The positive results of her work in San Lorenzo became well-known, with the news spreading across Italy, Europe, the US, Australia and India."*

Maria's work won her the right to set up her own schools that eventually spread across the world. She would later express some of her educational philosophy in the following quotations:

> *"Our aim is not only to make the child understand, and still less to force him to memorize, but so to touch his imagination as to enthuse him to his innermost core."*
>
> *"We must not dwell on his limitations but focus on his possibilities."*
>
> *"The teacher's task is not to talk, but to prepare and arrange a series of motives for cultural activity in a special environment made for the child."*

"The essential thing is for the task to arouse such an interest that it engages the child's whole personality."

"The first essential for the child's development is concentration. The child who concentrates is immensely happy."

"The first dawning of real discipline comes through work. Every action of the teacher can become a call and an invitation to the children."

"The more the capacity to concentrate is developed, the more often the profound tranquillity in work is achieved, then the clearer will be the manifestation of discipline within the child."

"Childhood passes from conquest to conquest in a rhythm that constitutes its joy and happiness."

Contribution to the strengths approach

Maria's work embodied many elements of the strengths approach. For example:

She created a pioneering approach that helped literally millions of students to build on their strengths.

They could pursue their interests, take responsibility for their learning and work until they reached their goal. They could flow, focus, finish and, as a by-product, find fulfilment.

She created attractive environments that encouraged students to use many senses when developing their skills.

This enabled them to pursue their preferred learning styles that improved their chances of success.

She encouraged each student to clarify their own philosophy and contribution to the world.

Maria invited them to begin thinking this way by providing a guiding compass – what she called *The Great Lessons* – that gave an overall framework. They could refer back to this compass to see how each new educational theme fitted into the big picture. Each student was later encouraged to develop their own life philosophy. They could then draw strength from this inner compass and choose how to make their best contribution to the world.

Maria invited us to focus on the potential of children and humanity. She wrote:

> *"We do not want children who simply obey and are there without interest, but we want to help them in their mental and emotional growth.*
>
> *"Therefore, we should not try to give small ideas, but great ones, so that they not only receive them but ask for more."*
>
> *"In serving the child, one serves life ... Within the child lies the fate of the future."*

John Dewey

John Dewey was an American writer and educational philosopher who lived from 1859 to 1952.

He believed that education should be relevant and rewarding, rather than only theoretical. It should also equip students to take a full and active part in shaping their future society. They may even be able to find their real vocation. He wrote:

> *"To find out what one is fitted to do, and to secure an opportunity to do it, is the key to happiness."*

Philosophy

America was shifting towards a different kind of economy and, John maintained, traditional schooling would not produce active, creative citizens.

'Traditional education', John believed, saw children as empty, passive receptacles to be filled with ideas. This helped to support the existing order. 'Progressive education', for which he – rightly or wrongly – became known, saw school as an opportunity for children to develop as individuals and citizens.

John believed education must be linked to the child's experience. Students were much more likely to embrace mathematics, for example, if they could see how it applied to their daily lives. He wrote in *My Pedagogic Creed:*

> *"I believe that the school must represent present life – life as real and vital to the child as that which he carries on in the home, in the neighborhood, or in the playground."*

Dewey was one of the first to promote this approach in America. Here are some – though not all – of the principles that run through his work.

People can learn by participating in relevant learning experiences.

People can develop their problem-solving skills, clarify the learning and apply the lessons in their daily lives.

People can take responsibility, think for themselves and take an active role as citizens.

People can follow their vocation and develop the habit of life-long learning.

A person's vocation is their calling: it is what they are here to do. Dewey railed against the concept of 'vocational training', however, which was being used to serve industry. Students were being prepared for jobs in which they might be trapped for life.

He had a different view of what a vocation entailed and also believed in life-long learning. Dewey wrote in *Democracy and Education:*

> *"The dominant vocation of all human beings at all times is living – intellectual and moral growth.*
>
> *"Put in concrete terms, there is danger that vocational education will be interpreted in theory and practice as trade education: as a means of securing technical efficiency in specialized future pursuits.*
>
> *"It is a conventional and arbitrary view which assumes that discovery of the work to be chosen for adult life is made once and for all at some particular date.*
>
> *"The preparation for vocations (should) be indirect rather than direct; namely, through engaging in those active occupations which are indicated by the needs and interests of the pupil at the time.*
>
> *"Only in this way can there be on the part of the educator and of the one educated a genuine discovery of personal aptitudes so that the proper choice of a specialized pursuit in later life may be indicated.*
>
> *"Moreover, the discovery of capacity and aptitude will be a constant process as long as growth continues."*

Dewey's views sparked controversy. Backed by humanists, his writings spread far and wide. He travelled the world, lecturing in places such as Europe, China and Japan.

His views, however, continue to appeal to those who aim to translate philosophy into practice. For example, people who focus on project work, action learning, workshops, simulation and community based learning.

Contribution to the strengths approach

John's work embodied many elements of the humanistic tradition that has contributed to strengths approach. For example:

> *He believed in enabling people to follow their vocation – their calling – and encouraged the concept of life-long learning.*
>
> *He focused on the student's real-life experiences and believed in making learning relevant and rewarding.*
>
> *He provided the philosophical foundation for 'learning by doing' and experiential education.*

This enabled people with different learning styles – multiple intelligences – to make use of these strengths when developing. People could then take responsibility for their learning, clarify the lessons and apply these in their future lives.

Rabindranath Tagore

Tagore and Gandhi in 1940

Rabindranath Tagore lived between 1861 and 1941. He is best known as a writer and poet, but he was also an educational pioneer. He believed that:

"The highest education is that which does not merely give us information but makes our life in harmony with existence."

Rabi – as he was known – believed we could use our talents to serve others. Writing on this topic, he explained:

I slept and dream that life was joy.

I awoke and saw that life was service.

I acted and behold, service was joy.

Philosophy

Concerned about the over-industrialisation of education, Rabi founded a school at Santiniketan, West Bengal. This was dedicated to encouraging children to develop as whole human beings. He wrote:

"But for us to maintain the self-respect which we owe to ourselves and to our creator, we must make the purpose of education nothing short of the highest purpose of man, the fullest growth and freedom of soul."

Rabindranath believed that:

People learn best when they experience real life, such as being connected to nature.

People often learn on a subconscious level when surrounded by stimulating influences. They learn from interesting people, art, music, dance, creativity, ideas and the humanities.

People gather strength from understanding their own heritage. They also learn from exploring and appreciating the best in other cultures. This helps to increase their humanity.

People learn by creating and doing, rather than being force-fed abstract concepts. By expressing themselves they develop their own aesthetic, intellectual and other qualities.

Tagore believed education could enable people to learn from different cultures and express their talents. They would then be more ready to choose their route in life. He wrote:

"Man's abiding happiness is not in getting anything but in giving himself up to what is greater than himself, to ideas which are larger than his individual self, the idea of his country, of humanity, of God."

Contribution to the strengths approach

Tagore contributed to the humanistic tradition, which has had a strong influence on the strengths approach. For example:

He created a pioneering school that encouraged many people to develop a more holistic approach to education.

He enabled people to learn on a subconscious level in a stimulating environment.

He encouraged people to explore, create and express their talents.

Rabi's work has enabled many people to appreciate life, be more humble and give their best to the world. He said:

"We come nearest to the great when we are great in humility."

Abraham Maslow

Maslow's work is known to virtually everybody who has been on a psychology or management course. He was one of the pioneers of humanistic psychology and inspired people to explore the positive aspects of human potential.

Abe, who lived between 1908 and 1970, is best known is his famous hierarchy of human needs. Perhaps his most pioneering work, however, is encapsulated in the title of one of his books *The Farther Reaches of Human Nature.*

Philosophy

Maslow was fascinated by people he called 'self-actualisers'. He believed that human beings were living systems that strove towards fulfilling their potential.

He felt that humanity's future lay in understanding healthy people. Looking back at history, he studied individuals such as Abraham Lincoln, Jane Addams, Albert Einstein and Albert Schweitzer.

Maslow found that such people were true to themselves. They saw reality clearly and used their creativity to solve problems. They had strong ethics combined with a sense of humility and respect. Paradoxically, they could be ruthless to achieve a desired goal.

Maslow first published his groundbreaking book *Motivation and Personality* in 1954. He then revised and reissued it in 1970. The book described the hierarchy of human needs and also outlined his views on human potential. He wrote:

> *"Musicians must make music, artists must paint, poets must write if they are to be ultimately at peace with themselves.* ***What human beings can be, they must be.*** *They must be true to their own nature. This need we may call self-actualization."*

Writing in another of his books, *Towards A Psychology of Health*, he explained:

> *"There is now emerging over the horizon a new conception of human sickness and of human health, a psychology that I find so thrilling and so full of wonderful possibilities that I yield to the temptation to present it publicly even before it is checked and confirmed, and before it can be called reliable scientific knowledge."*

Maslow's views attracted attention in fields beyond psychology. Advocates of humanistic approaches to education embraced the philosophy, as did some people in business.

Frederick Herzberg's book *The Motivation to Work* was published in 1959. Seen as complementing Maslow's approach, it highlighted the importance of what Herzberg called 'hygiene' and 'motivational' factors. The acknowledged 'companion volume' to Maslow's books on work, however, is considered to be Douglas McGregor's *The Human Side of Enterprise*.

Principles

Maslow's ideas have now become accepted in many fields, so let's explore some of the key principles.

People can grow in the right environment.

The hierarchy of human needs is his best-known concept. Put simply, this says that people have an ascending set of needs.

Individuals have an inbuilt drive to climb this hierarchy. Once they are satisfied on one level, they are then more likely to move onto the next level. These drives start with the physiological needs, then climb onwards towards self-actualisation.

Maslow believed that people are more likely to fulfil their potential if they are able to live, learn and work in an environment that enables them to satisfy their needs.

Maslow's views on creating the right climate for growth have spread to many fields. But there are some reservations. Certainly there are many people who have grown despite – or even because of – tough circumstances. Maslow also questioned his own views: but it now accepted that people are *more likely* to develop in an encouraging environment.

People can explore the further reaches of human nature.

Abe focused on 'self-actualisers' who used their talents to help other people. There are obviously some people who get their 'highs' by hurting others. But he studied people who, in the broadest sense, were committed to 'doing good'.

So how did such people achieve peak experiences? Here are some of the principles they followed.

Self-actualisers demonstrated some of the following characteristics

They followed their values. They were 'real' – being true to themselves rather than 'fake'. They had a strong sense of autonomy and resisted pressure to conform.

They found solutions – treating life's-problems as challenges to be solved. They frequently saw the 'means' – the journey – as being as important as the 'ends'.

They enjoyed solitude and preferred to have deep relationships with a few people. They also had a positive sense of humour, rather than laughing at others misfortunes.

They accepted themselves and, within limits, other people. At the same time, they wanted to improve themselves if they saw the benefits. They had a strong sense of respect towards others. Maslow called this quality 'human kinship'.

They believed in certain values – and were prepared to 'fight' for these – but also appreciated and enjoyed differences in others. They were prepared to draw the line, however, if people did not show respect to others or certain values. They had strong ethics. These were often 'spiritual' in nature, rather than 'religious'.

They had the ability to be creative, imaginative and original. They had a sense of wonder – a 'freshness of appreciation'. This stretched to seeing the extraordinary in ordinary things.

They had more peak experiences than most people. Such experiences sometimes gave them a sense of transcendence.

They worked well with other people to create synergy.

'Synergy' was a term coined by the anthropologist Ruth Benedict. She used it to describe the way that people co-operated in certain tribes that she studied. People worked well together and combined their talents to achieve common goals. This enabled them to develop a peaceful, satisfying and sustainable life-style.

Maslow used the word 'synergy' to describe organisations where:

People worked in an environment where they were able to satisfy their hierarchy of needs. This included doing meaningful work and gaining a sense of achievement.

People aligned their goals with those of the organisation.

People combined their talents to produce synergy, 'produce more than the sum of the parts'. This helped them to achieve their personal and organisational goals.

Maslow believed people could combine their talents in a way that benefited themselves, their colleagues, their organisation and, in some cases, their society. Everybody would win.

Contribution to the strengths approach

Abe seldom – if ever – referred to people's 'strengths'. But he laid the groundwork for the strengths philosophy. For example:

He pioneered the strategy of studying health – rather than sickness – and identified the principles people followed to become psychologically healthy.

He showed that people are more likely to grow if they are provided with an encouraging environment in the family, school, work and society.

He described how people could combine their talents to produce synergy.

Abe Maslow was one of the giants of positive psychology and his ideas made a great contribution to studying human development.

Carl Rogers

Carl Rogers was born in 1902 and died in 1987. His name is known to virtually everybody who has done a counselling course.

Today it is hard to realise how revolutionary his ideas were in the 1930s and

40s. In those days the medical profession treated people with psychiatric difficulties as 'patients'. The doctor saw the patient, made a diagnosis and prescribed a 'treatment'. Few sat down with a troubled person to encourage them to clarify their feelings, set goals and take responsibility for shaping their future. Carl Rogers changed all that.

Philosophy

He became known as the father of modern counselling and gave birth to the 'people-centered' approach in many areas of life. During his career he focused on certain key principles. Carl believed that:

People have an organic drive towards self-actualisation.

People who pursue this drive successfully are more likely to become psychologically healthy. Those who don't may experience 'problems of living'.

People can be helped to grow by participating in an encouraging relationship that enables them to pursue their drive towards actualisation.

Carl outlined what he saw as the core conditions for building a good therapeutic relationship. He saw the helper's role as:

To be 'congruent': to be genuine and honest with the client.

To show 'empathy': to understand and experience the world from the client's point of view.

To have 'unconditional positive regard': to show respect and accept the person as they are, rather than be judgemental.

Despite resistance from some quarters, Rogers' ideas gained wide acceptance and, in 1956, he was elected the first President of the American Academy of Psychotherapists. During the following years he wrote one of his best-known books, *On Becoming A Person.* Published in 1961, it attracted a worldwide audience. He spent the rest of his life sharing the person-centered approach with people across the world.

Contribution to the strengths approach

Carl's approach helped to give birth to many elements of the strengths philosophy.

> *He showed how to create a stimulating sanctuary – an encouraging relationship in which a person felt able to grow. This enabled the person to develop their inner strength and work towards fulfilling their potential.*
>
> *He wrote inspiring books that spread the message about these core conditions for growth. This enabled their clients to feel valued. They were then more likely to develop their inner strength and fulfil their potential.*
>
> *He encouraged people to believe in their individual uniqueness and also help others to fulfil their potential.*

Carl emphasised the importance of creativity, in its widest sense. For him this meant practising elements of 'generativity'. This called for doing one's best to encourage future generations. His work embodied many elements of the strengths philosophy.

Bernard Haldane

Bernard Haldane is recognised as one of the giants of the strengths philosophy. He began using this approach during the 1940s. His legacy lives on through his thought leadership, his protégés and the continuing work with what he termed 'Dependable Strengths'.

The following pages give a brief overview of Bernard's approach, which was enriched and supported by his wife, Jean.

Philosophy

Bernard was born in 1911, grew up in England and trained to be a doctor. He moved to New York in 1946, but found that his medical qualifications did not meet US standards. Choosing to go another route, he became an editor at the *New York Journal of Commerce*. Then came a career shift.

The job market was flooded by veterans returning from war, but organisations did not know how to employ their talents. Veterans were used to 'war jobs', many of which did not exist in the labour market.

Bernard was invited to help such people to find work. Adopting a different approach from other recruiters, he went through the following steps with the veterans.

> *He asked them to recall their best achievements and, in the process, clarified what they enjoyed doing and what they did well.*
>
> *He clarified their individual strengths and transferable skills that would be useful to an organisation.*
>
> *He helped people to market and present their offering in a way that showed the benefits to a potential employer.*

Bernard's 'inside-out' out approach was radical for the time. Most people who assisted job seekers adopted an 'outside-in' approach, trying to fit people into boxes. Richard Knowdell, a highly respected figure in career development and a friend of Haldane, said that:

> *"Bernard believed that he could reveal 'the excellence in each person' by analysing the skills that individuals had used in performing past accomplishments."*

People then needed help in marketing their strengths and conducting interviews. Bernard was highly skilled at helping individuals, but this approach was labour intensive. Richard Knowdell explains how Haldane tackled this challenge.

> *He asked the job seeker to enlist a small group of friends. The individual would relate past accomplishments and the group members would record the skills on a skills analysis checklist.*
>
> *He trained interested people to practise this approach with job seekers.*
>
> *He continued to expand his network of career counsellors. The demand became so great that he set-up Bernard Haldane Associates (BHA) in New York and Washington.*

Bernard published *Career Satisfaction and Success* in 1974. Eight years earlier he had married Jean, who added her skills to enriching the strengths approach.

BHA grew in size, spread across America and he sold the company in the 70s. With it he sold the rights to use the name and the methodology to work with people in the commercial sector. The company bore his name, but he had no connection to it. Bernard and Jean then focused on the 'not-for-profit sector', continuing to do superb work into the 21st Century.

Principles

Bernard developed many of the ideas now common in personal and professional development. Here are some of those principles.

People can explore their strengths by recalling their good experiences.

Peter Drucker called Bernard a "pathfinder in finding human strength and making it productive." Jean Haldane said that Bernard's methods stayed the same throughout his life, even though he refined the methodology.

He would "help people look at their experiences" and find "things you feel you do well, enjoy doing and are proud of." This approach was developed by many of his protégés.

People can clarify their dependable strengths and transferable skills by exploring these good experiences with other people.

The Center for Dependable Strengths is an organisation that applies Bernard's approach. People often work together in groups to help each other discover their strengths. Here is a description the Dependable Strengths Articulation Process that can be found on their web site.

> *DSAP is a peer-assisted, group process first developed by Bernard Haldane in 1945. The heart of the process is story telling. DSAP facilitators are trained to elicit the kind of stories that illustrate a person's Dependable Strengths® – each person's special talent for excellence.*
>
> *Participants in the process reflect on their experiences in life, identify their patterns of strengths, and learn how to talk about their Dependable Strengths in ways that demonstrate their value to an organization or community. We help people plan for successful futures!*

The Dependable Strengths Articulation Process (DSAP)

The following gives an overview of one process for uncovering Dependable Strengths. People are encouraged to explore this with each other in groups.

1) Remember

Think back and identify your Good Experiences. These are events that you did well, you enjoyed doing and feel proud of.

2) Prioritise

Using your own criteria, select and prioritise your most important Good Experiences.

3) Describe

Describe in detail your Good Experiences to identify how you made them happen.

4) Uncover

With the help of a team, uncover and prioritise the skills you've used repeatedly. These few skills could be your Dependable Strengths!

5) Reality Test

Share proof of your Dependable Strengths with your team and draft a special report that provides evidence of their effectiveness and your worth and growth.

People can be proactive and develop their skills for finding roles in which they can use their strengths.

Bernard did more than help people to find their strengths – he encouraged them to go out and find their perfect role. He also helped them to do what would now be called 'networking'. In an article titled *Bernard Haldane Was Ahead Of His Time,* Jerald Forster wrote:

> *"In his 1960 book, How to Make a Habit of Success, Bernard Haldane made the case for focusing on successes rather than mistakes ... He then described a series of activities wherein the person 'mines the gold' in his key achievements, searching for success factors.*
>
> *"As early as 1962, Bernard wrote: 'Seventy percent of all beginning jobs today are obtained through personal contacts with an employer or through friends.'"*

Contribution to the strengths approach

Bernard made an enormous contribution to the strengths philosophy. For example:

> *He pioneered thought leadership in the area of building on people's strengths. This was at a time when most people thought that development called for continually focusing on weaknesses.*
>
> *He developed practical approaches to focusing on 'the excellence in each person' and enabling them to find their strengths and transferable skills.*
>
> *His influence has contributed to millions of people finding and enjoying satisfying work.*

Jerald Forster says: "While the first part of Bernard's career was almost totally focused on the goal of facilitating job and career satisfaction, the latter part had a broader focus on what might be called life satisfaction."

Summarising Bernard's later work, The Center for Dependable Strengths says:

> *"Through a culmination of experiences, and with the assistance of his wife, Dr Jean Haldane, Dr Haldane evolved the idea of marketing one's strengths and potential in everyday life with a focus on helping children and the poor build their self-esteem.*
>
> *"This idea was the seed that blossomed into the Dependable Strengths Articulation Process, a process that has since spread worldwide."*

Peter Drucker, the renowned management writer, wrote the following in the Foreword to *Career Satisfaction and Success:*

> *"Bernie Haldane has, for twenty-five years or more, pioneered in finding human strength and in making it productive.*
>
> *"Long before it became fashionable, Mr Haldane realised that placing people is the most important help one can give them, whether they work in an organisation or for themselves. And understanding what one is good for and what one therefore should try to strengthen and develop is the key to self-development.*
>
> *"This book distills his experience, his achievements, his knowledge and his wisdom. It is more than a 'guide to the perplexed' – it is a guide to achievement and self-fulfillment, especially in the modern organisation."*

Bernard died in 2002, but his work continues. Many practitioners in the fields of job search and strengths identification acknowledge the debt they owe to him. Summarising his later work, The Center for Dependable Strengths says:

> *"Through a culmination of experiences, and with the assistance of his wife, Dr Jean Haldane, Dr Haldane evolved the idea of marketing one's strengths and potential in everyday life with a focus on helping children and the poor build their self-esteem. This idea was the seed that blossomed into the Dependable Strengths Articulation Process, a process that has since spread worldwide."*

Viktor Frankl

Viktor was an Austrian psychiatrist who lived between 1905 and 1997. His philosophy has helped many people to develop their inner strength.

This work reached millions through his book *Man's Search For Meaning.* The book described his harrowing journey through the Nazi concentration camps. Surrounded by terror, he wondered how to make sense of this madness. Viktor concluded that:

> *"Man is not free from his conditions, but he is free to take a stand towards his conditions."*

Philosophy

Frankl found that many of the survivors had something to live for beyond the immediate horror. They had a book to write, a relationship to rebuild or a dream to pursue. He later wrote:

> *"Everything can be taken from a man or a woman but one thing: the last of human freedoms to choose one's attitude in any given set of circumstances, to choose one's own way."*

Chance played an enormous part in the death camps, of course, but each person faced choices each day. Viktor describes how it was vital to look alert and ready to work. New arrivals found the ordeal began when the railway trucks drew into the camp sidings.

Recalling his own experience, he describes joining a long line which shuffled towards an SS Officer. The Officer looked at each person and casually pointed to the left or the right. In Viktor's words:

> *"It was my turn. Somebody whispered to me that to be sent to the right side would mean work, the way to the left being for the sick and those incapable of work.*
>
> *"My haversack weighed me down a bit to the left, but I made an effort to walk upright.*
>
> *"The SS man looked me over, appeared to hesitate, then put both his hands on my shoulders, I tried very hard to look smart, and he turned my shoulders very slowly until I faced right, and I moved over to that side."*

Viktor survived the Nazi camps, emigrated to America and worked as a psychiatrist. Working with suicidal people, he recognised the similarity between them and prisoners in the death camps. He recalled two prisoners who talked of committing suicide. Both men used the typical argument: that they had nothing more to expect from life. The challenge was to show the men that life was still expecting something from them. Viktor continues:

> *"We found, in fact, that for the one it was his child whom he adored and who was awaiting for him in a foreign country. For the other it was a thing, not a person. This was a scientist and had written a series of books which still needed to be finished. His work could not be done by anyone else, any more than another person could ever take the place of the father in his child's affections.*
>
> *"A man who becomes conscious of the responsibility he bears toward a human being who affectionately waits for him, or to an unfinished work, will never be able to throw away his life. He knows the 'why' for his existence, and will be able to bear almost any 'how'."*

Camp life showed that people do have a choice of action, said Viktor, and prisoners who lost faith in the future were doomed. As a result of his experiences, he created Logotherapy, a form of therapy that helps people to fulfil their meaning in life.

Viktor became fascinated with each individual's search to live a meaningful life. We need to create a meaning for our lives – a vocation to follow, a person to help, a deed to do, a legacy to leave. Happiness is often a by-product of doing our best during our time on Earth. Viktor also quoted Albert Schweitzer, who said:

> *"The only ones among you who will be really happy are those who have sought and found how to serve."*

Principles

Viktor's books pass-on the wisdom he gained from a life of service and suffering. Here are some of the key principles that run through his philosophy.

People can choose their attitude.

Human beings want to feel in control. Time after time we hear people say: "But I had no choice." Based on his experience in the death camps, Frankl maintains that there is always one final freedom. We can choose our attitude towards events. He wrote:

> *"We who lived in concentration camps can remember the men who walked through the huts comforting others, giving away their last piece of bread.*
>
> *"They may have been few in number, but they offer sufficient proof that everything can be taken from a man but one thing: the last of the human freedoms – to choose one's attitude in any given set of circumstances, to choose one's own way."*

People want to find and follow their personal sense of meaning.

Human beings long for a sense of purpose, said Frankl. He believed there were three ways to create meaning in life:

> *By doing a deed or creating a work.*
>
> *By appreciating the experience of someone or something.*
>
> *By choosing our attitude towards suffering.*

"Everyone has his own specific vocation or mission in life," he wrote. "Everyone must carry out a concrete assignment that demands fulfilment ... Therein he cannot be replaced, nor can his life be repeated, thus, everyone's task is unique as his specific opportunity to implement it."

People find 'happiness' as a by-product of following their meaning.

He believed that, providing we follow our meaning in life, happiness would happen as a by-product. The key was to follow our vocation each day. He wrote:

> *"I want you to listen to what your conscience commands you to do and go on to carry it out to the best of your knowledge ... Then you will live to see that in the long run – in the long run, I say – success will follow you precisely because you had forgotten to think of it.'"*

Contribution to the strengths approach

Frankl talked about 'meaning' and 'purpose', rather than strengths, and underlined we each have a mission to fulfil. This could mean, in some cases, fulfilling our duty to make full use of our talents. At the same time, he showed that people draw courage from pursuing their chosen path. (This aspect has since been developed through Martin Seligman's work on 'character strengths'.)

Here are several ways that Victor contributed to the strengths approach.

He emphasised that people can develop their inner strength by focusing on the concept of choice. People can choose their attitude in any situation.

He showed that each of us have something to give to the world. We may have a book to write, a legacy to leave, a talent to fulfil or whatever. We can do this by finding and following our vocation.

He showed that people draw tremendous strength from doing something that provides a sense of meaning.

Speaking towards the end of his life, Viktor said that, for humanity to survive, we needed to focus on a common purpose. We can choose our attitude and, if we wish, pass-on a better world to future generations. Faced by interviewers who asked what people should do when faced by economic crises or global challenges, he returned to his famous saying.

"Man is not free from his conditions, but he is free to take a stand towards his conditions."

Al Siebert

Al Siebert, who lived between 1934 and 2009, did pioneering work on resilience. His books such as *The Survivor Personality* and *The Resiliency Advantage* enabled many people to develop their inner strength.

He provided more than inspiring stories. He offered positive models and practical tools that enabled people to develop their resiliency skills. They could then apply these to overcome challenges when using their strengths.

Philosophy

Al spent over 50 years studying how people develop inner strength. A paratrooper in the 1950s, he remembered meeting the few remaining survivors from the 11th Airborne Division, a unit that had served in WWII and Korea. Something about them made him take notice. They weren't the 'gung-ho' types: they had unusual qualities. He wrote:

> *"During our training I noticed that combat survivors have a type of personal radar always on 'scan.' Anything that happens, or any noise draws a quick, brief look ... They have a relaxed awareness. I began to realize it wasn't just luck or fate that these were the few who came back alive. Something about them as people had tipped the scales in their favour."*

Returning to college after completing his military service, Al resolved to study psychology, but he grew frustrated by its emphasis on mental illness.

He decided to study life's survivors – those who grew when overcoming tough challenges. Scoping out the areas of study, he chose to focus on people that met four criteria:

> *They had survived a major crisis.*
>
> *They had surmounted the crisis through personal effort.*
>
> *They had emerged from the experience with previously unknown strengths and abilities.*
>
> *They had, in retrospect, found value in the experience.*

Al shared his knowledge by running workshops, giving keynote speeches and writing articles. He came to international prominence with his book *The Survivor Personality.*

This book contains many stories about people who had overcome extreme challenges. The situations they faced included sexual assaults, life-threatening illnesses, being prisoners of war, addictions, physical attacks and crippling accidents.

Principles Followed By Resilient People

How do people cope with such adversity? Some don't, says Al. They feel victimised, blame other people, become helpless or lash out at others. Some people do cope with adversity. Drawing on their inner strength, they stay calm, clarify the situation and chart their strategy. Committing to their course of action, they concentrate fully until they reach their chosen goal. Al wrote:

"They thrive by gaining strength from adversity and often convert misfortune into a gift. Are life's best survivors different from other people? No. They survive, cope, and thrive better because they are better at using the inborn abilities possessed by all humans."

Building on his research, Al outlined some of the strategies survivors adopt to overcome crises successfully. These include the following.

They quickly read the new reality.

Survivors have experience of overcoming difficulties in life. As a result, they have developed a particular kind of savvy or 'personal radar'. Al says:

"This quick comprehension of the total circumstance is 'pattern empathy'."

They read situations quickly and start considering the consequences. Other people ignore what is happening or bury their heads in the sand. Survivors click into awareness mode and take snapshots of what is actually happening.

They are positive realists and have life-competencies that helps them in emergencies.

Survivors are life-long learners. They love to explore and make sense of experiences. They prefer to take initiatives, rather than become institutionalised. Such people are often positive realists. They have a positive attitude, but also quickly read reality. They then use their repertoire of skills to see patterns and deliver the required results.

They stay calm.

Why? They realise it is vital to establish clarity. They must clarify what is happening – then make decisions about the way forward. Al gives examples of hijack survivors who stay calm. They gather information about how the hijackers behave, look for patterns and explore potential exits – not only for themselves, but also for other people.

They maintain a sense of perspective.

People who are diagnosed with a serious illness, for example, may then move to clarifying their assets. Some people reframe the difficulty as a 'project'. Looking at it from this perspective, they are able to 'remove themselves' and plan the path ahead.

They are open to doing anything.

Al Siebert found that survivors choose their strategies from a wide 'repertoire' of options. One contributing factor is that they have a quality common to many peak performers. Such people embrace what appear to be paradoxes. They are able to see the big picture *and* the small details, to be focused *and* flexible, to be serious *and* playful. They see a wider number of options than, for example, people who have been 'trained' to behave in one way.

They develop personal radar.

Al found a link between survivors and peak performers. Such people have a sixth sense in the areas in which they perform brilliantly. They seem to know 'what will happen before it happens'. This is called 'personal radar'. Reflecting on his time with the paratroopers who survived battles, Al talks about them quickly 'scanning' situations. Looking for patterns, they asked questions such as:

> *"What is happening? What isn't happening? Are events following their normal course or is something else happening?*
>
> *"What are the patterns I can observe? What will happen if these patterns continue? What will be the consequences?*
>
> *"How can I build on the successful patterns? How can I deal with the unsuccessful patterns?*
>
> *"What action do I need to take? Bearing in mind the patterns that are occurring – and the potential consequences – how can I do my best to achieve success?"*
>
> *They take responsibility and totally commit to doing their best.*

Survivors make their decision – then throw themselves into pursuing their chosen strategy. They employ every ounce of energy to reach the goal. Such people balance the apparent paradox of being simultaneously 'helicoptering' and 'hands-on'. They are completely committed to the task in hand, yet 'hover' above it to get perspective on what is happening. People then do everything possible to reach the goal. As Al Siebert wrote:

> *"The survivor way of orientating to a crisis is to feel fully and totally responsible for making things work out well."*

Al then expanded on the topic to produce another compelling book *The Resiliency Advantage.*

Building on the theme of survival, Al focused on how people can thrive in a fast-changing world. This calls for individuals, teams and organisations to develop their resiliency skills. Why? In the old days many people relied on 'institutions' to tell them what to learn and how to behave. Nowadays people must manage increasing information, complexity and unpredictability.

Such events may include personal setbacks, sickness, redundancy, market changes, reduced budgets, technological changes, economic downturns or whatever. People will need to deal with such challenges. This calls for them taking responsibility, seeing to the heart of the matter and making good decisions.

Even if they choose the right strategy, events may conspire to throw them off-track. They will need to recover quickly, practise 'course correction' and do everything possible to reach their goals. People who develop such resiliency skills are more likely to increase their chances of success.

Contribution to the strengths approach

Al made many contributions to the strengths philosophy. For example:

He provided positive models and practical tools that people can use to develop their resilience and inner strength.

He showed how survivors and peak performers are often positive realists. They have a positive attitude, but also quickly read reality. They then use their repertoire of skills to deliver the required results.

He introduced the concept of 'personal radar'. Exploring where a person has such radar provides valuable clues to finding their strengths.

Al Siebert was extremely generous with his knowledge. He passed-on many stories, strategies and skills that gave people the courage to express their personal strengths.

Don Clifton

Don Clifton was one of the pioneers in the modern strength movement. He is best known for playing a leading part in the Gallup Organization's work on strengths. This led to many best-selling books, such as *Now, Discover Your Strengths.* He also led the team of researchers that created the strengths profiling tool called *StrengthsFinder.*

Don was born in 1924 and served in the Second World War. He went on to achieve a degree in Mathematics and a doctorate in Educational Psychology. He became Professor of Educational Psychology at the University of Nebraska. There he began his revolutionary research into his key question:

> *"What would happen if we actually studied what is right with people?"*

Philosophy

During the late 1940s most funding for psychological research was geared to studying problems rather than potential. On the one hand this was understandable, because war veterans and others were suffering from difficulties. On the other hand several people tackled the challenge from a different angle.

Don chose to study what people did right to achieve top performance. This led to him identifying certain life themes that were later translated into strengths themes. His work provided solid recommendations for employers and individuals looking to develop fulfilling careers. So, in addition to his academic career, Don founded Selection Research, Inc.

Beginning as a small business in his basement, this grew to become a large human resources consultancy. So much so that, in 1988, it acquired the Gallup Organization, which was best known for its research and polling activities.

Don acted as the guiding lighted in developing Gallup's work on leadership, management and peak performance. He led teams of researchers whose work eventually led to creating the *Clifton StrengthsFinder* and *The Gallup's Q12.*

The latter is a set of 12 questions for assessing employee engagement. These questions continue to be used to measure and improve leadership in organisations. Gallup also produced a series of best selling books by writers such as Marcus Buckingham, Tom Rath, Curt Coffman and Paula Nelson.

Principles

The strength's work of Don Clifton and Gallup is based on certain key principles.

People can clarify their strengths.

Writing in *Now, Discover Your Strengths,* Don Clifton and Marcus Buckingham say:

> *"The definition of a strength that we will use throughout this book is quite specific: consistent near perfect performance in an activity."*

So how do you discover these abilities? Don and his colleagues at Gallup created an assessment tool called the Clifton StrengthsFinder. The latest version of this tool can be found on the Strengths Gallup site.

People can do an on-line analysis that highlights their top five 'signature themes'. What do the themes look like?

The following paragraph gives a taster of three – Achiever, Context and Futuristic. But it is vital to visit the official site to see the full definitions.

Somebody with an **Achiever** theme, for example, loves to set goals, work hard and achieve those goals. They enjoy making lists and get a kick from crossing-off each item.

Somebody who has **Context** as a theme will gather data about the past to build up a complete picture. They believe such research is required to plot the way forward.

A person who is **Futuristic** will automatically focus on possibilities. Faced by a setback or problem, they quickly move to envisaging a positive future, a quality that often inspires other people.

Every theme does, of course, have pluses and minuses. Similarly, working in a team calls for knowing how to communicate with people who demonstrate the different characteristics. Such skills are outlined by Tom Rath in his book *Strengthsfinder 2.0.*

People's greatest area for growth is in the area of building on their strengths.

Don Clifton spent much of his life studying great performers. Based on these findings, he challenged the traditional 'deficit' model of development – the idea that people develop by focusing on improving their weaknesses. Don turned this approach on its head. In *Now, Discover Your Strengths* he said:

"Each person's greatest room for growth is in the areas of his or her greatest strengths."

"'But what about a person's weaknesses?' somebody may ask. "Shouldn't these also be addressed?"

The Gallup approach was sometimes criticised for overlooking this area, but actually it didn't. *Now, Discover Your Strengths* says:

"You will excel only by maximizing your strengths, never by fixing your weaknesses. This is not the same as saying 'ignore your weaknesses' ... The point here is not that you should always forgo this kind of weakness fixing. The point is that you should see it for what it is: damage control, not development ... damage control can prevent failure, but it will never elevate you to excellence."

Peak performers are extremists. They perform brilliantly in a few areas, rather than being a complete human being. Again, some of the weaknesses may need to be addressed in terms of 'damage control'. Don Clifton and Marcus Buckingham wrote, however:

"When we studied them, excellent performers were rarely well rounded. On the contrary, they were sharp ... Whatever you set your mind to, you will be most successful when you craft your role to play to your signature talents most of the time."

People can build strengths-based organisations that achieve ongoing success.

The Gallup approach was well received. People were shocked to discover that in some companies less than 20% of the employees felt 'they had an opportunity to do what they did best each day'.

Many organisations adopted the ways forward suggested in *First, Break All The Rules; Now, Discover Your Strengths* and *Follow This Path.* The latter was written by Curt Coffman and Gabriel Gonzalez-Molina. This had the subtitle: *How The World's Greatest Organizations Drive Growth By Unleashing Human*

Potential. The Gallup Organization showed how companies could improve their profits, for example, by:

Providing clear direction.

Providing good leadership.

Engaging their people.

Mobilising people's strengths.

Managing by outcomes, rather than by tasks.

This final point was crucial. Don emphasised:

"Since each person's talents are unique, you should focus performance by legislating outcomes rather than forcing each person into a stylistic mould.

"This means a strong emphasis on careful measurement of the right outcomes, and less on policies, procedures, and competencies. This will address the 'in my role I don't have any room to express my talents' problem."

Gallup put forward in an integrated approach. Implemented properly, this could lead to improved employee engagement and performance.

Contribution to the strengths approach

Don made an enormous contribution to the strengths philosophy. For example:

He helped to pioneer the modern strengths movement by studying top performers, clarifying their successful patterns and creating StrengthsFinder. This helped people to find and express their strengths themes.

He mentored many people who became thought leaders in the strengths movement.

This led to both him and they producing best selling books. These books showed how building on strengths could benefit both the individuals and their organisations.

He acted as a Founding Father in creating and nurturing The Gallup Strengths approach. This has had a profound effect on organisations around the world.

Don died in 2003, but his legacy lives on. In *Now, Discover Your Strengths* he wrote:

"Rapid learning offers another trace of talent. Sometimes a talent doesn't signal itself through yearning. For a myriad of reasons, although the talent exists within you, you don't hear its call.

"Instead, comparatively late in life, something sparks the talent, and it is the speed at which you learn a new skill that provides the telltale clue to the talent's presence and power."

Don helped many people to discover their abilities much earlier in life. They then used these talents to help themselves and other people to give their best to the world.

Mihaly Csikszentmihalyi

Mihaly Csikszentmihalyi wrote the best-selling book *Flow.* Flow experiences are those in which you become completely absorbed and 'time goes away'.

You start by doing something stimulating – be it writing, skiing, solving a problem, tackling a challenge or whatever. You set a clear goal, employ your skills and stretch yourself to achieve success. Then something odd happens, says Mihaly.

> *"Your awareness of self disappears but, after completing the task, your sense of self emerges even stronger."*

You flow, focus, finish and, as a by-product, find fulfilment. Mihaly's work shows how people can find and follow certain principles to create flow in the future.

His books have had a profound effect in fields such as sports, education and work. They have also made a great contribution to the strengths approach

Philosophy

Mihaly was born in Rijecka, Croatia, in 1934. His family was Hungarian, and his father Alfred, a diplomat, had been posted to Italy. Living in cities such as Rome and Florence exposed Mihaly to different cultures and he became fluent in Hungarian, Italian and German. Despite being a child, he was interned in Italy for a while and tried to make sense of events.

Interviewed years later by Dava Sobel for *Omni Magazine*, he described how, a child in World War 2 Europe, he was dismayed to find that grown-ups seemed at a loss to deal with the mess they had created. Mihaly explained:

> *"I resolved to figure out how one could live a better life. I tried many things, such as art, fiction, philosophy and working in youth organisations.*
>
> *"I discovered psychology through the writings of C.J. Jung, and thought that perhaps this was the best way to understand behaviour and history ... I can't say I have, but in the process I learned a lot and had a good time."*

Choosing to study psychology at university level, he found the most attractive courses were in America. He applied to the University of Chicago and, despite speaking little English, was accepted.

He improved his English by reading comic books, but a greater difficulty was his parents losing their life-savings to a fraudster employed in their restaurant. Mihaly arrived in Chicago in 1956 with little more than a dollar in his pocket.

He did well at university and went on to study for a Masters. Explaining his chosen field of study, Mihaly told Elizabeth Debold of *Enlightenment Magazine* that he did his doctoral dissertation on young students at the Chicago Art Institute. He explained:

> *"One thing that I noticed – and I knew also from my own experience – is that when they started painting, they almost fell into a trance. They didn't seem to notice anything, and they just moved as if they were possessed by something inside themselves.*
>
> *"When they finished a painting, they would look at it, and they'd feel good for about five or ten minutes. Then they'd put the painting away and not look at it much after that. What became important was the next canvas ..."*

Mihaly moved on to studying chess players, rock climbers, musicians and basketball players. He asked them to describe what happened 'when what they were doing was really going well'. Despite coming from different fields, people reported similar experiences. Explaining this in an interview with Sarah Trevelyan, Mihaly said:

> *"Many of the interviewees described their feeling as 'being carried away by a force greater than myself,' or 'being in a current,' or 'being in flow.' I chose the last of these analogies as being the most simple."*

Principles

Mihaly's work explores peoples' experiences of feeling fully alive. So let's consider some of the principles it highlights.

People from all walks of life can experience a state of flow.

Beginning by asking artists, musicians and surgeons to describe their flow experiences, he then interviewed people from all walks in life. These have included factory workers in Chicago, farmers in Italy, teenagers in Tokyo and paraplegics recovering from accidents. He and his colleagues have talked with tens of thousands of people from all around the world and similar themes emerged. He says:

> *"Women who weave tapestries in the highlands of Borneo, meditating monks in Europe, also Catholic Dominican monks, and so forth. They all said these same things. So 'flow' seems to be a phenomenological state that is the same across cultures."*

People follow certain principles to achieve a state of flow.

So what do people do right to achieve flow? Mihaly identified certain principles they follow. They pursue these as individuals, but also sometimes as a team. He writes:

> *"Surgeons say that during a difficult operation they have the sensation that the entire operating team is a single organism, moved by the same purpose; they describe it as a 'ballet' in which the individual is subordinated to the group performance, and all involved share in a feeling of harmony and power."*

This involves taking certain steps – whether you are working as an individual or as part of a team. These include: tackling a stimulating task – *or one you make stimulating* – setting a clear goal, being fully concentrated, getting feedback, being creative, stretching yourself and, hopefully, achieving your picture of success.

Flow

Mihaly's study says that people enjoy a sense of flow when:

1) *They tackle a task which they have a chance of completing.*

2) *They concentrate on what they are doing.*

3) *They have clear goals.*

4) *They get immediate feedback.*

5) *They experience a deep and effortless involvement that removes the frustrations of everyday life.*

6) *They enjoy a sense of control over their actions.*

7) *They find their concern for self disappears, but paradoxically their sense of self emerges stronger.*

8) *They find the experience is so enjoyable that their sense of time disappears.*

People can follow these principles in the future to achieve a sense of flow.

Mihaly once invited an 84-year-old man to describe his flow experiences. The man recalled a time when, as 24-year-old, he was playing polo.

After identifying what the man did right at that time, Mihaly explained that he could follow similar principles to experience flow in other activities. The man had not previously made the connection. He thought the experience was exclusive to polo.

Making up for lost time, he immediately threw himself into new activities and, following the principles, enjoyed a sense of flow. As Mihaly writes in Flow:

> *"What I 'discovered' was that happiness is not something that just happens …*
>
> *"We have all experienced times when, instead of being buffeted by anonymous forces, we do feel in control of our actions, masters of our own fate.*
>
> *"On the rare occasions that it happens, we feel a sense of exhilaration, a deep sense of enjoyment that is long cherished and that becomes a landmark in memory for what life should be like … "*

A person's best moments occur when their body or mind is stretched to its limits in a voluntary effort to accomplish something difficult and worthwhile, said Mihalyi. Therefore: "Optimal experience is therefore something that we make happen."

Contribution to the strengths approach

Mihaly has made an enormous contribution to the strengths philosophy. For example:

He popularised the concept of flow with his best-selling books. These encouraged people to focus on their strengths, rather than continually discuss their weaknesses.

He encouraged people to learn from their flow experiences and follow similar principles to achieve flow in the future. This included identifying and building on their strengths.

He showed how people can apply the flow principles in the arts, sports, education and work. Many people – and organisations – have applied these principles successfully.

Mihaly describes his life's work as the effort: "to study what makes people truly happy." He believes true happiness calls for being part of something that goes beyond ourselves and, hopefully, builds a better world. He says:

"Each of us has a picture, however vague, of what we would like to accomplish before we die ... How close we get to attaining this goal becomes the measure for the quality of our lives. If it remains beyond reach, we grow resentful or resigned; if it is at least in part achieved, we experience a sense of happiness and satisfaction."

Thomas Armstrong is an American educator who has helped thousands of people to find their natural talents. His books are inspiring and also practical. They enable readers to find and develop their intelligences.

Whilst his books often focus on children, he provides insights that can be used by people at any age. Paying great tribute to Howard Gardner's work on multiple intelligences, he offers tools for translating these concepts into concrete actions.

Philosophy

Thomas believes that every child is gifted. The key is to find and develop their unique talents. He says:

> *"Each child comes into the world with unique potentials that, if properly nourished, can contribute to the betterment of our world."*

Introducing his book *In Their Own Way,* he explains:

> *"Six years ago I quit my job as a learning disabilities specialist. I had to. I no longer believed in learning disabilities ...*
>
> *"It was then that I turned to the concept of learning differences as an alternative to learning disabilities. I realised that the millions of children being referred to as learning disabled weren't handicapped, but instead had unique learning styles that the schools did not understand.*
>
> *"Everyone has (the different) kinds of intelligence in different proportions. Your child may be a great reader but a poor math student, a wonderful drawer but clumsy out on the playing field.*
>
> *"Children can even show a wide range of strengths and weaknesses within one area of intelligence. Your child may write very well but have difficulty with spelling or handwriting, read poorly but be a superb story-teller, play an excellent game of basketball but stumble on the dance floor."*

Thomas himself had a successful educational career – teaching right through from primary to doctoral level. During this time, however, he became increasingly passionate about the importance of encouraging the strengths within every child.

He began producing many books and videos on the topic. These included *The Myth of the A.D.D. Child* and *Awakening Your Child's Natural Genius.*

Principles

Thomas says that his writing is motivated by the desire to ensure that every child gets a chance to fulfil their potential.

His books help teachers spot each individual's strengths and preferred learning styles. They can then create enjoyable and effective lessons that give every child the opportunity to develop. So let's explore some of his key ideas, starting with those in his book *7 Kinds of Smart.*

People are 'smart' in different ways – there are Multiple intelligences.

Thomas embraces much of Howard Gardner's work on multiple intelligences. So what is the story behind these intelligences? Howard is a Harvard Professor who in 1983 published *Frames of Mind.* This challenged the academic establishment by expanding the conventional number of 'intelligences' measured by schools.

Howard believed there were many intelligences. There were, in his view, at least seven. In addition to 'linguistic' and 'logical-mathematical', these were 'interpersonal', 'spatial', 'bodily-kinesthetic', 'musical' and 'intrapersonal' intelligences.

Educational institutions tended to look for 'linguistic' and 'logical-mathematical' intelligences. They paid little attention to other talents unless, for example, a person was outstanding at athletics or art.

Children who had other talents had difficulty being recognised by the system. Certainly each student must take responsibility for shaping their future, but this might be easier in an environment that encouraged their talents. Some were actually punished or 'labelled' because their natural abilities did not fit into the system.

Gardner's treatise was somewhat academic, as were the names he coined. He later confessed to being deliberatively provocative by calling these 'intelligences' rather than, for example, 'styles'. He got his reaction. Academics debated the semantics, whilst practitioners applied the ideas in schools.

Thomas has translated these principles into practical approaches that can be used in daily life. Some of these ideas were outlined in *7 Kinds of Smart.* Since then he has expanded his view of the different intelligences. These include the following ways in which people are smart.

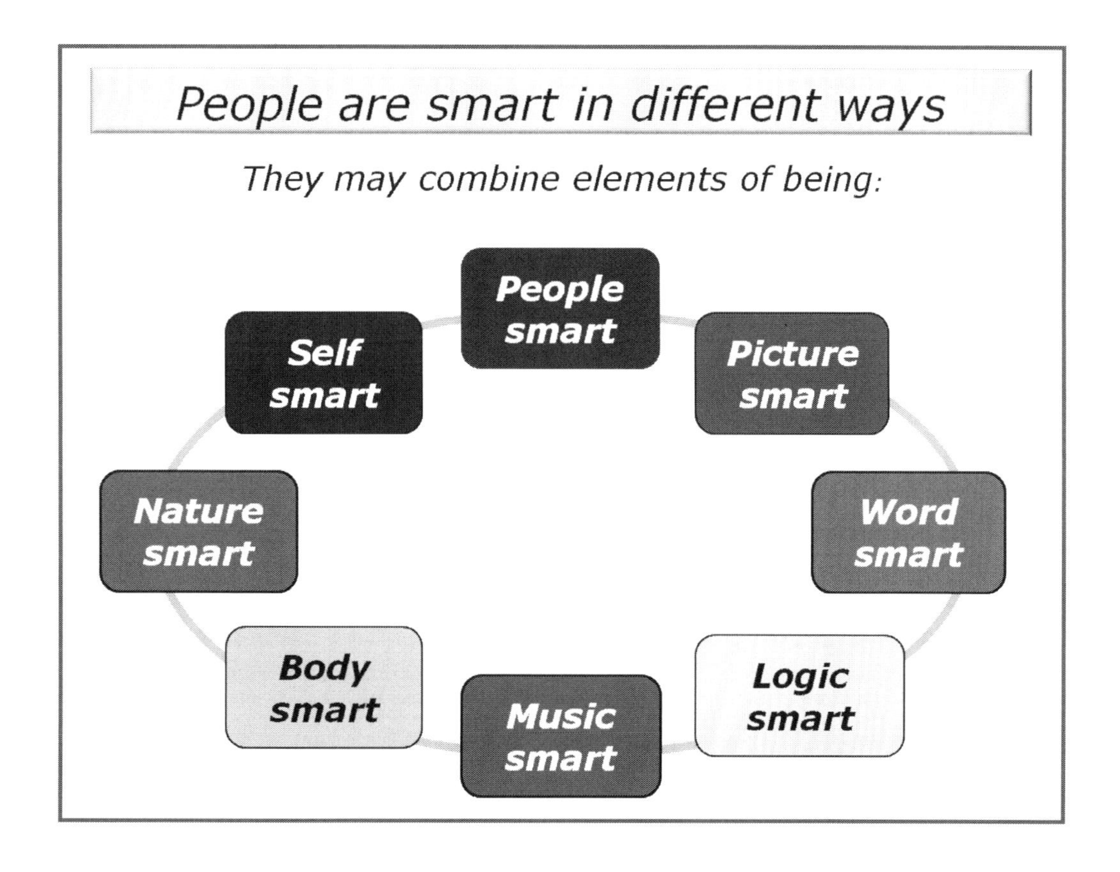

Thomas built on this approach with his book *Neurodiversity: Discovering the Hidden Strengths of Autism, ADHD, Dyslexia and Other Brain Differences*. He has also co-operated with Howard Gardner and Mihaly Csikszentmihalyi to work alongside teachers in State schools. Their work has produced excellent results.

Contribution to the strengths approach

Thomas' approach embodies many elements of the strengths philosophy. For example:

He has encouraged thousands of people to focus on children's talents. He has provided a framework they can use to focus on children's 'smarts' and clarify their strengths.

He has provided hundreds of practical tips that parents and educators can use to encourage children in the family, school and society. These show how multiple intelligences can be translated into daily practice.

He continues to show that education can play a vital part in human development. The approach he advocates enables people to identify their talents and fulfil their potential.

Thomas continues his journey. Returning to one of his quotes at the start of this article, he said:

"Each child comes into the world with unique potentials that, if properly nourished, can contribute to the betterment of our world."

Charles Garfield is the author of the best-selling books *Peak Performers* and *Second to None*. While best known for his work on peak performance, many of the themes he covers overlap with the strengths philosophy. His work also encourages people to become the best they can be. He wrote:

> *"Do not compete with anyone except yourself."*

Charles says it is vital for people to follow their values and translate these into a compelling vision. People, teams and organisations can also mobilise great strength when they pursue 'missions that motivate'. He wrote:

> *"Peak performers develop powerful mental images of the behaviour that will lead to the desired results.*
>
> *"They see in their mind's eye the result they want, and the actions leading to it."*

Philosophy

Charles has vast experience in many fields. He worked as a computer analyst and leader of a team of engineers, scientists, and support staff on the *Apollo 11* project.

He is the founder and CEO of Shanti Project. This is a volunteer organisation that focuses on delivering service excellence for patients and families facing life-threatening illness. He is also a clinical professor at the University of California Medical School in San Francisco.

Charles said he first heard the phrase 'peak performance' from a cancer patient who said:

> *"Staying alive these days is my peak performance".*

Remembering the phrase, Charles went on to study great workers in many fields. These included people in medicine, sports, business and the NASA work in which he was participating.

Charles said that, towards the end of the 1970s, he discovered a key trigger for peak performance.

People were often motivated by an external mission. But the key factor was for them to make an *internal decision* to perform at their best. He wrote:

> *"Now I began to understand what I was hearing and seeing, as one peak performer after another spoke of self-training, learning by experience, organizing that experience around a single theme, speaking and finding a purpose, a personal mission that represents something important.*
>
> *"They were talking about what management theorist Warren Bennis calls 'working near the heart of things.' ... They want to feel proud of themselves, to achieve something, to leave a mark and a contribution, and they follow their plans for doing all that purposefully and tenaciously. That is what I – and many others I knew – wanted.*

> *"So peak performers are not merely exceptions. They represent a kind of person any of us can be – once we find the capacity in ourselves."*

Charles' findings led to him writing *Peak Performers,* which was published in 1986.

Principles

He found that peak performers often followed six principles that enabled them to excel. His book explained each of these themes in great detail. Here are the phrases that he uses about each of these principles.

Missions that motivate.

This is the call the action, the 'click' that starts things moving.

Results in real time.

This is a purposeful activity directed at achieving goals that contribute to the mission.

Self-management through mastery.

This is the capacity for self-observation and effective thinking.

Team building/team playing.

This is the complement to self-management. It is empowering others to produce.

Course correction.

This is mental agility, concentration, finding and navigating a 'critical path'.

Change management.

This is anticipating and adapting to major change while maintaining momentum and balance within an overall game plan.

Charles also believes it is vital to build sustainable systems that nurture the human spirit and also deliver tangible success. The old kind of achiever was often seen as a rugged individualist, he says.

But the new peak performer learns to co-operate with others and channel their talents towards achieving a compelling goal. He said in an interview for *Educom.*

> *"The most powerful human motivator of all is the desire to be proud of ourselves in the pursuit of something we care about deeply.*
>
> *"The mission of the individual needs to align with the mission of the team, which needs to align with the mission of the organization.*
>
> *"In fact, I would take it further – the mission of the organization needs to align with the mission of the society in which it is embedded and the mission of the planet to which we are all indebted."*

Contribution to the strengths approach

Charles' work on peak performance highlights many themes that are also present in the strengths approach.

> *He showed the importance of working from the heart and mobilising our inner strength. People work best when they follow their values, translate these into a clear vision and do valuable work. These become missions that motivate.*
>
> *He provided positive models and practical tools that people could use to achieve peak performance. Many individuals, teams and organisations applied these tools successfully.*

He showed the importance of sustainability. Whether working as individuals, organisations or societies, we need to generate at least as many resources as those we use. This will give future generations the opportunity to enjoy enriching lives.

Many people have since developed new models for achieving peak performance. But it remains valuable to revisit the pioneering work done by Charles Garfield.

Appreciative Inquiry

Appreciative Inquiry is a positive model for helping people, teams and organisations to develop. AI focuses on what works. It invites people:

To clarify when they have performed brilliantly.

To clarify the principles they followed to perform brilliantly.

To clarify how they can follow these principles – plus add other elements – to perform brilliantly in the future.

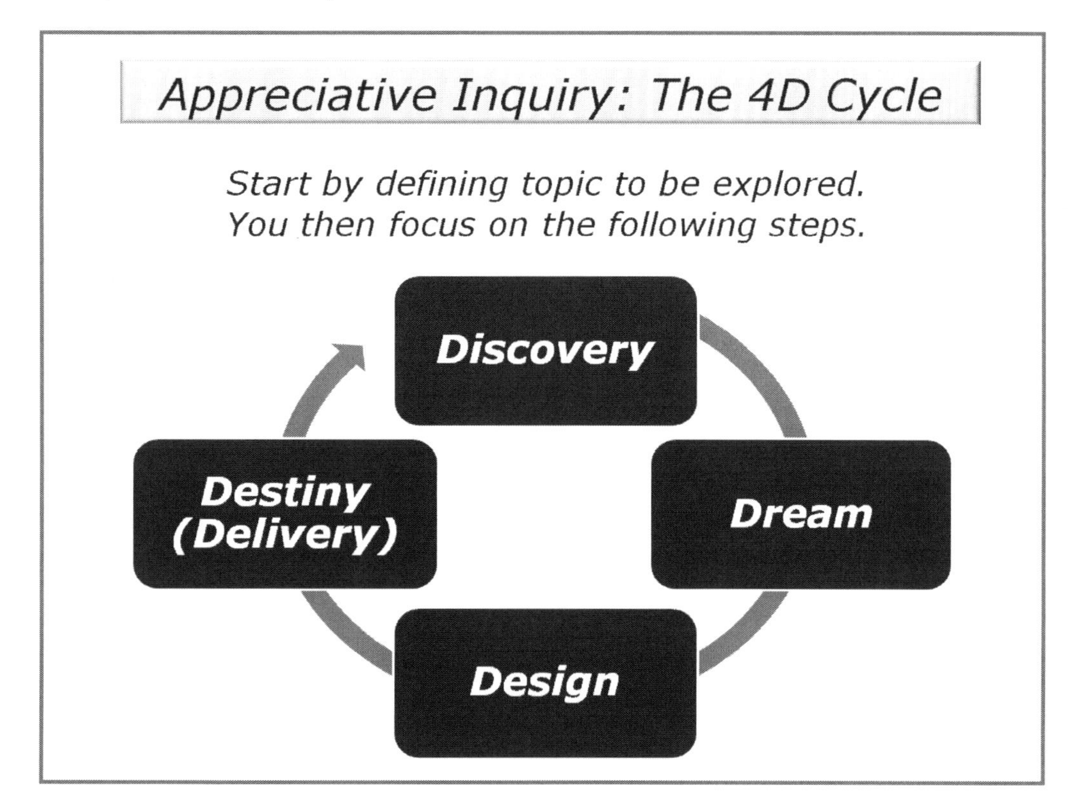

This approach can involve thousands of people in an organisation. They are asked to share their ideas – not simply participate in 'training' – to help shape the organisation's future.

People like the approach. They build on when they have performed brilliantly and aim to keep developing. AI has a track record of delivering success.

Philosophy

David Cooperrider helped to pioneer AI in the early 1980s. He is now a professor at the Weatherhead School of Management, Case Western Reserve University in Cleveland.

At that time he was a 24-year-old doing his doctorate and was focusing on organisational development work at The Cleveland Clinic. David began with 'traditional change management' questions, looking at 'deficits' and 'gaps' in performance.

Then something happened. Impressed by the positive co-operation and innovation he found in the hospital, David changed tack. He began focusing more on people's strengths. He asked employees about their best experiences in work. People found that revisiting their successes ignited their desire to create an even better future.

David and his team had discovered a gold mine. He asked the Clinic's Chairman, Dr William Kiser, if he could focus totally on this positive approach. The Chairman encouraged him to go ahead. David and his project supervisor, Suresh Srivastva, would later write:

> *"Human systems grow in the direction of what people study."*

This proved the case at the Cleveland Clinic. The staff loved learning from their past successes and wanted to follow these principles in the future. They translated these into tackling specific challenges and produced concrete results.

Diana Whitney also pioneered the way with Appreciative Inquiry. Working with David Cooperrider, she co-authored the first book on the topic called *Appreciative Inquiry: A positive revolution in change.*

Since then she has became a leader in the field and authored or co-authored many books, several with Amanda Trosten-Bloom. These include *The Power of Appreciative Inquiry* and *Appreciative Leadership.*

David Cooperrider and Diana Whitney

Principles

The AI approach starts by defining a challenge that people want to tackle. For example:

How can we provide great customer service?

How can we develop successful new products?

How can we communicate well inside our organisation?

People then follow the 4D cycle that goes through the stages of Discovery, Dream, Design and Destiny. (Some people call this last stage Delivery.)

The starting point when tackling any challenge is to formulate certain questions. These help:

To define the challenge and direction in which people channel their energy.

To define the real results they want to achieve.

The art of Appreciative Inquiry revolves around the art of asking the right questions

"But you can't frame every challenge in a positive way?" somebody may say. Some situations are difficult, but this is where AI excels. David believes it is vital to define the topic in a way that inspires people to achieve the goal.

The 'Definition' process is one that some people see as the 'Fifth D' in the AI framework. It comes before focusing on Discovery, Dream, Design and Destiny.

Defining the topic.

This is the process that AI calls 'Affirmative Topic Choice.' Creative people, for example, often frame their challenges in a positive way. They may move from saying:

"How can I stop feeling bad?" to: "How can I start feeling good?"

"How can we stop arguing?" to: "How can we, as far as possible, find a 'win-win'?"

"How can we reduce sexual harassment?" to: "How can we encourage women and men to work together successfully?"

David was actually confronted by this final topic. One day he received a phone call from a consultant who was helping a company to tackle sexual harassment.

During the previous two years the employees had been attending training designed to eliminate this issue: but the levels of sexual harassment were actually increasing, as were the lawsuits against the company.

The consultant in charge of the gender and diversity training asked David:

> *"How would you take an appreciative approach to sexual harassment?"*

David asked about the real results to achieve. The reply was:

> *"We want to dramatically cut the incidence of sexual harassment. We want to solve this huge problem."*

Going deeper, he asked what this would look like. The consultant said:

> *"What we really want is to see the development of a new century organization – a model of high quality cross-gender relationship in the work place!"*

Though this wording was somewhat awkward, it clarified a positive picture of success. So eventually the questions posed to people during the following Discovery stage were along the lines of:

> *"When have women and men worked together successfully in the company? What did they do right then? How can we follow those principles in the future?"*

The company introduced a small pilot programme on this theme. This exceeded everybody's expectations. Hundreds of pairs and teams nominated themselves to provide stories illustrating men and women working together successfully in the company.

Defining the topic is crucial. It creates the framework within which people can channel their positive energy. Once the topic is chosen, they can then embark on the 'Discovery' part of the AI process. Here are some themes for defining the topic.

Defining The Question

* *Start by asking:*

"What is the challenge we want to tackle?"

"What is the theme we want to explore?"

"How can we frame the question in a positive way? What are the real results we want to achieve? What is the picture of success?"

Define the question in terms of -
The challenge we want to explore is:

* *How to*

Discovery.

The Discovery phase taps into the positive core – the life-giving forces of a team, organisation or community. AI can be applied in teams or across literally thousands of people. (The latter is sometimes called an AI Summit.)

AI invites people to discover what works. It explores the stories, strengths and successful principles already within the system. Here is a framework you can use during the Discovery stage and, if appropriate, to present these findings back to the team.

Discovery

* *Looking back, ask: "When have we tackled similar challenges successfully?" Describe specific situations.*

  Ask: "What did we do right then? What were the principles that we followed? What were the practical things people did to translate these into specific actions?"

* *Describe:*

  a) The principles people followed to do successful work.

  Try to give some specific examples.

  b) The things people can do to follow these principles in the future.

Discovery Presentation

The specific examples chosen were:

*

*

*

Principles. The principles people followed were:

* *They*

  For example: They

* *They*

  For example: They

* *They*

  For example: They

Principles in The Future.

The things we can do to follow some of these principles in the future are:

*

*

*

Dream.

AI is different from most 'visioning' approaches in a crucial way. *It builds on the stories, strengths and successful principles that have already emerged.* People are then doing several things.

They are building on what they know works. They are building on the organic soul of the organisation. They are then more confident about extrapolating these principles into the future – seeing how these might be expressed in the picture of success.

People may be dreaming but, because they are following successful principles, they have a hunch they can deliver. This is because they have 'started from within'. It is something that is rooted in both their intellect and intuition.

AI practitioners find the Dream and Design parts sometimes start to overlap. This is okay, because there is often a moving forwards and backwards between the two elements. Here is a framework you can use during the Dream stage and, if appropriate, present these findings to the team.

Dream – The Picture of Success

* *Describe the picture of success – the real results to achieve.*

The real results we want to achieve are:

* *To*

* *To*

* *To*

* *Make sure:*

- *The dream is an expression of the principles.*
- *The dream is within the scope of your controllables.*
- *The dream is stimulating and stretching.*
- *The dream has an absolutely clear picture of success.*

* *Describe the pluses and minuses for each group of stakeholders. Describe how to build on the pluses and minimise the minuses.*

* *Ask: "Are we really serious? Are we prepared to accept the whole package?" Describe the extent to which you are serious: ____ / 10*

* *Describe the specific things that will be happening that will show you have achieved the picture of success.*

The Dream

Here is a vision – a representation - of the specific things that will be happening when we reach the goal.

Design.

The Dream is the 'What' – the real results to achieve – and the 'Why' – the benefits of achieving the goal. The Design is the 'How' – the strategies and systems for achieving the goal. People ask questions such as:

"What are the key strategies we can follow to give ourselves the greatest chance of success? What support will people need to do the job? 'Who' will need to do what and 'When'? What structures and systems need to be in place? How can people get some early successes?"

Sometimes this calls for radical approaches to redesigning an organisation. David explains:

> *"People are encouraged to 'wander beyond' the data with the essential question being this:*
>
> *'What would our organization look like if it were designed in every way possible to maximize the qualities of the positive core and enable the accelerated realization of our dreams?'*
>
> *"When inspired by a great dream **we have yet to find an organization that did not feel compelled to design something very new and very necessary.**"*

Here is a framework you can use during the Design stage and, if appropriate, present these findings to the team.

Design

* *Strategies.*

Ask: "What are the 3 key things we can do to give ourselves the greatest chance of success?"

Describe the key strategies you want to follow.

* *Strengths.*

Ask: "What are people's strengths? How can we use these strengths to achieve the goals? How can we manage the consequences of our weaknesses?"

Describe how to build on the strengths.

* *Support.*

Ask: "What support do people need to do the job? How can we get some early wins?"

Describe the support required.

* *Solutions.*

Ask: "What are the specific challenges we may face on the journey? How can we find creative solutions to these challenges?"

* *Specific action plan.*

Describe the action plan in detail. Describe 'What' must be done by 'Who' and 'When'.

Design Presentation

The key strategies we aim to follow to achieve the picture of success are:

*

*

*

The support required to do the job is:

*

*

*

Specific Action Plan

The specific action plan – including milestones – for delivering the picture of success is:

*

*

*

Destiny – Sometimes called 'Delivery'.

The Destiny phase translates the dream into reality. People throw themselves into the work and get some early wins. Maintaining the momentum is crucial: so it is vital to have follow-up meetings.

If you are running such follow-up sessions, start by giving the big picture. Remind people of the Dream, then invite them to present the following:

The specific things they have delivered in, for example, the past two months towards achieving the goal.

The specific things they plan to deliver in the next two months.

The challenges they face, their plans for tackling these and the support they would like to do the job.

The other topics they would like to explore regarding how to achieve the goal.

Celebrate the successes and develop the habit of constant improvement. People will then get into a virtuous circle.

Encourage them to generate more stories, build on their strengths and follow their successful principles. This will increase the chances of fulfilling the organisation's Destiny.

Delivery

Set the dates for people reporting progress on working towards the goals. Each person/team is to present:

The specific things I/we have delivered in the past _____ towards achieving the picture of success have been:

*

*

*

The specific things I/we plan to deliver in the next _____ towards achieving the picture of success are:

*

*

*

The challenges I/we face and the strategies for tackling these are:

*

*

*

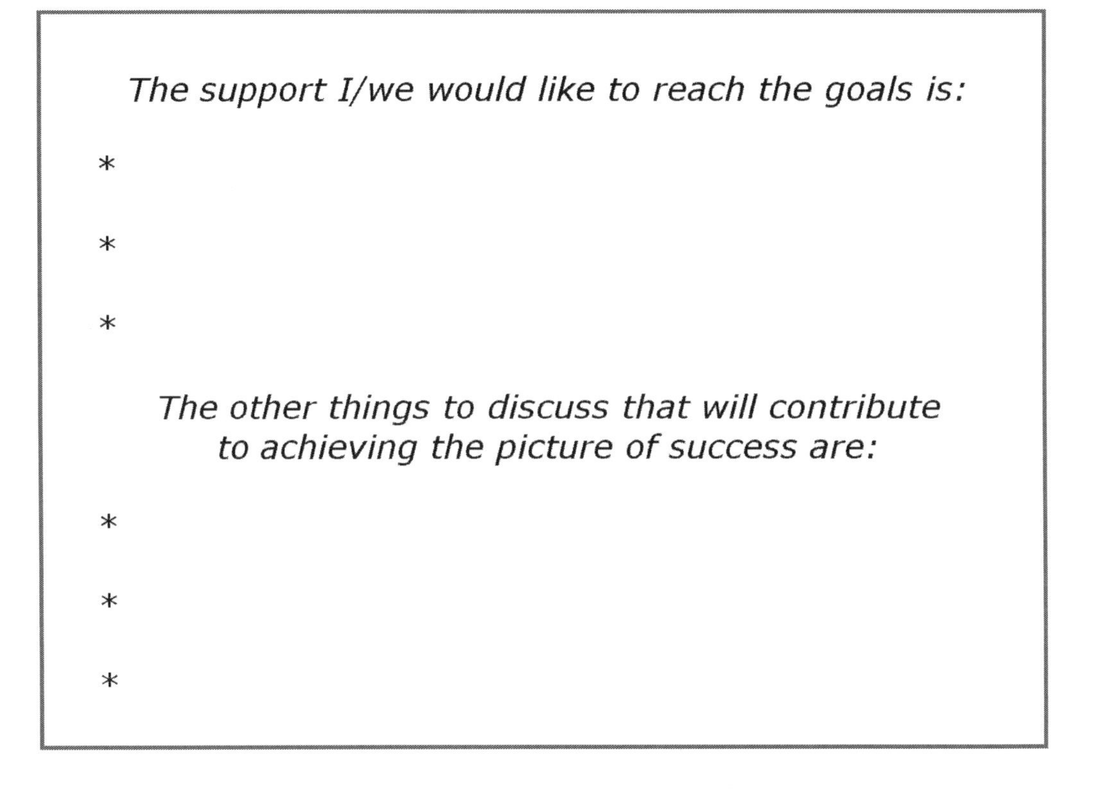

The support I/we would like to reach the goals is:

*

*

*

The other things to discuss that will contribute to achieving the picture of success are:

*

*

*

Starting from the work in Cleveland, AI has spread far and wide. Its philosophy has been translated into action in both the commercial and 'not-for-profit' sectors. The results have been outstanding.

Contribution to the strengths approach

AI has made an enormous contribution to the strengths philosophy. For example:

It has applied the strengths questions – such as revisiting one's best performances – to working with teams, organisations and communities.

It has enabled many thousands of people to build on their strengths, follow their successful principles and achieve their picture of success.

It has shown great generosity of spirit in the way it has shared the knowledge and tools with other people, particularly in vehicles such as the Appreciative

Inquiry Commons web site. This has enabled millions of people to access and apply the knowledge in their own ways.

David Cooperrider and his team started something special at the Cleveland Clinic. Appreciative Inquiry shows us how to build on our strengths, follow our successful principles and achieve our picture of success.

Marcus Buckingham

Marcus Buckingham has introduced literally millions of people to the strengths movement. His books include *Standout, Now, Discover Your Strengths* and *Go Put Your Strengths To Work.* He has reached people through his books, keynote speeches and appearances on television.

Say the word 'strengths' to most business people and they will associate it with Marcus. The first part of his career has been spent building this platform. The second part promises that he will deepen and expand what he calls 'the strengths revolution.'

Philosophy

Marcus grew up in England, went to Cambridge University and joined the Gallup Organization. He spent over a decade researching organisations before gaining international recognition with *First, Break All The Rules*, co-authored with Curt Coffman.

This book focused on employee engagement and described the habits of great managers. As the title suggests, it challenged the prevailing 'rules' regarding how to encourage people to perform outstanding work.

The Gallup Q12

The book explores what became known as the Gallup Q12. These are twelve 12 questions that measure employer engagement. Employees give ratings regarding statements such as:

> *"I know what is expected of me at work ... At work, I have the opportunity to do what I do best every day ... There is someone at work who cares about my development ... The mission or purpose of my company makes me feel my job is important ... My associates or fellow workers are committed to doing quality work ..."*

The research did more than measure overall organisational culture: it revealed that there were 'cultures within cultures'. It also highlighted managers who achieved outstanding results both on the 'bottom-line' and in relation to the questionnaire.

The research showed 'Four Keys' continually displayed by great managers. These were:

They select for talent – not simply experience or intelligence.

They excel at the art of interviewing. They are able to see recurring patterns that show where the person delivers.

They define the right outcomes – not the right steps.

They are crystal clear on the 'What', but give people freedom, within parameters, on the 'How'.

They focus on strengths – not weaknesses.

They encourage people to do what they do best and manage around their weaknesses.

They help employees to find the right fit – not simply the next rung up the ladder.

Casting is crucial. It must be a win for the person and a win for the organisation.

Curt and Marcus expanded on these themes, describing how the best managers got high ratings on the Q12. The companies that scored highest were those where people gave a high rating to the statement:

> *"At work, I have the opportunity to do what I do best every day."*

This laid the groundwork for the next book.

Now, Discover Your Strengths

Now, Discover Your Strengths was co-written with Don Clifton, the originator of *StrengthsFinder.* Based on massive research, the book describes the characteristics of great performers.

Readers were also introduced to the *StrengthsFinder* tool, which covers 34 recurring talent themes. People can do an on-line analysis that highlights their top five 'signature themes'.

The book was well received. People were taken aback to discover that in some companies less than 20% of the employees felt 'they had an opportunity to do what they did best each day'.

Marcus focused on leadership in his next book *The One Thing You Need To Know.* During this period he also moved on from Gallup to set up his own company.

He then returned to his main theme in what many see as his most practical book *Go Put Your Strengths To Work.* This went into great depths about how people could apply their strengths. Since then he has produced a book and assessment tool called *StandOut*. This helps people to focus more on their specific strengths and best contribution to work.

Principles

Marcus has communicated the strengths approach in ways that have reached millions of people. Here are some of the themes he continues to express in his books, seminars and media appearances.

Everyone has unique strengths.

Everyone can find and use their strengths.

Everyone wins when people play to their strengths.

The final theme provides one of his most compelling arguments, especially to businesses. People obviously feel better when they use their strengths. They are more likely to get positive energy and gain a sense of fulfilment.

When it comes to teamwork, it is vital to harness people's talents. Few would succeed if, for example, less than a quarter of their people felt fully engaged in their work: but this is a percentage common in organisations.

Marcus and his colleagues maintain that building on strengths is more likely to produce engagement. This can benefit everybody: ourselves, our children, our schools, our work places and our societies.

Contribution to the strengths approach

Marcus has made an enormous contribution to the strengths philosophy. For example:

He has introduced the concept of strengths to millions of people.

He has begun developing and spreading a system that may well enable more people to build on their strengths.

He has shown how building on strengths can benefit individuals, schools, teams, organisations and societies.

Marcus continues with his research, writing and speaking. Whatever he does in the future, he has already had a great impact on the way people think about strengths.

Dr Peter L. Benson

Dr Peter Benson had a profound influence on the way many people encourage children, teenagers and adults. He and his colleagues at Search Institute®, for example, focused on the times that children came alive. Much of his work was around the theme of 'Sparks'. He wrote:

> *"A spark is something that gives your life meaning and purpose. It's an interest, a passion, or a gift."*

Children want to be known for their sparks, said Peter. When you see these sparks, then affirm them. He maintained that:

> *"You shall know them by their sparks."*

So let's explore the work done by Peter and Search Institute. You can discover more at their official website: *http://www.search-institute.org*

Philosophy

Peter looked for the good in everybody and everything. Whilst being a rigorous researcher, he conveyed his findings about people in a compassionate and inspiring way.

Joining Search Institute in 1985, he played a key part in pioneering Positive Youth Development programmes in the United States and across the world. Peter and his colleagues at the Institute focused on children's Sparks. What does this mean? Here is an extract from the Institute's web site.

> *Sparks are the hidden flames in kids that excite them and tap into their true passions.*
>
> *Sparks come from the gut. They motivate and inspire. They're authentic passions, talents, assets, skills, and dreams.*
>
> *Sparks can be musical, athletic, intellectual, academic, or relational; from playing the violin to working with kids or senior citizens.*
>
> *Sparks can ignite a lifelong vocation or career, or balance other activities to create an emotionally satisfying, enriched life.*
>
> *Sparks get kids going on a positive path, away from the conflicts and negative issues – violence, promiscuity, drugs, and alcohol – that give teens a bad name and attract so much negative energy.*

Principles

Peter and his colleagues at Search Institute developed ways to encourage these drives. Here are some of the principles they have followed.

People have Sparks.

Search Institute did research with American teenagers. Here is a list of what were found to be the ten most common sparks. These were the activities and areas in which young people felt most alive, joyful and inspired.

Creative Arts
Athletics
Learning (e.g., languages, science, history)
Reading
Helping, serving
Spirituality, religion
Nature, ecology, environment
Living a quality life (e.g., joy, tolerance, caring)
Animal welfare
Leading

Peter and his colleagues produced many books, materials, courses and other tools that focused on how to enable people to find their sparks.

"That sounds fine," somebody may say, "but what do you do after you have found somebody's sparks?" This takes us to the next principle.

People can grow with the help of Developmental Assets®.

People can take responsibility for shaping their lives, but they can also be helped by getting support. After surveying over 2 million young people in the United States, Search Institute discovered 40 key factors that enabled young people to thrive. These became known as Developmental Assets.

Search Institute has identified these assets, which it describes as the 'building blocks of healthy development. These factors are sorted into External Assets and Internal Assets.

Some assets are needed at every stage of development, whilst some are specific to particular ages. Below is an overview of the assets that enable young people aged 12 to 18 to grow. More details about these can be found on the Institute's web site.

External Assets

* *Support.*

* *Empowerment.*

* *Boundaries and Expectations.*

* *Constructive Use of Time.*

Internal Assets

* *Commitment To Learning.*

* *Positive Values.*

* *Social Competencies.*

* *Positive Identity.*

What percentage of young people benefit from these assets? Search Institute says:

> *"The Gap – The average young person experiences fewer than half of the 40 assets. Boys experience three fewer assets than girls (17.2 assets for boys vs. 19.9 for girls)."*

Bearing this in mind, Search Institute has produced many resources, trainings, materials, programmes that enable parents, teachers, schools, youth organisations and communities to provide these assets for young people.

People can Thrive.

Peter and his colleagues believed it was important to begin developing a different definition of health. They focused on the idea of 'Thriving'. This means feeling fully alive, happy and, hopefully, giving to others.

Search Institute has identified indicators of Thriving. This provides a different definition of success – for individuals, communities and societies.

Contribution To The Strengths Approach

Peter's philosophy can be seen in many elements of the strengths approach. Working together with his colleagues at Search Institute, for example:

He encouraged people to focus on Sparks.

He produced many books, practical tools and programmes that encouraged people to grow by focusing on Developmental Assets.

He encouraged individuals, parents, schools, communities and societies to focus on enabling people to Thrive.

Peter died at the age of 65 in 2011. Announcing his passing under the title of *Remembering A Life Well Lived*, Search Institute described him as:

"An inspiring leader who devoted his own life to making the world a better place for families, schools and communities."

Martin Seligman

Photo by Daniel Burke Photography

Martin Seligman was born in 1942 in the USA. He is acknowledged as one of the great figures of the modern positive psychology movement. He has written several best-selling books, such as *Learned Optimism, Authentic Happiness, Flourish* and *Character Strengths and Virtues,* the latter co-written with Christopher Peterson.

Philosophy

Marty – as he is known – says he spent the first part of his psychological career studying misery. Partly this was because psychology adopted a 'disease model'. It identified how people went wrong and tried to correct these failures. Partly it was because the funding for psychologists was mainly based around treating those labelled 'sick'.

He says that psychology now has many ways of helping people to overcome such challenges. But many of our institutions continue to encourage people to become passive and adopt the role of 'victims'.

Bearing this in mind, Marty moved on from treating 'learned helplessness' to studying 'learned optimism'. He asked questions such as:

> *"Who never gets helpless? Who resists collapsing?"*

Such people focused on what they could control and saw setbacks as temporary. They had a positive outlook, saw possibilities – whilst also being realistic – and proactively took charge of shaping their lives.

Studying optimism was rewarding, but Marty then passed over a threshold after being elected president of the American Psychological Association.

He was asked to pick the 'themes' he wanted to work on during his Presidency. After a period of reflection, he chose to focus on positive psychology.

Marty decided to make this his life mission. He defined this as:

> *"My aim is that psychology and maybe psychiatry will increase the tonnage of happiness in the world."*

This led to him and several colleagues founding The Positive Psychology Center. Here is a summary of the introduction to their web site.

> *Positive Psychology is the scientific study of the strengths and virtues that enable individuals and communities to thrive. The Positive Psychology Center promotes research, training, education, and the dissemination of Positive Psychology.*
>
> *This field is founded on the belief that people want to lead meaningful and fulfilling lives, to cultivate what is best within themselves, and to enhance their experiences of love, work, and play.*
>
> *The Center focuses on the scientific study of three key themes.*

Positive emotions.

This entails the study of positive emotions. It covers contentment with the past, happiness in the present, and hope for the future.

Positive individual traits.

This entails the understanding of positive individual traits. It consists of the study of the virtues and strengths, such as the capacity for love and work, courage, compassion, resilience, creativity, curiosity, integrity, self-knowledge, moderation, self-control, and wisdom.

Positive institutions.

This entails the study of positive institutions. It covers the study of the strengths that foster better communities, such as justice, responsibility, civility, parenting, nurturance, work ethic, leadership, teamwork, purpose, and tolerance.

Principles

Marty believes the word 'happiness' does not do full justice to the study of enriching lives, but it does provide a useful label. More recently he has moved to the concept of people living Flourishing Lives.

Looking back, however, here are some of the principles highlighted by him and his colleagues.

It is possible to study three kinds of lives that bring happiness.

"What's workable within happiness are three different kinds of lives," says Marty.

Happiness:

Three kinds of lives that can bring happiness

* *The Pleasant Life.*

  This is the 'life of enjoyment'. It is one where people get positive feelings from pursuing their interests and other pleasurable experiences.

* *The Good Life.*

  This is the 'life of engagement' or absorption. It is one where people immerse themselves in certain activities and experience a state of flow. This happens when there is a positive match between a person's strength and the task they are doing.

* *The Meaningful Life.*

  This is the 'life of affiliation'. It is one where people experience a sense of purpose by using their higher strengths to serve or be part of something greater than themselves.

The first is the pleasant life. This consists of doing the things that give you enjoyment and pleasure. People can keep doing these things but, like taking scoop after scoop of ice cream, there may be a limit to the pleasure.

The second is the good life. This consists of knowing your highest strengths and re-crafting your life to use them more.

"What you get out of that is not the propensity to giggle a lot," says Marty. "What you get is flow, and the more you deploy your highest strengths the more flow you get in life."

The third is the meaningful life. This consists of again using your highest strengths – but employing these to serve something bigger than yourself.

So what is the magic combination? Looking at it empirically, says Marty, the fulfilling life appears to be: The Meaningful Life + The Good Life + some aspects of The Pleasant Life. In that order.

It is possible to identify people's virtues and character strengths.

Marty and his fellow researchers looked across 70 nations and various cultures to define what they see as 'human virtues' and character strengths. He says:

> *"When we look we see that there are six virtues, which we find endorsed across cultures, and these break down into 24 strengths.*
>
> *"The six virtues that we find are non-arbitrary – first, a wisdom and knowledge cluster; second, a courage cluster; third, virtues like love and humanity; fourth, a justice cluster; fifth a temperance, moderation cluster; and sixth a spirituality, transcendence cluster.*
>
> *"Indeed, we're beginning to have the view that those six virtues are just as much a part of human nature as walking on two feet are."*

As mentioned earlier, within each virtue there are a cluster of strengths. Christopher Peterson and Marty then published their book, *Character Strengths and Virtues,* which provides a complete picture of these qualities.

Virtues

The 6 virtues and
24 character strengths are:

1) *Wisdom and Knowledge:*

   creativity, curiosity, open-mindedness, love of learning, perspective.

2) *Courage:*

   bravery, persistence, integrity, vitality.

3) *Humanity:*

   love, kindness, social intelligence.

4) *Justice:*

   citizenship, fairness, leadership.

5) *Temperance:*

   forgiveness and mercy, humility, prudence, self-control.

6) *Transcendence:*

   appreciation of beauty and excellence, gratitude, hope, humour, spirituality.

It is possible to make positive interventions that people can use to develop their happiness.

Marty and his fellow practitioners aim to go beyond collecting data. They aim to use the research to:

> *"Work to increase positive emotion and positive traits."*

This has resulted in building-up a body of coaching materials that can be used to enhance people's happiness.

The Positive Psychology Center, for example, runs many coaching programmes designed to improve happiness. Marty himself has conducted a 6-month twice-a-week course. This is aimed at coaches, clinical psychologists, teachers, professors, social workers and parents.

Marty believes the adventure has only just started, however, and the interventions need more testing – complete with placebos and comparative measurement.

Contribution to the strengths approach

He is one of the great figures behind the spread of the positive psychology, which includes elements of the strengths approach. For example:

> *He has put positive psychology on the map and popularised strengths with his best-selling books.*
>
> *He has promoted rigorous research that has focused on areas such as Happiness, Character Strengths and Virtues, and living a Flourishing Life.*
>
> *He and his colleagues have shown it is possible to make positive interventions that enable people to improve their happiness.*

The Positive Psychology Movement

There is a strong link between the strengths approach and aspects of Positive Psychology. At the moment, however, Positive Psychology covers a much wider field. It focuses on topics such as human virtues, happiness and how people live flourishing lives.

As mentioned earlier, Martin Seligman's work led to creating the Positive Psychology Center at The University of Pennsylvania. The Center says:

> *Positive Psychology is the scientific study of the strengths and virtues that enable individuals and communities to thrive.*

Christopher Peterson, a key figure in the movement, writes:

> *Positive psychology is the scientific study of what goes right in life, from birth to death and at all stops in between.*

Senia Maymin, Publisher and Editor-in-Chief of Positive Psychology News Daily, writes:

> *Positive Psychology studies what is right with people and how people live the good life.*

There are many themes that are studied under the umbrella of Positive Psychology. These include, for example:

* *Happiness.*

* *Hope.*

* *Positive Experiences in Teams, Organisations and Society.*

* *Character Strengths and Virtues.*

This is obviously a broad church. But one key theme runs through each of the topics. *Positive Psychology* ***is the scientific study*** of what people do right to live healthy, happy and fulfilling lives. So let's explore some of these themes.

Happiness

Many researchers have explored this topic. This has led to many popular books being produced by people such as Martin Seligman, Ed Diener, Robert Biswas-Diener, Sonja Lyubomirsky and Tal Ben-Shahar.

Positive psychologists recognise that people have studied these themes for centuries. The Ancient Greeks, for example, studied how to follow certain virtues and live in a state of *eudaimonia*.

There are, however, many different definitions for this state. These cover themes such as following one's spirit, flourishing and, as a result, experiencing health and happiness.

Christopher Peterson has also pointed out that many Eastern spiritual leaders, such as Confucius and Lao-Tsu, focused on the importance of living in harmony with one's spirit, nature and serving a greater calling. This could also result in a state of peace or happiness.

We have already looked at the work on Martin Seligman, so let's explore that of other authors.

Ed Diener and Robert Biswas-Diener

Ed is the Joseph R. Smiley Distinguished Professor of Psychology at the University of Illinois in Urbana-Champaign. He is also a senior scientist for the Gallup Organization. His research focuses on happiness and well-being. This includes the following themes:

* *The measurement of well-being.*

* *The temperament and personality influences on well-being.*

* *The theories of well-being.*

* *The impact of income on well-being.*

* *The cultural influences on well-being.*

Ed is the co-author of a well-known questionnaire that people can use to measure their life satisfaction. He has made this publicly available and it was used, for example, during the BBC Television series *The Happiness Formula.*

Robert Biswas-Diener is a key figure in the positive psychology movement. An inveterate traveller, he has researched well-being around the globe. He is a gifted story teller who brings this work to life. For example, he talks about researching happiness with:

* *Victims of land mine explosions in Cambodia.*

* *Refugees in Bangladesh.*

* *Maasai tribes in Kenya.*

* *Inuit people in Greenland.*

* *Homeless people around the world.*

Building on this rich resource, he collaborated with his father, Ed Diener, to publish *Happiness: Unlocking the mysteries of psychological wealth.*

They say that, while many cultures across the globe seem different, virtually all people prize happiness.

Interviewed about their book on various talk shows, the authors were often asked: "So how can people be happy?" Robert and Ed outlined some of the common principles.

We can enjoy happiness by having enriching relationships.

It is good to have people we care about and who care about us.

We can have a positive attitude to life.

It is helpful to practise gratitude, to savour the happy times and to extend these by remembering them.

We can have realistic expectations about emotions.

It is a reality that sometimes we will not be happy, but that is part of life's tapestry.

We can do work that gives us a sense of meaning.

It is good if we can do fulfilling work. This provides a sense of purpose and stimulation each day.

We can do simple things to increase our happiness.

It is quite possible to get a boost by doing simple things like exercising, helping others or 'waking up' – practicing mindfulness – to enjoy the moment.

We can see happiness as a process, rather than a destination.

It is about enjoying the journey as much as the prize. Paradoxically, this can increase our happiness.

Robert and Ed underline one key point. *The things we pay attention to affect our emotions.*

If we focus on positive things, then this can affect our system in a healthy way. If we constantly listen to bad news, this can have a debilitating effect.

Nobody is suggesting we go into denial. People prefer to have hope and positive solutions, however, rather than a constant diet of problems.

Robert has authored several books on Positive Psychology Coaching and done a great deal of work on strengths. He sees using these talents as sometimes providing a 'back door' to happiness. This led to him co-authoring *The Strengths Book,* which we will look at later.

Sonja Lyubomirsky

Sonja is a Professor at the University of California. She believes in studying happiness from a scientific basis, but also has the ability to get ideas across in everyday language. She describes her current research as focusing on three key areas:

What makes people happy?

Is happiness a good thing?

How and why can people learn to lead happier and more flourishing lives?

Writing on her official site, Sonja says:

> *"My empirical findings over the years have revealed that chronically happy and unhappy individuals differ systematically and in a manner supportive of their differing temperaments in the particular cognitive and motivational strategies they use.*
>
> *"For example, my students and I have found that truly happy individuals construe life events and daily situations in ways that seem to maintain their happiness, while unhappy individuals construe experiences in ways that seem to reinforce unhappiness.*
>
> *"In essence, our research shows that happy individuals experience and react to events and circumstances in relatively more positive and more adaptive ways."*

The Benefits of Happiness

Sonja asks if being happy simply leads to feeling good or does it have other benefits? She and her students have found it has many benefits for individuals, families, communities and the wider society. These include:

> *Higher income and superior work outcomes. For example, greater productivity and higher quality of work.*
>
> *Larger social rewards. For example, satisfying and longer marriages, more friends, stronger social support and richer social interactions.*
>
> *More activity, energy, and flow, and better physical health. For example, a bolstered immune system, lowered stress levels, and less pain. It can also lead to a longer life.*

The How of Happiness

So how do people become happy? And how can they maintain happiness?

Sonja's book on this topic has on its cover a Cherry Pie with a 40% slice cut ready to eat. This highlights the research done on individual happiness, which often falls into the following percentages.

50% is influenced by our Character – our Genes.

10% is influenced by our Circumstances.

40% is within our Control.

How To Increase Happiness

Sonja is frequently asked how people can increase their happiness. She often answers by saying that she is a scientist and tends to avoid self-help books.

Nevertheless, she says, the research seems to show that some of the 'corny' advice that Grandma gave may well be true. These include some of the following activities.

Gratitude.

Regularly setting aside time to count one's blessings. Other researcher's studies of individuals who set aside half an hour a day to count their blessings show that such people increase and maintain their happiness.

Kindness.

Being kind to others. The act of giving to others creates a good feeling in both oneself and, hopefully, in others. This creates a positive circle in one's life.

Positive Attitude.

Developing positive scripts. Reflecting on positive experiences, recalling times of overcoming difficulties, talking to oneself in a positive way regarding future opportunities.

Sonja and her students are also looking at the following themes regarding increasing one's happiness.

Life Goals.

Listing and taking action on 'baby steps' towards these goals.

Forgiveness.

Forgiving people in one's life, but not at the expense of becoming a victim.

Savouring Positive Experiences.

Such as using one's five senses to relish daily moments.

Using one's Signature Strengths in New Ways.

Continuing to develop doing the things one does best.

Sonja continues to study happiness in a scientific way and spread the knowledge to wider audiences.

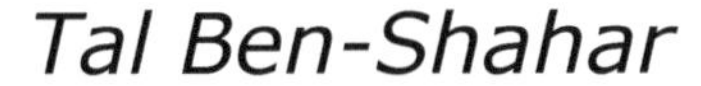

Tal came to prominence in America when the *How To Be Happy* course he taught at Harvard University attracted over 800 students. The programme the taught aimed:

To provide an introduction to the research in the field of happiness.

To provide practical ways the students can apply these ideas in their lives and communities.

Backed by scientific research, Tal aims to: "Provide the bridge between the Ivory Tower and the Main Street". Once all the academic research is reviewed, however, how can people be happier?

Like other researchers, Tal says some of the messages can sound obvious, but the secret is in actually translating these into action. Here are some of the messages.

Accept painful emotions.

These are part of being alive. The only people who don't feel pain are psychopaths and those who are dead.

Spend time with people you care about.

This quality time is enjoyable and also gives us energy to do other things.

Enjoy 'time affluence'.

Appreciate life and the specific thing you are doing. Enjoy the moments, rather than try to do several things at once.

Simplify your life.

This makes it easier to appreciate life. At the moment we are trying to cram more into our days.

Exercise.

This is equivalent to some of the most powerful drugs that deal with depression or anxiety.

Breathe.

Learning to breathe deeply and properly can improve our sense of well-being.

Cultivate gratitude.

Research shows that people who keep a Gratitude Journal are more positive, says Tal. This involves spending a few minutes each night writing down five things for which they are grateful. Such a simple exercise increases their optimism and even their health.

Barbara Fredrickson and Positivity

Positivity

People who have positive emotions in a ratio of 3:1 in relation to negative emotions are more likely to flourish.

Barbara Fredrickson has done pioneering work that demonstrates how developing positive emotions can improve our lives. Twenty years of research into emotions culminated in her book *Positivity.*

The book was based on solid research, but it also captured the imagination. Why? Interviewers and readers focused on a key theme that provided a signpost to the future. This was:

> *People who have positive emotions in a ratio of 3:1 in relation to negative emotions are more likely to flourish.*

Barbara believes in humanity's ability to shape a successful future, but she is a scientist, rather than a self-help guru. Her work is based on rigorous interviewing and testing. She says:

> *"As a scientist, accepting things on faith – or on mere hints within the data – is not in my bones. My mission is to unearth, test and then share the hidden value of positivity."*

What is Positivity?

Writing in her book, Barbara explains that positivity is more than simply being happy. And it certainly isn't putting on a smiling face to grin and bear things.

Positivity is based on being true to ourselves. It embodies gratitude, love, playfulness, curiosity and adventure. These emotions trigger each other and create an upward spiral. They 'broaden and build', helping us to make breakthroughs and bring new things into being.

Such emotions provide the basis for creativity, problem solving and even evolution. They enable us to open our hearts and minds. Negativity, on the other hand, closes down our ability to think, create and grow. Barbara explains that:

> *"(Positivity) consists of the whole range of positive emotions – from appreciation to love, from amusement to joy, from hope to gratitude, and then some.*

"The term is purposely broad. It includes the positive meanings and optimistic attitudes that trigger positive emotions as well as the open minds, tender hearts, relaxed limbs, and soft faces they usher in.

"It even includes the long-term impact that positive emotions have on your character, relationships, communities and environments."

The Ratio 3:1 – Where Does That Come From?

Barbara says the ratio came about via an introduction from her good friend, Jane Dutton, a Professor at Michigan's Ross School of Business. She describes Jane as 'matchmaker' who connects people with unrelated ideas.

Jane saw the connection between Barbara's work and that of Marcial Losada, who was born and raised in Chile. Marcial was in an unrelated field, that of industry and consulting. Barbara records, however, that he was pursuing his passion for the mathematical modelling of group behaviour.

When they eventually met Marcial described his work studying 60 business teams. These consisted of high, mixed and low performing teams. Barbara takes up the story:

"High-performance teams stood out with their unusually high positivity ratios, at about 6 to 1. By contrast, low-performance teams had ratios well below 1 to 1, and mixed-performance teams sat just above that, at around 2 to 1."

Barbara explains that Marcial analysed the numbers and eventually:

"Losada's maths led to his brave prediction that only when positivity ratios are higher than 3 to 1 is positivity in sufficient supply to seed human flourishing."

She explains that the ratio was in fact 2.9013 to 1, but 3 seemed an easier number. She began to test this by asking people to fill in a Positivity Test each day. She found:

"The consistency here is extraordinary. For individuals, marriages and business teams, flourishing – doing remarkably well – comes with positivity ratios above 3 to 1.

"By contrast, those who don't overcome their depression, couples who fail in their marriages, and business teams that are unpopular and unprofitable each have ratios in the gutter, below 1 to 1."

People Can Raise Their Positivity Ratio

So how do you raise your positivity and reach the tipping point? Barbara maintains it is a lot like physical health. If we eat good food this helps to nourish us. We also need a daily diet of psychological health. This forms the basis of her Broaden and Build Theory.

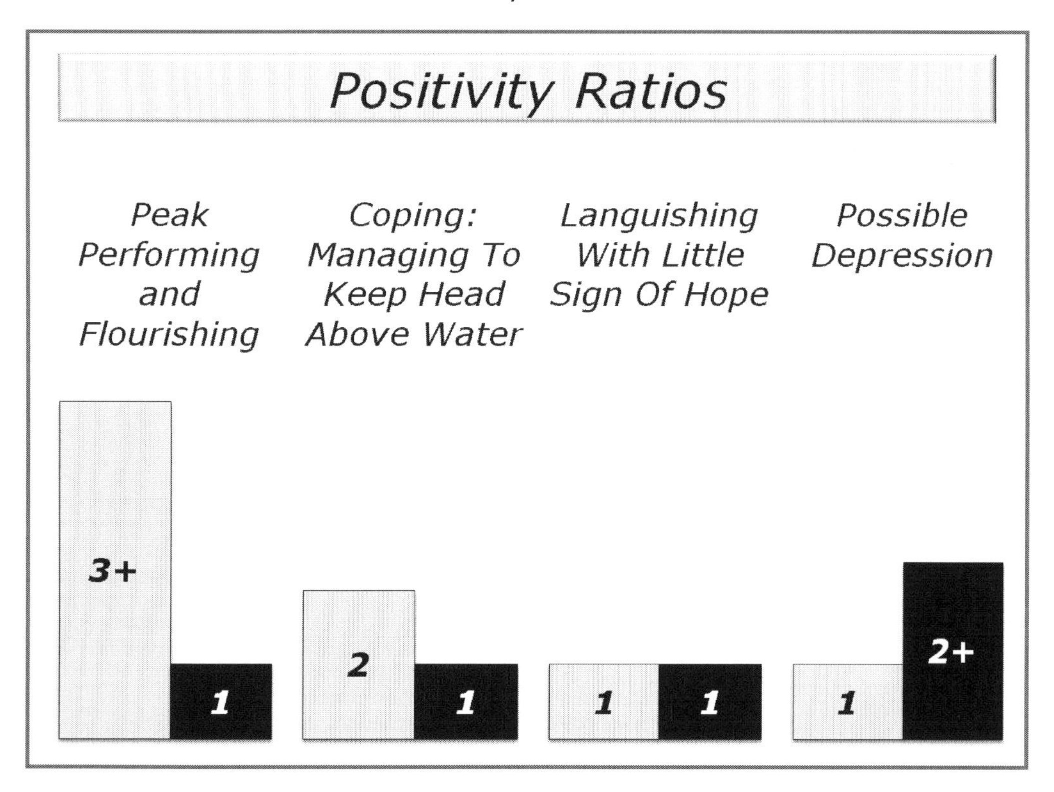

It is like putting ourselves on a diet of healthy food. If we eat just one meal of healthy food, we will not see an immediate difference. If we make this a daily habit, however, eventually the healthy food will change our system.

The same approach applies to positivity. Broadening and building the positive things we do – and expose ourselves to – will increase our sense of well-being. Similarly, it will also give use strength to find solutions to challenges.

Barbara lists ten forms of positivity that can nourish our soul. These will be familiar to readers who have studied the characteristics of those who enjoy a sense of happiness.

Ten Forms of Positivity

* *Joy.*
* *Serenity.*
* *Hope.*
* *Amusement.*
* *Awe.*
* *Gratitude.*
* *Interest.*
* *A Sense of Pride.*
* *Inspiration.*
* *Love.*

People can do simple things that embody some of these qualities. Eventually they will accumulate enough positivity that creates an upward spiral. This can take them beyond the tipping point.

So it can be useful to develop habits that embrace some of the following forms of positivity.

These are big words, but they can be broken down into small actions. Such habits then feed our development. As Barbara says, the aim is: "To increase your quantity of positivity over time." This is based on two core truths. She explains these in the following way.

> *Positivity opens us. The first core truth about positive emotions is that they open our hearts and our minds, making us more receptive and more creative.*
>
> *Positivity transforms us for the better. This is the second core truth about positive emotions. By opening our hearts and minds, positive emotions allow us to discover and build new skills, new ties, new knowledge, and new ways of being.*

Mihaly Csikszentmihalyi, the author of *Flow,* highlighted Barbara's contribution in the following review of *Positivity.*

> *"Written by one of the most influential contributors to this new perspective in science, Positivity provides a wonderful synthesis of what positive psychology has accomplished in the first decade of its existence ... It is full of deep insights about human behaviour as well as useful suggestions for how to apply them in everyday life."*

Alex Linley

Alex Linley is the Founding Director of Capp – the Centre of Applied Positive Psychology. He is an expert on positive psychology and helping people to find their strengths. His books include *Average To A+* and *The Strengths Book.* He has also been instrumental in developing and validating many tools for strengths assessment, such as the Capp tool called Realise2.

Alex has taken the strengths philosophy out into the wider society. He wrote the business case that helped launch the National Talent Bank, an initiative of the Council on Social Action, chaired by the Prime Minister, and launched at Downing Street in July 2009.

He subsequently served as a member of the Steering Committee for the National Talent Bank from 2009-2010. In 2011, he was appointed as a member of the Expert Group supporting the charity *Action for Happiness*.

The Strengths Book is the product of a decade of research into strengths by the team at Capp and is written by Alex, Janet Willars and Robert Biswas-Diener. The book is divided into three parts:

Part 1

This presents five character case studies. These show how the Realise2 model of strengths has been used by different people to achieve success. It also includes Alex's *Top Ten Strengthspotting Tips* and the empirical evidence base for strengths.

Part 2

This introduces the Realise2 model. The model is built on the three elements of energy, performance and use. These are core to defining a strength, which is:

> *A strength is something that energises us, that we are good at, and that we use (at least to some extent).*

Part 3

This provides the strengths library for each of the 60 strengths in Realise2. It includes:

A definition and catchphrase for each strength.

A case example of someone who has the strength.

A Hall of Fame of famous people who demonstrated the strength.

Advice about the strength in relation to leisure, careers and relationships.

Advice about the strength being overplayed.

Alex continues to be a pioneer in the field of applied positive psychology. His leading strengths are *Legacy, Catalyst, Innovation* and *Strategic Awareness.* He continues to express these in pursuing the Capp purpose of *Strengthening the World*.

Paul Brewerton and James Brook

Many other people are doing superb work with strengths. Paul Brewerton and James Brook, for example, have created a tool called *Strengthscope360™*, which also incorporates an optional 360 feedback function. This helps people to understand:

Their personality and performance strengths.

The tasks and activities that are most likely to energise them and lead to high levels of engagement.

The likely consequences of using their strengths too much, too little or in a way that isn't appropriate for the situation.

The extent to which they apply they strengths optimally in the way they approach their work.

The visibility of their strengths to co-workers and key stakeholders.

Paul and James have also produced the book *Strengths For Success – Your Pathway To Peak Performances.* This provides excellent exercises that enable people to build on their strengths.

C.R. Snyder and Hope

C.R. Snyder explored many areas of positive psychology, but he is renowned for his work on hope. He authored or co-authored books such as *The Psychology of Hope* and *Making Hope Happen.*

Ricky, as he was known, spent much of his academic career at The University of Kansas. Describing himself as a 'greying and absent-minded professor', he also had a gift for translating academic research into practice.

One example is *The Hope Scale,* which is an exercise that people can use to measure their present level of hope. The Hope Scale invites a person to measure two things.

* *Their Will Power.*

This is their will to shape their future.

* *Their Way Power.*

This is their ability to see ways to shape their future.

Ricky died in 2006, but he left an inspiring legacy. He provided practical tools that people could use to develop both their will power and way power. He helped many people to increase their sense of hope.

The Positive Psychology Movement – Some Headlines

Positive psychology continues to research how people can experience a sense of happiness and fulfilment in their lives and work. The strengths approach starts by inviting people to clarify their aims. So it can be useful to know the common themes that emerge regarding people who live happy lives.

Here is an overview of those themes that have been highlighted by the positive psychology movement. These can be explored in greater detail, of course, but they can be worth remembering when helping people to set their personal or professional goals.

Characteristics of happy people

* *Gratitude*

- *Being humble and having a sense of gratitude.*
- *Counting their blessings, rather than counting their burdens.*

* *Positivity*

- *Choosing to have a positive attitude.*
- *Giving and getting positive energy.*

* *Encouragement*

- *Experiencing love and affirmation.*
- *Spending time with kindred spirits.*

* *Aliveness*

  - *Feeling fully alive.*

  - *Enjoying the moment with all their senses.*

* *Authenticity*

  - *Being true to themselves – but in a way that helps, rather than hurts, other people.*

  - *Following their values in their daily lives and work*

* *Purpose*

  - *Having a sense of purpose, following their vocation or serving something greater than themselves.*

  - *Seeing the connection between their daily actions and their long-term goals.*

* *Control*

  - *Focusing on what they can control and maintaining a sense of hope.*

  - *Organising and simplifying their lives.*

* *Creativity*

  - *Doing things that are stimulating and creative.*

  - *Continuing to learn and develop.*

* *Potential*

  - *Being the best they can be. Accepting who they are, rather than comparing themselves with others.*

  - *Building on their strengths and managing the consequences of their weaknesses.*

* *Peace*

    - *Enjoying a sense of peace.*

    - *Doing things that enable others to enjoy a sense of peace.*

* *Wisdom*

    - *Seeing the big picture and having perspective.*

    - *Knowing what works.*

* *Generosity*

    - *Being generous and helping others.*

    - *Encouraging future generations.*

The Peak Performance Approach

Charles Garfield encouraged people to learn from the times they and others had performed great work. The Sports Psychology movement also has a tradition of encouraging athletes to learn from their best performances. Sports psychologists frequently invite people to focus on:

The specific times they have performed brilliantly.

The specific things they did right then – the principles they followed – to perform brilliantly.

The specific things they can do to follow these principles – plus add other elements – to perform brilliantly in the future.

The strengths philosophy adopts a similar approach. It aims to study, simplify and share what works. During my early work with people, for example, it made sense to focus on what people did right:

To be happy and successful.

To build super teams.

To build superb organisations.

People achieved success by following certain strategies. Looking at these strategies, however, most were based on building on their strengths. People were operating from something organic within. They therefore found it natural to keep following certain habits, overcome setbacks and achieve their goals.

So what did people do right to achieve peak performance? Looking at these people, teams and organisations, I found that many took the following steps towards achieving their picture of success.

Peak Performers

Peak performers often take the following steps. They build on their strengths and manage the consequences of their weaknesses. They then:

* *Clarify their Picture of Success.*

* *Clarify the strategies and road map for achieving their Picture of Success.*

* *Clarify and do whatever is necessary to achieve their Picture of Success.*

At the time I was working with Recovery Programmes, such as running therapeutic communities. Later I ran 5 day programmes on strengths building for people from all walks of life. This led to working with sports psychology and, from the late 1970s onwards, aiming to help people to build super teams and superb organisations.

The sessions started by clarifying people's goals. The aim was then to pass on practical tools that people could use in their daily lives and work. It was to enable people to achieve ongoing success. This became the basis for the work I have done with strengths coaching.

Looking back on this chapter we have travelled from Heinrich Pestalozzi to Happiness and on to Peak Performance. There are, of course, many other people who have contributed to the strengths approach. These include, for example:

Dennis Saleeby with his focus on applying strengths in social work. He wrote *The Strengths Perspective in Social Work Practice.*

Jenifer Fox who focuses on strengths in education. She wrote *Your Child's Strengths.*

Jenny Eades Fox who works with educators and students in schools. She wrote *Celebrating Strengths.*

There have also been significant contributions by people in the fields of career development, coaching and mentoring. These include authors such as Richard Bolles, William Bridges, Barrie Hopson, Mike Scally, Katie Ledger, Nick Williams and Sue Moore, co-author of *Strengths Coaching in 90 Minutes.* Many others continue to add to the philosophy and principles.

Earlier we talked about education involving the whole person – the heart, head and hands. So how can strengths coaching put tools in people's hands that they can use to shape their futures? Let's explore some ways to make this happen.

Part 2

The Practice

Introduction

There are many approaches to strengths coaching. You will obviously have your own model.

Some coaches use various assessment tools to help people to build on their strengths. Some include ideas from Dependable Strengths and Appreciative Inquiry. Some employ principles from Humanistic Psychology, Existential Psychology, Positive Psychology or other approaches.

Looking at the various methods, however, it is possible to clarify some of the core principles that people focus on during the sessions. These often resemble the seven steps outlined in the illustration.

This is not to say that there is a certified 'Seven Step' model. The overview simply provides a guide to some elements that may be covered in the various approaches to strengths coaching.

For example, I always start by clarifying people's picture of success and their strengths. Depending on the situation they face, we then focus on the most appropriate steps. The goal is to enable people to achieve success.

Here is an introduction to the steps. We will be exploring these in greater detail in the chapters on helping individuals, teams and organisations to achieve their goals.

Strengths Coaching

Start by setting the scene and clarifying people's picture of success. You can then help individuals, teams and organisations to take the following steps towards achieving their goals. They can focus on their:

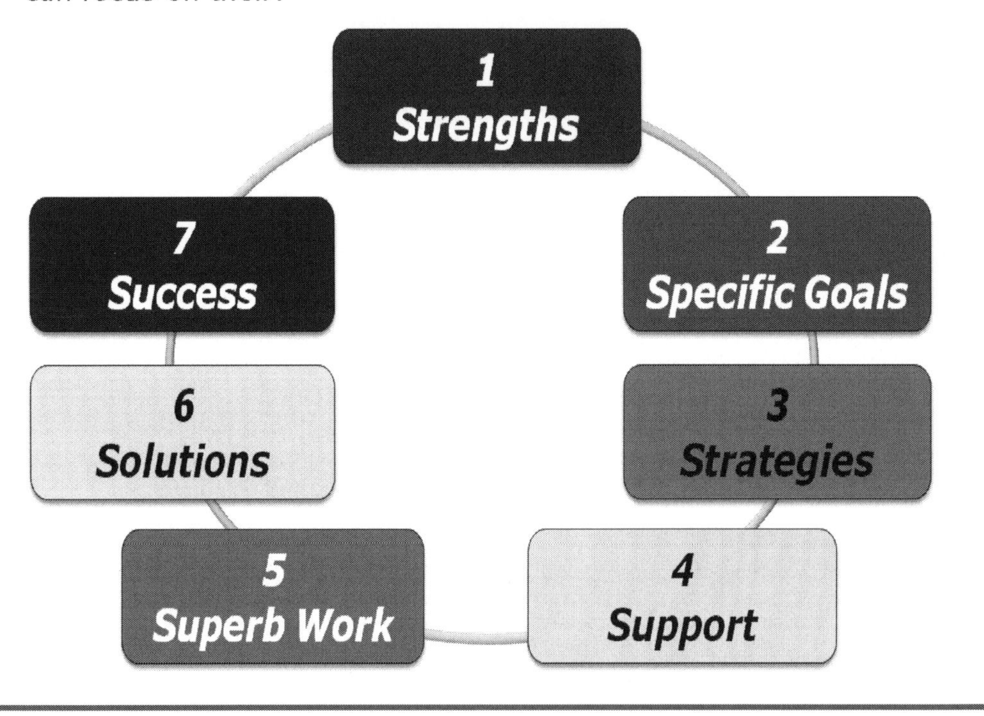

Setting The Scene

This involves creating an encouraging environment and clarifying people's picture of success. It also involves making clear working contracts on how the coach and the people involved will work together to achieve the goals.

Strengths

This involves focusing on people's strengths and successful style. It then looks at how they can use these to achieve their goals.

Specific Goals

This involves focusing on people's specific goals on the road to achieving their overall picture of success.

Strategies

This involves focusing on the key strategies people can follow to give themselves the greatest chance of success.

Support

This involves focusing on the support people can gather to help them to achieve their goals.

Superb Work

This involves focusing on how people can do superb work and, where appropriate, provide great service to customers.

Solutions

This involves focusing on finding creative solutions to challenges and overcoming setbacks.

Success

This involves focusing on people doing whatever is required to achieve the picture of success.

Different coaches have different styles of coaching. They may concentrate on being results focused, being facilitative, providing practical tools or whatever.

If you are a coach, it can be useful to explain your style to the people with whom you are working. People will know what they can and can't expect from the sessions. It is then possible to make clear working contracts.

Good Coaches Practise the Art of Generosity

Great coaches are often similar to great educators. Such people practise the art of generosity. Generous people love to create an environment that encourages people and things to grow.

They love to pass on knowledge that helps others to succeed. They believe that learning must be personal – relevant to the person – practical and, in the widest sense, profitable. So they start by clarifying the learner's agenda.

Great educators focus on the 3 Is: inspiration, implementation and integration. They create an inspiring environment, provide implementation tools that work and help people to integrate the learning in their daily lives. They help learners to go through the stages on awareness, action and achievement.

Such educators often move from the 'concept' to the 'concrete'. They translate the principles into practical tools that people can use to achieve their goals. Great coaches often follow these steps in their own way. They encourage, educate and enable people to achieve ongoing success.

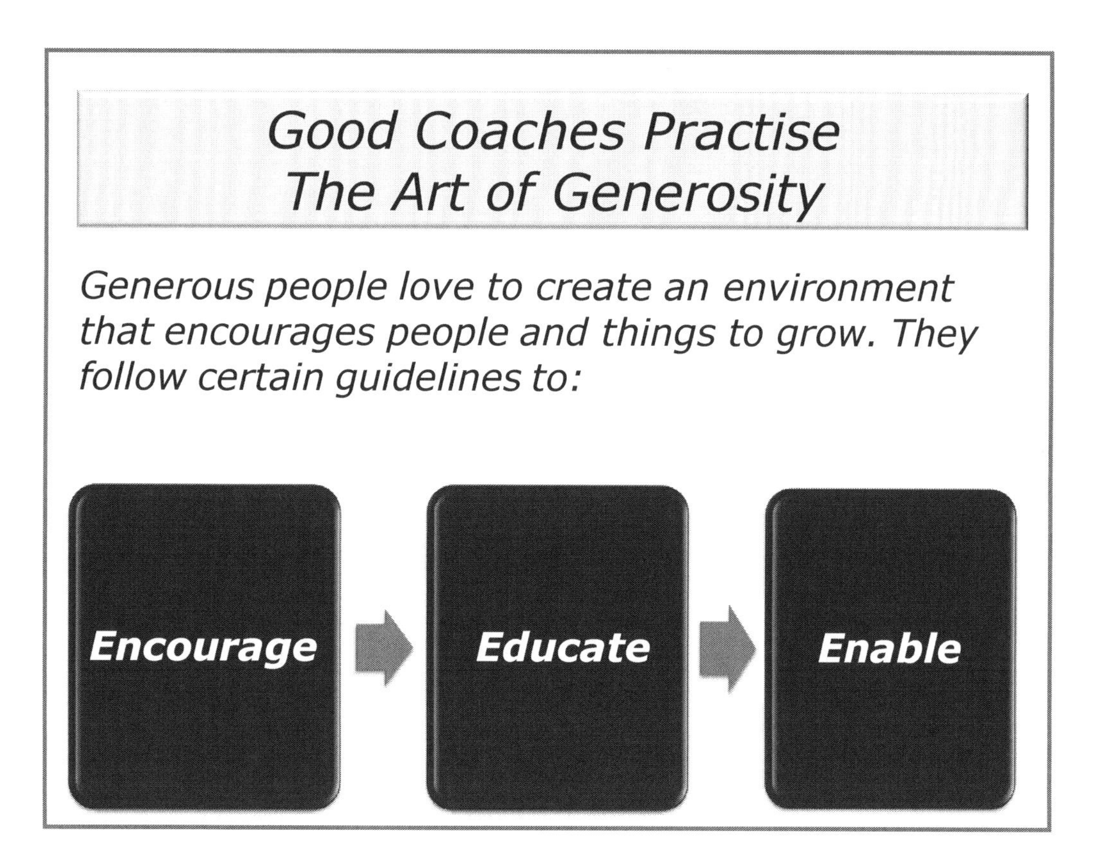

Let's move on to the actual work. The rest of the book focuses on how strengths coaching can help individuals, teams and organisations to achieve their goals. The first section focuses on working with individuals.

The Art of Helping People to Build on Their Strengths

This section focuses on helping individuals to build on their strengths and achieve their picture of success

Setting the Scene

–

Clarifying the Picture of Success

"Coaching is one of the best jobs in the world," said one of my mentors. "You get the chance to encourage people, but that is also a great responsibility. So do your best to enable them to achieve their aims."

Great coaches often create a stimulating sanctuary in which people feel able to explore challenges and focus on their future goals. You will do this in your own way, but let's consider some steps towards creating such an environment.

Imagine that you are going to meet somebody who may want you to work with them as a coach. You will have done your research and discovered more about:

The person's background, their specific goals and the challenges they may face.

The person's past successes, strengths and successful style.

The person's personality style – including the pluses and minuses of their style.

The person's passions – such as business, sports, the arts or whatever.

The person's philosophy – their beliefs – about how they think people achieve success.

"That sounds a lot," somebody may say. Maybe, but it is important to find out what you can ahead of the meeting. Sometimes you can find this information by asking around in a discreet way. Sometimes you may simply need to use your imagination and check these things in the meeting. Remember:

The meeting is about the person and how you can help them to achieve success – it is not about you 'selling' yourself.

Let's assume you have done your research. You will then mentally rehearse the meeting. There are many models for mental rehearsal, some of which we will be covering later in the book. During such a preparation session, however, you will rehearse focusing on the following areas.

Credibility

You can aim to connect with the person to show you understand their world and agenda. This can help to establish credibility.

Clarity

You can aim to establish the results they want to achieve and the challenges they face.

Concrete Results

You can aim to immediately share some know how and practical tools the person can use to get concrete results.

Helping The Person To Clarify Their Goals

Imagine that you have created an encouraging atmosphere and shown the person that you understand their world. The next step is to clarify their goals. This may, of course, also include exploring some of the challenges they face on the way to achieving their goals.

Different coaches use different questions for uncovering the topics to explore. Here are some they may ask the person before agreeing on the specific goals for the first session.

What are the specific things that you would like to take away from the session? What for you would make it a successful session?

Looking at the wider picture, is it okay to explore some of your medium and longer-term goals? What are your professional goals? What are your personal goals? What is your long-term picture of success?

Let's return to the present day. What are the key challenges you face? Can you give an example of these challenges? Would it be helpful to explore solutions to these challenges?

There are many approaches to helping people to explore their challenges and goals. You can, for example, simply ask questions. Another approach is to invite them to tackle exercises on these themes. You will obviously have your own methods, but here are some well-known exercises you may want to use.

Clarifying Challenges

You can invite the person to clarify the specific challenges or other themes they would like to explore in the sessions. They may, for example, say something like:

I would like to explore:

How to make better use of my strengths.

How to manage the consequences of my weaknesses.

How to take the next step in my career.

How to regain a sense of control in my life.

How to deliver results in an organisation that believes in 'matrix management' where many people avoid taking responsibility.

How to manage my boss.

How to lead my team to success.

How to help my son to focus on what he does best and also cope with school.

You can then translate these into specific goals the person wants to achieve.

The challenges – or other themes – I would like to explore in the sessions are:

1) How to

For example:

2) How to

For example:

3) How to

For example:

Clarifying Goals

You can invite the person to clarify the specific goals they would like to achieve over a certain time frame. This could be over the next three months, one year, three years or whatever.

If appropriate, you can invite them to also describe the benefits of achieving the goals.

The specific goals I want to achieve in the next _____ are:

1) To

For example:

2) To

For example:

3) To

For example:

The benefits of achieving these goals will be:

1) To

For example:

2) To

For example:

3) To

For example:

So a person might, for example, describe their goals as something like the following:

The specific goals I want to achieve in the next 12 months are:

To find or create a role where I can do satisfying work and also earn a reasonable salary.

To learn how to build more self-managing teams so that I can be released to do more of the things I do best.

To help my partner to make the transition to working three days a week.

Clarifying Longer-Term Goals

People like to see a connection between their daily actions and their overall life goals. So, if appropriate, you can invite the person to do the following exercise.

Invite them to imagine they are looking back on their life in later years. For example, when they are 80 years old.

What are the things they would like to have done by then that for them would mean they have had a successful life? What is their personal picture of success? People often focus on three themes when doing this exercise.

Positive Relationships

They may want to feel they have been a good parent, partner or friend. So they may say something like:

I want my partner and I to have given our children the opportunity to enjoy a happy childhood. For example, for them to say things like:

"Our parents were always there for us. They encouraged us, helped us to develop our talents and also learn how to make good decisions."

Positive Difference

They may want to feel they have made a positive difference in the world. So they may something like:

> *I want to have used my strengths to have done positive work that has encouraged other people. The specific ways I want to have achieved this is by doing the following things:*
>
> *
>
> *
>
> *
>
> *(Each person will obviously complete this part in their own way.)*

Positive Memories

They may want to feel they have enjoyed life and have had few regrets. So they may say something like:

> *I want to have lived life fully.*
>
> *For example, I want: To have visited many countries; To have completed the book I promised myself I would write; To have made full use of my talents.*

People can then ensure they are doing something each day towards achieving their life goals. This will provide a sense of meaning in their daily lives.

Looking back in future years, I will feel my life has been successful if I have done the following things:

1) *I have*

For example:

2) *I have*

For example:

3) *I have*

For example:

Clear Contracting

Let's assume you have clarified the person's goals. It will soon be time to start focusing on the first theme they want to explore. Before doing so, however, it may be important:

To communicate what you can and cannot offer as a coach.

To make clear working contracts.

Clear contracting is crucial in any relationship, especially if you are providing a service. There are many ways to make such agreements, but it is normally good to cover the following things. It can be useful:

To clarify the specific goals the person wants to achieve.

To clarify the person's responsibility in working to achieve the goals.

To clarify the coach's responsibility – your responsibility – in helping the person to achieve the goals.

To clarify the specific things that will be happening that will show the person has achieved their goals.

You may or may not create such a formal agreement, but here is the kind of template that some people use to make clear working contracts.

The Coaching Contract

The Specific Goals

The specific goals the person wants to achieve are:

1) To

For example:

2) To

For example:

3) To

For example:

The Specific Responsibilities

The person's responsibilities in working towards achieving the goals are:

1) To

For example:

2) To

For example:

3) To

For example:

The Specific Responsibilities

The coach's responsibilities in helping the person to work towards achieving the goals are:

1) To

For example:

2) To

For example:

3) To

For example:

The Specific Measures

The specific things that will be happening that will show the person has achieved the goals will be:

1)

For example:

2)

For example:

3)

For example:

Good contracting provides the basis for achieving future success. You can return to the contract if there is ever confusion about the respective responsibilities in achieving the goals.

Moving Forwards

Let's assume the client has explained the various challenges they face and their specific goals. At this point it can be useful to settle on the goals for the session. So you may say something like:

> *Looking at the various topics we have mentioned, which would it be the most helpful to tackle? Let's agree on the agenda for today.*

Agree with the client on the things they would like to take away from the session. If appropriate, you can then 'play back' your understanding. So you may say:

As far as I understand it, you would like to focus on the following topics during the session:

* *How to*
* *How to*
* *How to*

So it is important to be crystal clear on the person's goals for the session. You can achieve this by completing the following exercise:

The specific things the person would like to explore in the session are:

* *How to*

  For example:

* *How to*

  For example:

* *How to*

  For example:

Let's assume that the person wants to work towards their overall picture of success. Some coaches will immediately focus on the strategies that people can use to achieve these aims.

Strengths coaches often take this approach after the first session. Before then, however, they believe it is useful to utilise a person's assets to achieve their aims. Bearing this in mind, during the first session they may say something like the following to the person.

> *Looking at the topics you want to explore, I am sure that we can cover all these. Before exploring the first one, however, I would like to know a little more about your strengths. We will then explore the strategies and solutions you can use to achieve success. Is that okay?*

Some people may, of course, want to go straight into tackling a key challenge, rather than look at their strengths. If this is the case, you will follow the client's agenda and help them to find creative solutions to the challenge.

You will have lots of opportunity to find the person's strengths at a later stage. As ever:

> *The session is about the person and what they want to achieve – it is not about you.*

Let's imagine, however, that the person wants to discover more about their abilities. This takes us to focusing on their strengths.

Strengths

Peak performers do what they do best and do it brilliantly. They build on where they deliver As and manage the consequences of their Bs and Cs. Such people pursue the right strategies, perform great work and overcome setbacks. They keep improving and aim to achieve ongoing success.

Imagine that you want to help a person to clarify their talents. You may meet somebody who says, for example:

> *"I have a rough idea of what I am good at, but it is hard to be specific. Looking into the future, I would also like to make a living doing work I love. Have you any suggestions?"*

It is quite possible to help such a person to, for example, focus on the following areas.

Strengths

To build on their strengths, follow their successful style and set specific goals.

Satisfying Work

To perform superb work, find solutions to challenges and provide great service to customers.

Success

To achieve their specific goals, pass on their knowledge and help other people to achieve success.

There are many ways to help a person to clarify what they do best. One approach is to use Strengths Assessment Tools. Another approach is to invite the person to answer certain questions. The next few pages provide an overview of some potential topics to explore. If you invite somebody to talk about these themes, it can be useful to look for when:

They 'come alive' and become excited about the topic they are exploring.

They demonstrate the equivalent of a photographic memory and describe things in great detail.

You will, of course, have your own approach to helping people to find their talents. But here are some questions you may wish to consider.

Strengths

Some questions you can explore with a person to help them to find their strengths

1) *What are the deeply satisfying activities in which you deliver As, rather than Bs or Cs?*

2) *When do you feel in your element – at ease and yet able to excel?*

3) *Where do you have a natural feeling for an activity? Where do you feel at home and say: "This is where I was meant to be?"*

4) *When do you flow, focus and finish? Where do then, as a by-product, get a sense of fulfilment?*

5) *What are the activities that give you positive energy – even when you just think about them?*

6) *When do you follow your passion, translate this into a clear purpose and achieve peak performance?*

7) *What are the specific activities in which you do things you find stimulating, set stretch goals and achieve your picture of success?*

8) *Where do you have the equivalent of a photographic memory?*

9) *When do you see the destination quickly? When do you go 'A, B ___ then leap to ___ Z'? Where do you have a track record of delivering Z?*

10) *What are the situations in which you quickly see patterns?*

11) *Where do you have good personal radar? Where do you seem to know what will happen before it happens? Where do you also have the repertoire to deliver the right results?*

12) *Where do you make complicated things look simple?*

13) *What are the situations in which you are calm?*

14) *When are you good at dealing with 'crowdedness' – many things happening at the same time?*

15) *What are the activities in which you continually do creative problem-solving by focusing on clarity, creativity and concrete results?*

16) *What are the activities where you naturally do mental rehearsal?*

17) *What are the activities in which you have natural self-discipline? Where do you score highly on drive, detail and delivery?*

18) *What are the activities in which you enjoy the journey as much as reaching the goal - the process as much as the prize?*

19) *Where do you always do the basics and then add the brilliance?*

20) *Where do you reach the goals by adding that touch of class?*

21) *What is your successful style of working?*

    Looking back at your positive history, what for you have been the most satisfying 'projects'? What was satisfying about them?

    What were the principles you followed to be successful? How can you follow these principles again in the future?

22) *What do you think may be your vocation?*

    How can you express this vocation through various vehicles on the route to doing valuable work?

23) What for you would be the most stimulating kind of Project, with stimulating People in a stimulating Place?

24) Who are your perfect customers – the kinds of people with whom you work best?

What would be the specific things you could deliver to your perfect customers to help them to achieve success?

25) How can you do satisfying work?

How can you build on your strengths, find sponsors - people who will pay you - and help them to achieve success?

Clarifying A Person's Strengths

Different people obviously have different talents. Here are some examples that illustrate some of these themes.

A sales person may be in their element when selling technology to particular kinds of customers. They feel at ease and able to excel. Such people love rising to the occasion and making the sale when it matters.

An interior designer may walk into a scruffy building and, in their mind's eye, see the finished rooms. They go 'A, B then leap to Z.' They may also have a track record of delivering 'Z' – the completed design.

A technical problem-solver may feel calm in the midst of computer chaos. They have the ability to deal with 'crowdedness' – many things happening in this area at once. They focus on how to solve the problem by going through the following stages.

Clarity: they establish the real results to achieve.

Creativity: they quickly explore all the possible options finding solutions.

Concrete Results: they do whatever is necessary to deliver the required results.

A great footballer may quickly see patterns during a game. They have the radar to 'know what will happen before it happens'. This gives them more time and space than the other players. They also have the professional repertoire required to deliver positive results.

A coach may have the ability to tune into a client's strengths. They help the person focus on the activities they find stimulating, to set stretch goals and to do what is necessary to achieve success. Such a coach may work well with certain kinds of people, but not with others.

"That sounds fine," somebody may say. "But what if a person is relatively young or setting out on their journey. How can you spot when somebody has the seeds of a talent?"

One approach is to focus on where they follow the process of absorption, adventure and achievement. It is to focus on when:

They come alive and have a natural feeling for an activity.

They follow the process of absorption, adventure and achievement.

They have the ability, if they apply themselves, to deliver As, rather than Bs or Cs.

The person may go through this process when writing an article, gardening, cooking, mastering a skill, learning a language or whatever. Becoming completely absorbed in the subject, they go on a journey of adventure.

They keep working hard and enjoy a sense of fulfilment when reaching the destination.

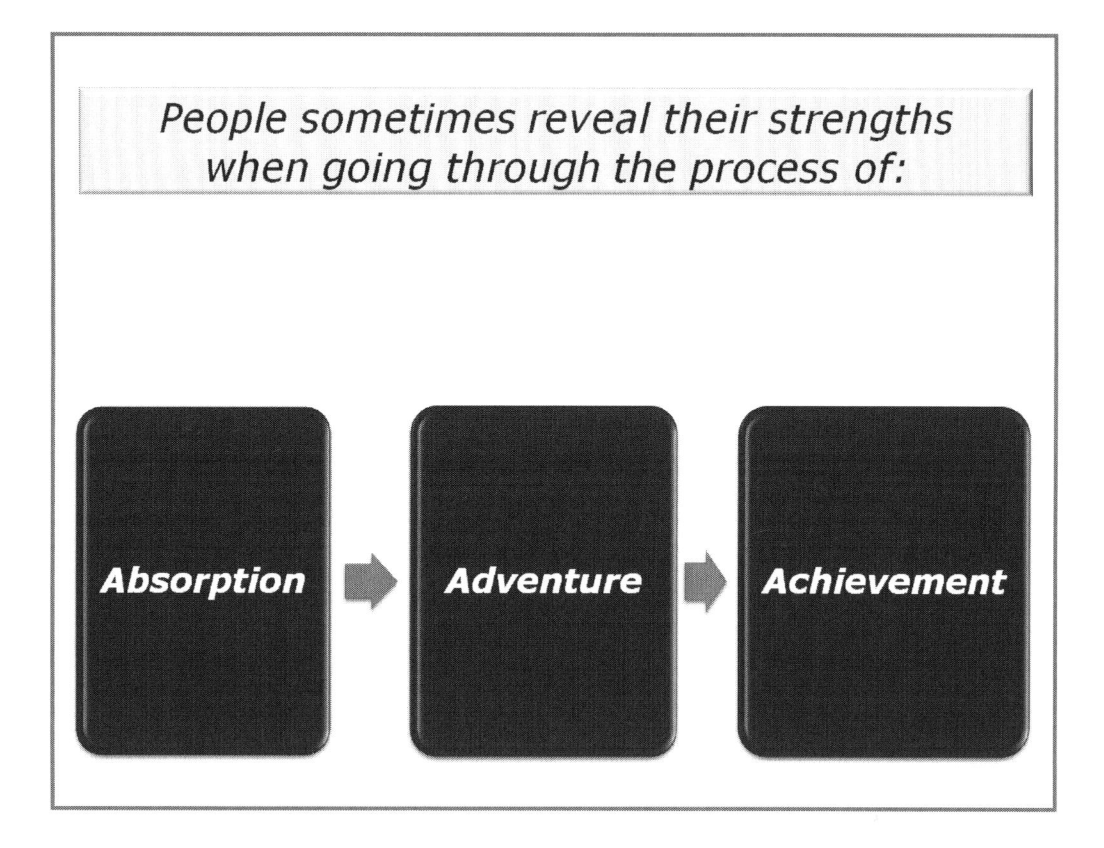

How to discover where a person has this ability? The best way is obviously to watch a person in action. You can then spot if they have a feeling for an activity.

Sometimes this is not always possible. So another approach is to invite the person to talk about the activities they find fulfilling and to listen to their language. They may use some of the following words under each of the headings.

Absorption

> *"I was fascinated by the subject ... I was doing something I really cared about ... I found that things came easily for me."*

Adventure

"I loved solving that kind of problem ... I felt as if I was learning ... I looked forward to each day, even when I knew it was going to be hard work."

Achievement

"It felt really satisfying to finish ... It was great to make things work ... I rested for a while, but then went looking for a similar kind of challenge."

Let's imagine that you have done a lot of work on exploring a person's talents. At some point you can invite the person to do the following exercise to clarify their strengths. Encourage them to provide specific examples that highlight when they have used these abilities. Here is the exercise, complete with the introduction that sets the scene.

My Strengths

Introduction

This exercise invites you to clarify your strengths. Please be as honest as possible when doing the exercise.

* *Describe the deeply satisfying activities where you deliver – or have the potential to deliver – As rather then Bs or Cs.*

  These may be particular kinds of projects, tasks or other activities. Try to be as specific as possible. Give concrete examples. Please note. The emphasis is on the word 'Deliver'.

* *Describe where you deliver Bs or Cs.*

The B activities are probably those that you can do reasonably well. They are not your As, however, or maybe they once were but now you get bored doing them.

The C activities are those where you have little aptitude or desire to learn.

* *Describe how you can build on your strengths and manage the consequences of your weaknesses.*

Later we will explore how you can translate these strengths into a specific contribution to a potential employer.

My A Strengths

As. The deeply satisfying activities, projects or other tasks where I deliver – or have the potential to deliver - As are:

1)

For example:

*

*

*

2)

For example:

*
*
*

My Bs and Cs

Bs. The activities where I deliver Bs are:

*
*
*

Cs. The activities where I deliver Cs are:

*
*

Building On My Strengths

The specific things I can do to build on where I deliver As are:

*

*

*

Managing My Weaknesses

The specific things I can do to manage the consequences of my Bs and Cs are:

*

*

*

A person may find it useful to keep returning to the exercise and refining it over the years. This can help them to clarify their strengths and, if appropriate, communicate what they can offer to a potential employer.

Clarifying A Person's Successful Style

Everybody has abilities, but the key is to see how they apply these in action. There are many ways to clarify a person's potential contribution to, for example, a potential employer. But one of the best is to identify their successful style.

The person's strengths are 'What' they do best. The person's successful style is 'How' they work best. Combining these elements can identify the specific activities in which they are able to deliver great work.

When doing strengths coaching, I move on to this approach fairly quickly by inviting people to explore the exercise *My Successful Style.*

Everybody has a positive history. Everybody has a successful style of working. They can find this by looking back at what for them have been the most satisfying 'projects' in their life. The word 'project' is used in its widest sense. They may have gained the greatest satisfaction when:

Creating a beautiful garden.

Competing in an athletic tournament.

Encouraging other people.

Writing a book.

Renovating a house.

Passing an exam.

Solving a particular kind of problem.

Designing a web site.

Trading goods on a market place.

Organising a Fun Run.

Showing a new way of doing business.

Or whatever.

Because this pattern is organic, it can be useful for the person to find and follow this successful style. So what were the things that made each project satisfying? What did they do right then? What were the principles they followed? How can they follow similar principles – plus maybe adding other elements – in the future?

Sometimes people have two successful styles. One when working with other people; one when working alone. It can be useful to find each approach. Here is the exercise that can be used to help a person to find their best way of working.

My Successful Style

Introduction

Everybody has a successful style of working. Clarifying this style is often the clue to finding their real strengths.

This is a long but important exercise. It invites you to describe three satisfying 'projects' you have done in your life.

The word 'project' can be used in its widest sense. For example: writing an article, organising a fun run, launching a web site, solving a particular problem, leading a team or whatever.

* *Describe each of these projects in turn and what made them satisfying.*

Try to be as specific as possible, especially about the things that made them satisfying. Looking at these projects, can you see any patterns? These often provide clues to your preferred style.

* *Describe your successful style – your preferred way of working.*

(Sometimes we have two successful styles: one when working alone, one when working with other people. See what the exercise reveals.)

* *Describe the things you can do to follow these principles in the future.*

The first satisfying project was:

* *When I*

The things that made it satisfying were:

*

*

*

*

*

The second satisfying project was:

* *When I*

The things that made it satisfying were:

*
*
*
*
*

The third satisfying project was:

* *When I*

The things that made it satisfying were:

*
*
*
*
*

My Successful Style

Looking at the patterns that have emerged, I believe my successful style – my preferred way of working – is:

* *To*

* *To*

* *To*

* *To*

* *To*

My Successful Style: Following it in the future

The things I can do to follow these principles in the future are:

* *To*

* *To*

* *To*

* *To*

* *To*

What do these styles look like in action? Each person will obviously have their own preferred way of working, but here are some examples.

A person may have a pattern of building successful prototypes. They may have shown such skills when piloting new approaches in technology, providing customer service, creating a fresh way of doing business or whatever. They may say, for example:

> *"I like to build new things that show people a better way. Once these have succeeded, however, I get bored and look for another project. I like to make the new rules for the game."*

A person's may have a pattern of being a co-ordinator or implementer who makes things work. They may have shown such skills when organising social events, raising money for charity, introducing a new computer system or whatever. They may say, for example:

> *"I am not a visionary myself, but I like to make things work. There is nothing more satisfying then when a plan comes together."*

A person may have a pattern of turning around ailing teams. They may have shown such skills when revitalising existing companies, even though the process was difficult. They may say, for example:

> *"I like to fix problems and can take an organisation from 3/10 to 8/10. But then I get bored and look for the next big problem. Maybe one day I will want to stick with an organisation long enough to take it to 10/10. In the meantime, however, there are enough organisations that need fixing."*

A person may have a pattern of providing healing environments that enable people to grow. They may have shown such skills when counselling troubled children at school, being a nurse, running their own clinic or whatever. They may say, for example:

> *"I like to create a space where people can feel at ease and encouraged. They must provide the will-power themselves, of course, but I can help them to pursue their road to recovery."*

A person may have a pattern of passing on knowledge that helps other people to succeed. They may have shown such skills when educating young musicians, running workshops for people who want to change careers or writing training manuals that actually work. They may say, for example:

> *"I have always loved helping other people to develop. At sports camp I was always given the job of coaching the difficult kids. Even though I was only a few years their senior, I seemed to get through to them. Maybe it was because they heard that my previous teams of difficult kids had gone on to win the trophies."*

Recognising The Three Kinds of Builders

Sometimes you may work with individuals who like to do pioneering work in organisations. If so, it can be useful to recognise the three ways that people may try to make this happen.

Sometimes the different approaches can be likened to building a house. Some people renovate an old house. Some build a new house that is connected to an old house. Some build a new house in a new place.

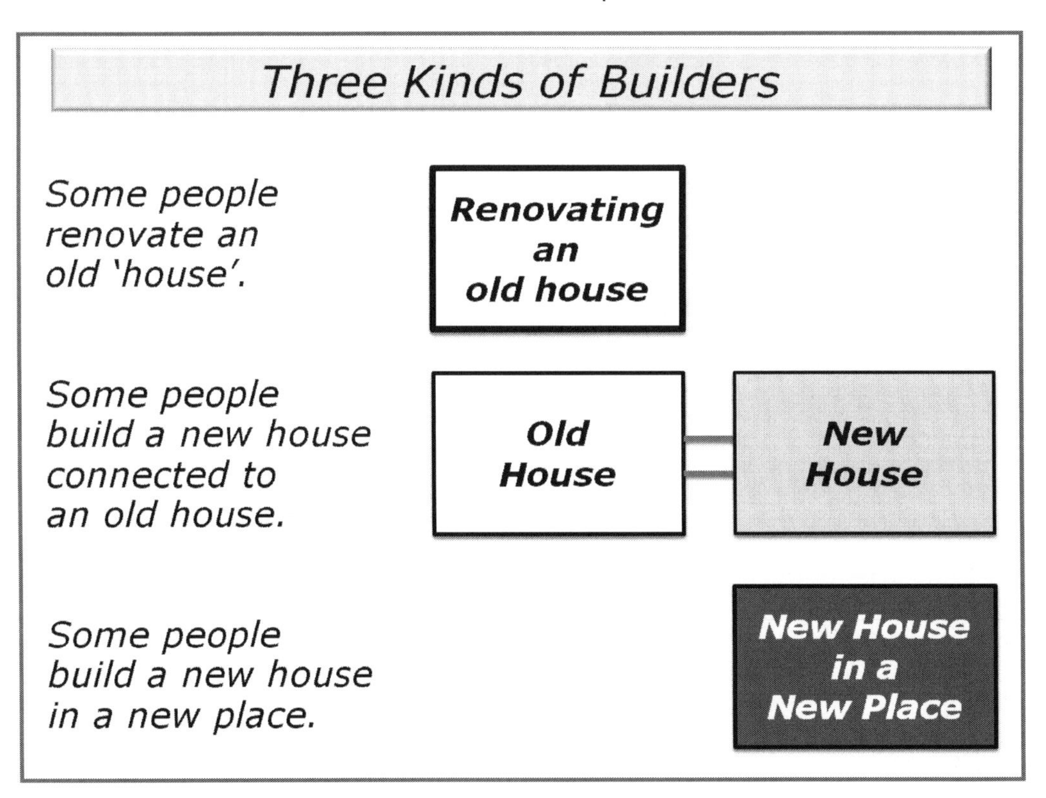

It is vital for the person to choose the route that matches their strengths. So let's explore these three ways.

Renovating an old house

Revitalising an existing house – or an organisation – can be challenging. Sometimes changing a system meets resistance. Too much time can be spent trying to 'persuade' people, rather than delivering the required results.

Imagine a person is taking this approach to revitalising an organisation. They may choose to pursue or combine some of the following options.

They can try to build on the good parts of the business and turnaround the rest.

They can put everybody through a 'change programme' and hope they develop the urgency required to achieve success.

They can clarify the organisation's strengths and successful patterns – by using methods such as Appreciative Inquiry – and develop these to build a successful future.

They can maintain the present business but simultaneously develop prototypes that show how the business can be successful in the future.

They can close the business and start again.

It is possible to 'renovate an old house'. But this can be an arduous process. The person will need to implement the right strategy with the right people in the right way. This can call for many tough decisions along the way.

Building a new house that is connected to an old house

This is an approach used by many people who want to help an organisation to develop. They may aim to introduce a new way of delivering customer service, doing business or whatever.

They build a new house – a new way of doing things – that has a long 'connecting corridor' to the existing organisation. The new method may differ radically from the previous approach – so they need distance from the old house. A person may take the following steps to deliver the goods:

They get a clear picture of success and a clear mandate from the Board.

They clarify what had worked best in the organisation and show respect for its heritage.

They connect the new approach to the existing organisation by creating some kind of 'corridor' – but they develop the new approach separately.

(They do not go back to the old house to sit in committees and ask if it is okay to paint the walls a certain colour.)

They build the new house, deliver superb work and show the bottom-line results.

They hand-over the new approach to people who they have coached to run it successfully.

This is often the most effective way of shaping the future. Once the new way is established, the 'existing house' – the old way of doing things – is sometimes demolished.

Building a new house in a new place

Pioneers often take this route. They go out and build a 'house' – a new business, new idea or new project – on the prairie. Sometimes they find gold; sometimes they go bankrupt.

Such people go beyond having a big idea. They move forward through the stages of imagination and implementation to achieve the desired impact.

Different people adopt different approaches to shaping an organisation. Some combine elements of all three approaches that have been mentioned. If you are working with somebody who wants to improve an organisation, it is important they take the route that plays to their strengths.

Imagine that you have helped a person to clarify their successful style. This can lead to helping them to find their vocation and the kinds of projects they find stimulating. Let's explore these themes.

Clarifying a Person's Vocation

A person's vocation is their calling. It is what they are here to do. Their vocation remains constant throughout their life, but they may express it through various vehicles on the way towards doing valuable work.

So how can a person begin to clarify their vocation? One approach is to look back at the *My Successful Style* exercise and see if there are any recurring themes.

The 'red thread' in these projects could be, for example, encouraging people, inventing products, leading pioneering teams, solving problems, creating beauty, making the world a better place or whatever.

Imagine that a person's vocation may be: 'To create enriching environments in which people grow.' They can express this theme through many different vehicles. They may choose:

To be an educator.

To be an interior designer.

To create inspiring music.

To do landscape gardening.

To lead a successful team in which people grow.

Or whatever.

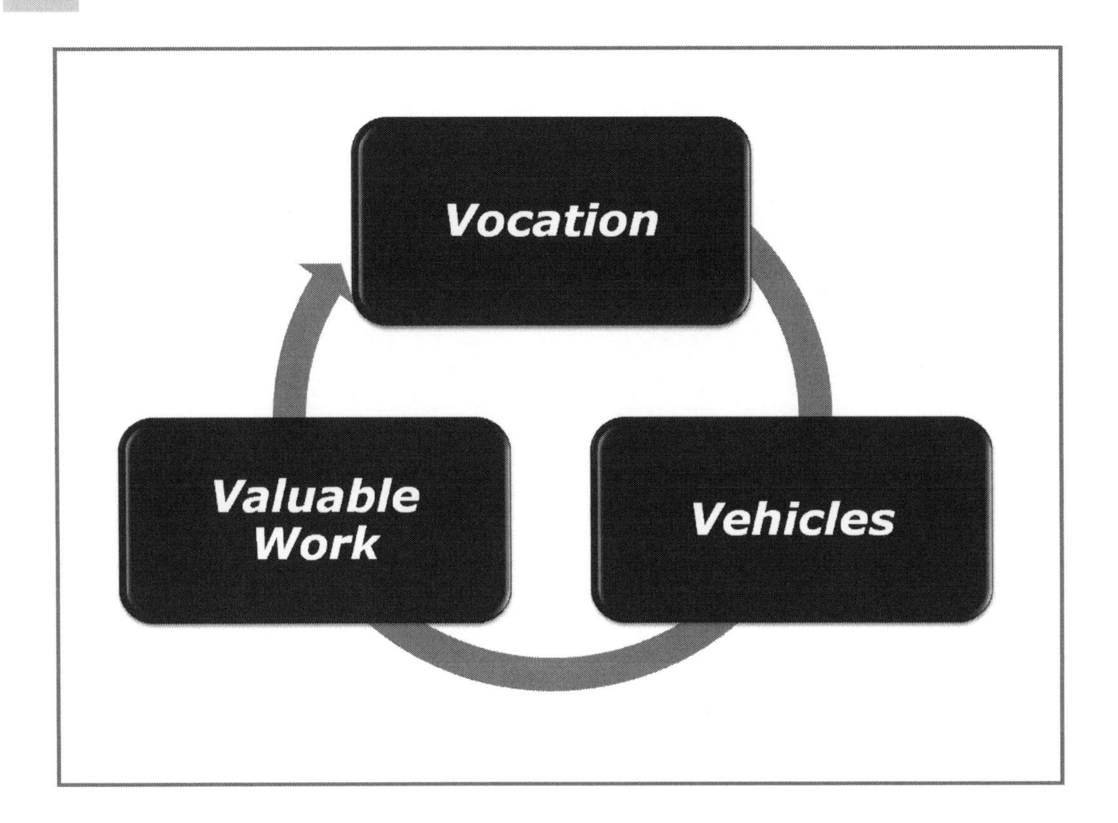

There are many different ways a person can express their vocation. So how to find the right vehicle? It is important to find the field and form of activity in which they can excel. Let's explore these two areas.

The Field of Activity

The person may feel at home working with technology, business, science, sport, the arts, food, music, people management or whatever. It is good for them concentrate on a field where:

They have a feeling for the activity.

They find the work fulfilling.

They have a track record of finishing.

How to find such a field? They can again focus on the deeply satisfying activities in which they deliver As, rather than Bs or Cs.

They can choose a field they find fascinating where, for example, a person would pursue this activity even if they did not get paid for doing it.

The Form of Activity

The person can choose a form of activity that fits their successful working style. They may prefer to express their talents by doing, teaching, leading, managing, writing, speaking, designing, making films or whatever. They may prefer to work alone, to be a leader, to work in a team, to work in an organisation or whatever.

There are many ways for a person for follow their vocation. Here are examples from five people I have worked with in the past.

One person's vocation is encouraging people to care for nature. They now express this by making pioneering – and sometimes controversial – wildlife films for television.

One person's vocation is enabling people to communicate in a compelling way. They now express this by running a company that educates people to connect with their audiences.

One person's vocation is creating beautiful environments. They express this by running their own interior design company. They got their first customers by doing weekend work for family and friends. Fifteen years later they have a highly successful business.

One person's vocation is making things work – something that has fascinated them ever since they were a child. They now express this by working as the Chief Operating Officer in a high-tech company. Others may find this boring; but they find it satisfying to make things work properly.

One person's vocation is enabling people to take charge of their lives. They now express this by writing career development books that, in their words: 'Enable people to become architects of their own futures.'

The Vocational Themes

One point is worth remembering. There are relatively few vocational themes, but the way a person expresses these themes will be unique to them. In this way they will give their best to the world.

Most of the vocational themes revolve around the eternal human activities. These include, for example:

> *Encouraging, Nurturing, Caring, Healing, Educating, Developing, Researching, Exploring, Navigating, Mapping, Creating, Designing, Leading, Building, Implementing, Problem Solving, Trading, Communicating, Performing, Entertaining, etc.*

Clarifying one's vocation can be a lifetime search, but there are some clues that can be found reasonably quickly. The key is for a person to focus on the activities that give them positive energy and 'make their heart sing'.

While the theme may remain constant, the way a person expresses it will change over the years. So you can, if you wish, invite the person to tackle the following exercise called *My Vocation.*

My Vocation

Introduction

A person's vocation is their calling. It is what they are here to do.

Their vocation remains constant in life, but they may express it through various vehicles on the way towards doing valuable work.

Finding one's vocation can take years. But it is possible to make a start by looking back at the 'satisfying projects' you have done in your life.

Looking at each of these projects in turn, what made them satisfying? Can you see any patterns?

Sometimes there is a 'red thread' that runs through these projects. This key theme could be, for example, activities such as:

** Encouraging people.*

** Creating beautiful environments.*

** Making things work.*

** Passing on knowledge.*

** Showing a better way.*

** Or whatever.*

The following exercise assumes you have already done some work on clarifying the themes that run through your most satisfying projects. It invites you to do the following things.

* *Describe what you believe may be your vocation. Also describe when you have expressed this theme in the past.*

* *Describe the ways you can express this vocation through various vehicles in the future.*

* *Describe the steps you can then take to do valuable work.*

As mentioned earlier, getting the right wording can take years. But this exercise offers a starting point.

My Vocation

Looking at the themes that run through the satisfying projects I have done in my life, I believe my vocation may be:

* *To*

The specific situations where I have expressed this theme - or similar themes - in the past have been:

*

*

*

My Vehicles

The specific things I can do to express this vocation through various vehicles in the future are:

* *To*

* *To*

* *To*

My Steps To Doing Valuable Work

The specific things I can therefore do to try to do valuable work are:

* *To*

* *To*

* *To*

Clarifying a Person's Perfect Role

Imagine that you have helped a person to find their strengths and successful style. You may also have done some work on clarifying their vocation. It may be that the person wants to focus on where they can do satisfying work and, for example, earn a salary.

There are many approaches to helping a person to find or craft such a role. We will explore more of these later in the book. One approach that can be helpful, however, is to focus on the things they want in their perfect role.

Here is an exercise you can invite a person to do on this theme. It invites them to clarify the characteristics of the Project, People and Place they find stimulating. Let's explore these three areas.

Project

Invite the person to describe the characteristics of the kind of 'project' they find stimulating.

They may enjoy launching prototypes, doing turnarounds, leading superb teams, fixing particular problems, selling to certain kinds of customers or whatever. One person said:

> *"Looking back on my satisfying projects, I can identify several patterns. For example, I love doing work that contributes to improving the quality of people's lives.*
>
> *"At university I organised the first ever sponsored 'Fun Run', raising £10k for charity. Early in my IT career I launched software that enabled students to take charge of their own learning.*
>
> *"The projects I enjoy normally have a deadline. This forces me to get my act together and make sure I deliver on time."*

What are the characteristics of the kinds of projects that the person find stimulating? They can try completing the first part of the following exercise.

My Perfect Role

Project

The kind of project I find stimulating is one where:

*

*

*

People

Invite the person to describe the characteristics of the people – both the customers and colleagues – that they find stimulating. The person mentioned above said:

> *"If I am working for a company, I must have a boss I respect.*
>
> *"It's best if we agree on the 'What': the goals to achieve. But then I need to have lots of freedom regarding the 'How'.*
>
> *"When leading a team, I must have positive team members who are prepared to work hard.*
>
> *"The customers I like are those who are at the forefront of their field. They may be demanding, but they can also make quick decisions."*

What are the characteristics of the colleagues and customers who the person finds stimulating? What are the qualities they want in their ideal boss? Invite them to try completing the following sentence.

My Perfect Role

People

The kinds of people – manager, colleagues and customers – I find stimulating are:

*

*

*

Place

Invite the person to describe the characteristics of the place – the culture and environment – they find stimulating. One person said:

> *"I like working in pioneering businesses. They are professional and yet informal. They are also results focused and fast paced, which suits my style. It also feels like we are creating the rules for the future."*

What are the characteristics of the kind of work places that the person finds stimulating? Invite them to complete the following sentence.

My Perfect Role

Place

The kind of place – the culture and environment – I find stimulating is one where:

*

*

*

Making it Happen

If appropriate, invite the person to make their action plan. Bearing in mind the answers they have already given, the following exercise invites them to do several things.

Describe their perfect project.

Describe the specific results they could deliver to a sponsor – an employer or customer – by doing this kind of project.

Describe the specific benefits to the employer or customer.

Describe the specific things they can do to find or create such a project.

Invite the person to complete the following sentences. They can then do their best to craft their perfect role.

Making It Happen

Bearing in mind the answers I have written, my perfect project would be one where:

*

*

*

The specific results I could deliver to a sponsor – an employer or customer – by doing this kind of project would be:

*

*

*

The specific benefits to the sponsor – the employer or customer - would be:

*

*

*

The specific things I can do to find or create such a project are:

*

*

*

In this section we have focused on the specific things you can do to find a person's strengths. There are, of course, many other methods you can employ.

You now know what the person does well. The next step is to use this information when revisiting their picture of success. It is then to focus on the specific goals they want to achieve in the short, medium and long term. Let's explore how to make this happen.

Specific Goals

Peak performers continually focus on the 'What' – the real results to achieve and the 'Why' – the benefits of achieving the goals. They then move on to the 'How, Who and When'. Albert Einstein is reputed to have had a similar approach to creative problem solving. He said:

> *"If I had only one hour to save the world, I would spend fifty-five minutes defining the problem, and only five minutes finding the solution."*

Peak Performers often focus on the 'What, Why, How, Who and When'

They keep asking:

What	***What are the real results I want to achieve? What is the picture of success?***
Why	***Why do I want to achieve these results? What will be the benefits?***
How	***How can I do my best to achieve these results? What are the key things I can do to give myself the greatest chance of success?***
Who	***Who are the people who will need to be involved – and what roles will they play – in delivering the results?***
When	***What are the specific things that will be happening – and when – on the road towards achieving the picture of success?***

Bearing in mind the person's strengths, you can return to the first theme they want to explore and translate it into a specific goal. This will often be something related to achieving their long-term picture of success. One key thing is worth bearing in mind at this point.

Clarifying the person's strengths often re-affirms their long-term aims. But sometimes it can lead to revisiting and revising their plans.

Different people will, of course, have different goals. So what might be the theme that somebody wants to explore? Here are some questions that individuals have asked coaches during sessions.

How can I give up drugs and live a happy life?

How can I manage my difficult boss?

How can I make a living doing what I love?

How can I take care of my partner who has just got a life-threatening illness?

How can I spend more time with people who are positive and deal with the feelings caused by those who are negative?

How can I feel more in control and manage my panic attacks.

How can I build a great team?

How can I turn around an ailing organisation?

How can I build an organisation that really lives its values?

How can I manage the problems that a star player is causing in my professional football team?

How can I make the most of the remaining years I have to live?

How can I pass on my knowledge to people?

Different coaches will feel more or less equipped to explore some of these topics. Good coaches, however, recognise their own strengths and limitations.

So it is vital for them to be professional about what they can and can't offer. This is a crucial part of the coaching contract.

Looking at my own background, for example, it has involved strengths coaching in certain areas. This has included work with Recovery Programmes, Career Development, Entrepreneurship, Education, Teams, Organisations, Businesses and some aspects of Sport.

For me, however, there are certain topics that are off limits. If medical, legal or certain other issues appear, I advise the person to seek qualified advice.

Good coaches aim to fulfil their part of the coaching contract. At the same time, however, they emphasise they are offering positive models and practical tools. It is up to the person to take the ideas they like and use them to reach their goals.

Let's return to the coaching session. Imagine that the person you are working with wants to focus on a theme that relates to achieving their lifetime picture of success. They may say something like, for example:

How can I find a job that isn't draining?

We will consider how to explore this theme, but many of the steps we cover can also be applied to working towards other specific goals.

Clarity is Crucial

Good coaches often go through certain steps when helping a person to, for example, tackle a challenge. They help the person to explore the challenge, establish clarity and recognise the controllables. Let's consider these steps.

Different people will want to tackle different challenges. Whatever challenge they present, it can be useful to encourage them to frame this in positive terms. For example, the person can clarify their goal as:

"I want to be healthy," rather than "I want to stop smoking."

"I want to build a successful team," rather than "I want to solve the problems in my team."

"I want to help my teenage son to find work he loves," rather then "I want him to overcome his frustrations at school."

Why? Channelling one's energy towards achieving a positive goal is more likely to achieve success. It is hard to achieve a negative goal.

The next step is to establish clarity. Good decision makers spend a lot of time clarifying the real 'What'. They clarify this before moving on to the 'How'. Sometimes the person may have several aims they want to achieve. If so, encourage them to list these goals in order of priority.

Encourage the person to list the 'controllables.' These are the things they can control in the situation – such as their attitude and professionalism. They can focus on what they can control, rather than worry about what they can't control.

This final step can sometimes lead to a person refining their goals. For example, an athlete may choose to focus on achieving their personal best time in a 100 metres final. They can control their own performance, but they cannot always control whether they win a Gold Medal.

Bearing this in mind, it can be useful to revisit the goal. Ensure the person is crystal clear on the real results they want to achieve. So you can invite them to use the following three-part framework.

Challenge

The specific challenge I want to tackle is:

How:

Clarity

The real results I want to achieve – in order of priority – are:

*

*

*

Controllables

The things I can control in the situation are:

*

*

*

Imagine that the person has gone through these steps and restated their original aim. Originally they said:

"How can I find a job that is less draining?"

They may now frame this as:

"How can I do satisfying work that also earns a good salary?"

You can then move on to helping them to setting an even more specific goal.

Clarifying The 'What' and The 'Why'

Peak performers often translate their goal into the equivalent of a picture of success. 'Equivalent' because, while some visualise their goal, other people use other senses. Their creative style may be kinaesthetic, audio or have various combinations of synaesthesia.

One person I worked with, for example, was a Trader. He talked about 'smelling' a deal. At first I thought he was speaking metaphorically. But later I learned that he could literally smell a good deal. Another person talked about 'hearing' pictures when they went to an art gallery. So a person may say things like:

"I am crystal clear on the goal. I know what it looks like, feels like, sounds like, tastes like, smells like. I can already experience the end result. So now I will work backwards and work out how to reach the goal."

Here is the exercise you can use to invite the person to focus on the 'What' and 'Why'. They are to do the following things.

Describe the specific goal they want to achieve by a certain date.

Describe the benefits of reaching the goal.

My Specific Goal
The 'What' and 'Why'

The 'What' – The Picture of Success

The specific goal I want to achieve by ______ is:

** To*

The specific things that will be happening then that will show I have reached the goal will be:

*

*

*

The 'Why' – The Benefits

The benefits of achieving the goal – both for myself and for other people - will be:

*

*

*

Let's assume the client you are working with has clarified the 'What' and the 'Why'. This then provides the springboard for moving on to the strategies for achieving success – the 'How'.

Strategies

Good coaches move on to helping the client to explore strategies for achieving their picture of success. This is the creative part and people often enjoy brainstorming possibilities regarding the 'How'.

Sometimes people can hit a wall, however, or get bogged down by intricacies of making things work. The coach can then encourage them to keep returning to the 'What' by saying:

> *"Let's return to the goal. As far as I understand, the real results you want to achieve are:*
>
> ** To*
>
> ** To*
>
> ** To*
>
> *"Bearing this in mind, what are all the possible options for working towards achieving the goal?"*

There are many methods for generating strategies. So let's explore some of these tools for reaching a specific goal.

Strategies For Success

Strengths coaches build on what works. So they follow certain principles when focusing on the 'How'.

> *They encourage the person to focus on the strategies that will give them the greatest chance of success.*

This sounds obvious. But some people spend their time focusing on what does not work or become paralysed by worrying about problems.

Strength coaches obviously employ the normal methods for generating possible strategies. But they do this from a certain viewpoint. This involves encouraging the person:

To build on their strengths.

To follow their successful style.

To focus on the strategies that we know work – for them and for other individuals, teams and organisations – to deliver success.

Good coaches do more than facilitate answers. They share positive models and practical tools the person can use to reach their goals. When sharing knowledge, however, they look for which ideas resonate with the person. They then help the person to apply the ideas in their own way.

Generating Strategies

There are many ways to generate potential strategies. You will have your own approach, but let's explore some of these methods.

The classic approach is to do exercises like *My Possible Options.* This invites people to describe the following things.

The specific goal they want to achieve.

The possible choices – the various options – for working towards achieving the goal.

The consequences – the pluses and minuses – of each option.

The attractiveness of each option.

The option they want to follow towards achieving their goal.

My Possible Options

The Choices and the Consequences

Introduction

People often follow a certain approach when developing their decision making skills. They start by focusing on the goal they want to achieve. They then explore all the possible choices, consequences and creative solutions.

They often make the decision based on the consequences of the particular option. They then build on the pluses and minimise the minuses.

This exercise invites you to focus on the possible options you have for tackling a challenge or working towards reaching a specific goal.

It invites you to do the following things.

* *Describe the goal you want to achieve.*

* *Describe the possible options you have for going forward.*

Describe all of the options. Even though some may seem outlandish. Remember also that doing nothing is also an option.

* *Describe the pluses and minuses of each option.*

* *Describe describe the attractive of each route. Do this on a scale 0 – 10.*

People often start this exercise by listing the obvious options.

After a while, however, they start exploring other possibilities. For example, is it possible to combine the best parts of each road into a new option?

* *Describe your preferred option.*

Finally, if appropriate, describe the route you want to travel.

My Specific Goal

The challenge I want to tackle or
the specific goal I want to achieve is:

I want:

* *To*

The specific things that will be happening
that will show I have reached the goal will be:

*
*
*

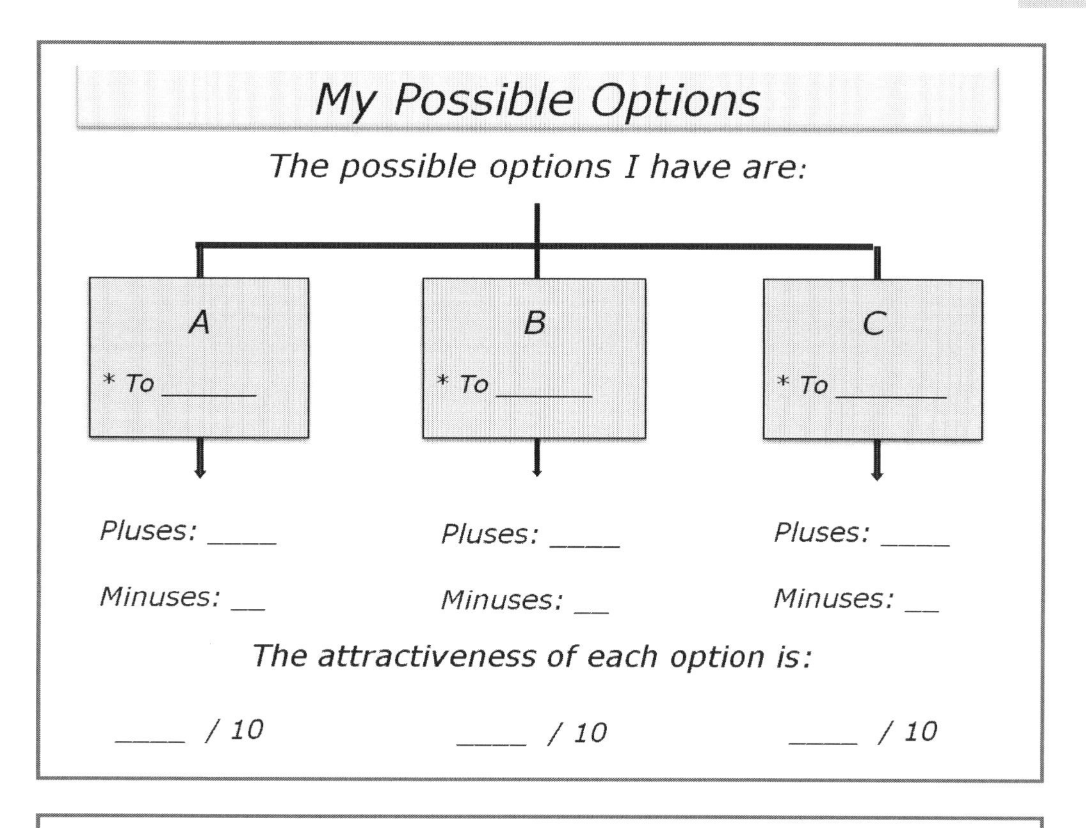

My Possible Options

The Possible Options Are:

a) To

The pluses will be:

*

The potential minuses may be:

*

The attractiveness rating is: __________ / 10

b) To

The pluses will be:

*

The potential minuses may be:

*

The attractiveness rating is: __________ / 10

c) To

The pluses will be:

*

The potential minuses may be:

*

The attractiveness rating is: __________ / 10

My Preferred Option

The Route – Or Combination Of Routes - I Want To Take Is:

* *To*

The pluses will be:

*

The potential minuses may be:

*

The specific things I can do to build on the pluses and minimise the minuses are:

*

Strategic Intuition

Experts apply the analytical approach early in their careers. But later they seem to act quickly without comparing the options. They adopt an approach called *Strategic Intuition.*

Hubert and Stuart Dreyfus referred to this ability in their book *Mind Over Machine: The Power of Human Intuition and Expertise in the Era of the Computer.*

After studying superb practitioners in several fields, they described five stages that people go through to progress from being Novices to Experts. There stages are:

1. *Novice.*
2. *Advanced Beginner.*
3. *Competent.*
4. *Proficient.*
5. *Expert.*

People who become Experts start by focusing on a field where they have a natural feeling for an activity. They then spend many years mastering the principles that will enable them to be professional. At a certain stage, however, they move into another dimension. According to the Dreyfus Brothers, Experts reach a stage where:

> *They go beyond rules and guidelines. They work primarily on intuition based on deep understanding.*
>
> *They do return to analysis, however, when facing new situations.*
>
> *They see what is possible, pursue their chosen strategy and deliver success.*

Experts actually do follow the book they have written, but they skip lots of pages. Going into a situation in which they excel, they go 'A, B ______ and then leap to ______ Z.' They actually 'read the book' quickly and do what is required to deliver success.

The Expert

* *They 'write the book', but they don't seem to follow it.*
* *They actually do, but they skip lots of pages.*
* *They 'read the book' quickly. They go 'A, B _____ Z' and deliver success.*

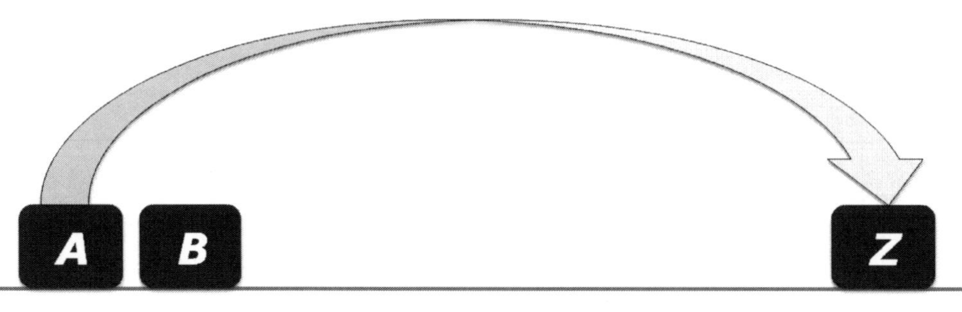

Gary Klein has also written extensively on this topic in books such as *The Power of Intuition.* He researched how firefighters, medical staff and others make decisions in pressure situations. Interviewed by Bill Breen in an article for *The Fast Company Magazine,* Gary explained how such people make decisions.

> *"I noticed that when the most experienced commanders confronted a fire, the biggest question they had to deal with wasn't 'What do I do?' It was 'What's going on?'*
>
> *"That's what their experience was buying them – the ability to size up a situation and to recognize the best course of action."*

Gary goes on to outline the steps such people then take in difficult situations.

> *They reach into their experience – going through it on 'hyperdrive' – to scan previous scenarios and see what lessons might apply to the present situation.*
>
> *They are, at the same time, fully present: they look for patterns and clues to piece together what is happening.*
>
> *They choose what they believe would be the best course of action and play scenarios about how this might work in practice.*

Bill's article outlines what such people do next. Once they make a decision, they evaluate it by rapidly running a mental simulation. They imagine how a course of action may unfold and how it may ultimately play out. The process is akin to building a sequence of snapshots and then observing what occurs. Bill continues his article by reporting what Gary says next.

> *"If everything works out okay, the commanders stick with their choice. But if they discover unintended consequences that could get them into trouble, they discard that solution and look for another one.*
>
> *"They might run through several choices, but they never compare one option with another. They rapidly evaluate each choice on its own merits, even if they cycle through several possibilities. They don't need the best solution. They just need the one that works.*
>
> *"Experienced decision makers see a different world than novices do," concludes Klein. "And what they see tells them what they should do.*

Ultimately, intuition is all about perception. The formal rules of decision making are almost incidental.

"We used to think that experts carefully deliberate the merits of each course of action, whereas novices impulsively jump at the first option," says Klein. "It's the novices who must compare different approaches to solving a problem. Experts come up with a plan and then rapidly assess whether it will work. They move fast because they do less."

Successful Strategies

Strengths coaches often use elements of these approaches when sitting alongside the person and working with them to generate possible options. Sometimes they then move to the exercise called *Successful Strategies.* They may introduce it by saying something like:

"Looking at the options we have considered, let's move on to clarifying your chosen way forward. Bearing in mind what works, what do you believe are the three key things you can do to give yourself the greatest chance of success?"

This approach invites the person to bring their ideas together and begin focusing on their action plan for achieving their goal.

SuccessfulStrategies

Introduction

Good decision makers focus on the key things they can do to give themselves the greatest chance of success.

This exercise invites you to do the following things.

* *Describe the specific goal you want to achieve.*
* *Describe the three key strategies you can follow to give yourself the greatest chance of success.*

  Also, if appropriate, give examples of how you can follow those strategies.

The Specific Goal

The specific goal I want to achieve is:

* *To*

The specific things that will be happening that will show I have reached the goal will be:

*

*

*

The Three Key Strategies I Can Follow To Give Myself The Greatest Chance Of Success Are:

1) To

For example

*

*

*

2) To

For example

*

*

*

3) To

For example

*

*

*

How does this work in practice? One of the keys is to study what works in a particular field. We know many of the principles that people often follow:

To achieve success.

To build super teams.

To build superb organisations.

People can then apply this knowledge in their own way. They translate the principles into practice and get positive results – rather than just talk. It is to move from awareness to action to achievement.

Let's consider how learning from success might apply, for example, when helping a person to do work they love.

Doing satisfying work that earns a salary

"The world of work keeps changing," people may say, "so how can we help people to shape their futures? It is hard to know what skills they must learn to be successful."

Perhaps, but as the saying goes: 'the more things change, the more things stay the same.' Creative people throughout history have followed certain themes to get paid for their work.

They have built on their strengths, found sponsors who paid them and delivered success. People who develop such eternal skills are more likely to shape their futures. So you can help a person to do satisfying work and earn a salary by focusing on the following themes.

Strengths

Michelangelo, Anita Roddick and Steve Jobs had at least one thing in common. They did what they did best and got somebody to pay them for doing it. This is a key skill for getting funding. Some customers will always be interested in buying quality. And the best way of producing quality is to develop one's top talents.

You may have already helped a person to find their strengths. So let's move on to the next stage.

Sponsors

Anybody can do work they love, the art is to get somebody to pay them for doing it. Creative artists have faced this challenge throughout history. They have asked themselves:

> *"Shall I be true to my art, stay in a garret and wait to be discovered?*
>
> *"Shall I publicise my services, sell my soul and do whatever is necessary for money?*
>
> *"Shall I be true to myself, find sponsors and try to get a 'win-win' solution?"*

So how can you help a person to find sponsors who will pay them for doing what they do best? We have explored some of these guidelines earlier, but it is useful to help a person:

> *To clarify their 'perfect customers' – the kinds of employers or customers with whom they work best.*
>
> *To clarify the challenges these people face and their picture of success.*
>
> *To clarify how they can use their strengths to help these people to achieve success.*

"That sounds logical," somebody may say. "But how do you find sponsors? I am not good at selling myself."

Getting work by going out and helping other people to succeed

I have not got any work. So I will go home, polish my CV and put it out to recruitment agencies. That should produce some work.

That is one approach. Another is to go out, give to people and perform superb work that helps people to succeed. That will lead to work.

There are many ways to find potential sponsors. As Bernard Haldane pointed out in the 1940s, however, most work comes from our network. It comes from people that one knows or from being recommended by those people.

Different people will try to find work in different ways. The key is for them to do it in way that fits their values. The old proverb says: "Some people make things happen, some watch while things happen, and some wonder 'What happened?'"

Certainly this was true during the recession. Some people who lost their jobs tried to figure out what had happened and looked for somebody to blame. Others adopted different strategies when pursuing their job search.

"I know my strengths," said one person. "There are lots of projects out there where people need help. You can't tell me that every project and every piece of work in the UK is on time, on budget and on course to reach its goals.

Somewhere there are bound to be unsatisfied customer needs. So I am going to go out and help other people to succeed."

They went out, offered to help in various offices and made themselves indispensible. Because they were on hand, they were given the first opportunity to help on future projects.

"The recession taught me a lot," said another person. "Looking back, my first reaction was to worry about maintaining an income. But the second reaction was more interesting. I reframed it as an opportunity to help people.

"Over the years I have built a business as a mentor, but that suddenly became a 'luxury purchase'. Despite funds being cut, I offered my time to meet clients five days a week.

"Mentoring is often about helping people to make good decisions. So my clients and I explored the tough choices they needed to make regarding finances, people and shaping their future businesses."

"On the practical side, the first aim was to cover my weekly costs. After a month or so several clients asked me to do various project work. This included helping teams to complete internal projects, improve customer service and develop new business.

"These projects were funded from the technology and marketing budgets. Previously my work had been paid by HR. Nowadays my diary is full. But I am concerned about the next possible dip in the market. So it is time to go out and give to people again."

"That sounds fine, but rather idealistic," somebody may say. "What if you have to earn money quickly?" Then you follow the golden rule:

Make getting a job a full time job

Successful job seekers follow this path. They cram their days with activities most likely to get them in front of people. Then comes the thorny part. Many people still say: "I am no good at promoting myself." But they forget the real point.

Real networking is about helping other people to succeed

Sounds crazy? Perhaps. But it is the most effective way of getting work. People buy people. Whilst CVs may look good, most buyers in the market want somebody who they can trust, somebody who they know can deliver. As one person said:

"Every job I have had over the past 20 years has come from my network. Twice during that time the company where I worked was taken over and my job disappeared. So it was then time to reconnect with people who knew what I could deliver.

"The hard part was getting started. I spent masses of time visiting people. A long time ago I recognised that the conversation should be about them and their company, not about me. I followed up every visit with an email framing possible ideas they could use to tackle specific challenges.

"Several times this led to contract work and somebody saying: 'How can we take this further?' This is how I have got my last two roles. I started by doing pieces of project work, then moved into full-time employment."

Another person reported: "Ten years ago when setting up my business somebody said: 'Do what you do best and use those talents to help other people to succeed.' At the time I thought it did not sound much of a business plan. But ten years later it is still working."

So how can a person give to others? It is important for them to follow their natural style, rather than force themselves to do 'cold calling'. They need to do things that put a spring in they step. They might want to recommend books, offer to provide a pair of hands or connect people by putting them in touch with each other.

Like an actor, it's vital to 'keep working'. They need to do something every day to reach people in their network. But it is important to be patient. Like gardening, it can take time for the seeds to grow. You can invite the person to do the following exercise on this theme.

They are to draw a map of their network – the names of potential sponsors, customers, colleagues, friends and other people.

They are to describe the specific challenges that each person faces.

They are to describe the knowledge, tools or services they can offer to help each of them to succeed.

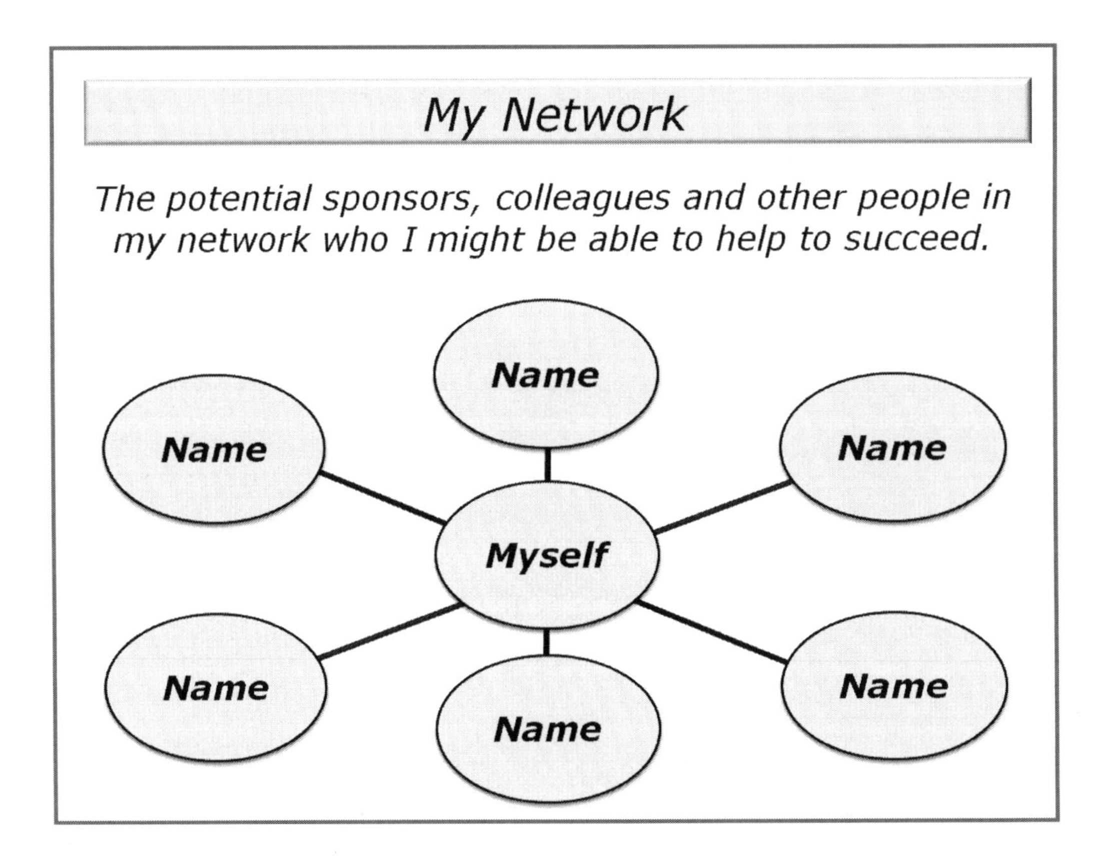

The name of the person is:

The specific challenges they face are:

*

*

*

The specific things I can do to help them to succeed are:

*

*

*

Clear Contracting With Sponsors

Providing a person keeps giving – without becoming a victim – at some point a potential sponsor will say: "How can we take this further?"

Great service givers recognise they are in the business of helping other people to succeed. Clear contracting is crucial, however, so they often take the following steps. They make agreements with the sponsor in the following areas.

Clarity

They clarify and agree on the 'What' – the specific results to be delivered.

Contracting

They clarify the 'How' – the overall principles to follow to reach the goal.

This also involves clarifying the Dos and Don'ts for working well with the sponsor. They reassure the sponsor by saying how they will proactively keep them informed about the progress towards the goals. Finally, they agree on the support required to achieve success.

Concrete Results

Great workers then take some of the following steps. They deliver some quick successes, because this reassures the sponsors. They perform superb work, provide great service and proactively keep the sponsors informed about the progress towards achieving the goals. They find creative solutions to challenges and do whatever is required to deliver the picture of success.

Crafting One's Best Contribution To An Employer

"This approach sounds logical if you are a freelancer," somebody may say. "But what happens if you want to work for an organisation or company? Is it possible to apply any of those principles when looking for a role?"

As we discussed before, we are all freelancers now. There are no jobs anymore, there are only projects. Even if a person is a applying for a role in an organisation, it can be useful for them to adopt the freelance mentality. They can focus on how they can use their strengths to help the employer to achieve success.

If appropriate, you can invite somebody to tackle the following exercise before going for an interview. The first step, of course, if for them to clarify their strengths.

The exercise then invites them to 'craft their script' for making their best contribution to an employer. They can prepare for the interview by clarifying what they believe to be:

The organisation's picture of success.

The contribution they would like make towards helping to organisation to achieve success.

The specific benefits of making this contribution.

Going for the interview, they can then focus on how they can help the employer to succeed. Here is the exercise.

My Best Contribution To An Employer

Introduction

This exercise invites you to do something rather challenging before going for an interview for a specific role. Before tackling it, however, it is vital to be aware of your strengths.

The following pages then invite you focus on the certain themes during the interview for your desired role.

** Success.*

Describe what you believe to be the goals – the picture of success – of the organisation, the team or employer you want to join.

This may be difficult, because you are not privy to lots of information. But focus on what you believe may be the goals. If possible, try to give some specific examples.

Great workers gear their strengths towards helping their employer to achieve their picture of success. So it is good to put some the effort into clarifying these aims.

* *Specific Contribution.*

Bearing in mind the organisation's goals and your strengths, describe the specific contribution you would like to make towards helping the employer to achieve the picture of success. Again, try to give some specific examples.

* *Specific Benefits.*

Describe the benefits of making this contribution. These can be benefits for the organisation, customers, colleagues and yourself.

* *Summary.*

Finally, there is a space to summarise the contribution you would like to make. Also add any other things that you would like to mention.

Enjoy the exercise. It will be challenging. But it can help you to clarify your potential best contribution to an employer.

Success

As far as I understand it, the goals of the organisation - together with some examples - are:

1) To

For example:

2) To

For example:

3) To

For example:

Specific Contribution

Bearing in mind the organisation's goals and my strengths, the specific contribution I would like to make towards achieving this picture of success would be:

1) To

For example:

2) To

For example:

3) To

For example:

Specific Benefits

The benefits of making this contribution would be:

For the Organisation

*

For the Customers

*

For the Colleagues

*

For Myself

*

Summary

So, in summary, this is what I would like to contribute towards achieving the picture of success. Plus any other things I would like to mention.

*

*

*

After finding a job, some people stop giving. But the best time to really 'network' is when they are successful, rather than when they want something. Paradoxically, they may find that even more opportunities come their way.

There are many models for finding work. One approach is to polish the CV and place it in the hands of others. Another is to get out there and help other people to succeed. The second approach is more likely to find work.

Let's assume that you have worked with the client on clarifying their successful strategies. The example we have explored relates to helping somebody to do satisfying work that earns a reasonable salary. But it is possible to apply a similar approach when helping a client to tackle many different challenges.

Good coaches often do more than just facilitate. Like a trusted advisor, they 'sit alongside' the client and, when appropriate, ask: "Is it okay if I share some ideas?" They aim to share knowledge and practical tools that the client finds relevant and rewarding.

Imagine that you have taken some of these steps. It is then time to bring everything together and, if appropriate, for the client to make their action plan for achieving their goals. There are obviously many ways to make such a plan. The following exercise invites a person to focus on the 'What, Why, How, Who and When'.

The exercise also includes making a road map for achieving their goals. We will be looking at this concept much more in the later section on building super teams. Here is the exercise that you can invite the person to tackle.

It will then be time to move on to the next section. This focuses on a person getting the required support to reach their goals.

My Action Plan

The 'What, Why, How, Who and When'

Introduction

This exercise is in several parts. It invites you to focus on the following steps when making an action plan for reaching a specific goal.

** The 'What'.*

The specific goal you want to achieve and by when.

The specific things that will be happening then that will show you have reached the goal.

** The 'Why'.*

The benefits of achieving the goal – both for yourself and for other people.

** The 'How'.*

The key strategies you can follow to give yourself the greatest chance of success.

** The 'Who'.*

The specific responsibilities of various people in working towards achieving the goal.

You will, of course, be responsible for doing your best to achieve the goal. But there may be other people who you involve in playing certain roles.

** The 'When'.*

This is the road map towards achieving the goal.

Some things to bear in mind when making the Road Map

Good decision makers often have a certain way of making a road map. They start from their destination and work backwards.

They keep their eyes on the end goal – rather than just look ahead to the next week. They clarify what is happening at the end and for the times preceding that date.

But then comes a complication. People sometimes find they are not certain what will be happening around the middle of the road map.

People solve this by returning to the beginning of the map and making their plans for going forward.

They often find this brings most of the plan together. Though there may still be areas that need to be settled around the middle.

The road map is a living document, however, and can be updated as they proceed along the journey.

Bearing this in mind, you may want to do some of the following things when making your road map.

* *Start from the destination and work backwards. Then, when appropriate, begin from the beginning.*

* *Describe the milestones – the specific things that you want to have achieved and by when – on the road to achieving the goal.*

* *Describe, if appropriate, the actual words you would like to hear various people saying on the road to achieving the goal.*

  This can help to bring the road map to life.

The following pages provide the first parts of the goal setting exercise. The further parts come later.

The 'What' – The Picture of Success

The specific goal I want to achieve by _____ is:

* *To*

  The specific things that will be happening then that will show I have reached the goal will be:

*

*

*

The 'Why' – The Benefits

The benefits of achieving the goal – both for myself and for other people - will be:

*

*

*

The 'How'

The key strategies I can follow to give myself the greatest chance of success are:

*

*

*

The 'Who'

The specific responsibilities of various people on the road to achieving the goal are:

*

*

*

The goal I want to achieve by _____ is:

To ____

Dates	Milestones. The specific things that I will have achieved by then will be:	Quotes. The words I want to hear people saying then are:
* End Date Then work backwards	* ____________ * ____________ * ____________	"____________" "____________" "____________"
* ________	* ____________ * ____________ * ____________	"____________" "____________" "____________"
* ________	* ____________ * ____________ * ____________	"____________" "____________" "____________"
* ________	* ____________ * ____________ * ____________	"____________" "____________" "____________"
* ________	* ____________ * ____________ * ____________	"____________" "____________" "____________"
Today		

Support

Imagine the person has clarified their strategies for achieving their goal. Some people choose to set off climbing their chosen mountain straight away. Other people pause for a while to rehearse their strategy and clarify the support they will require to reach the summit.

Peak performers are prepared to sweat, but even the toughest people need encouragement. Some coaches therefore help their clients to clarify the practical and personal support they need to deliver the goods. So you may the person some of the following questions.

> *Looking at the strategies you are going to pursue, what help do you need to make them happen? What would you like in terms of practical and personal support? Who are the people from whom you need support? How can you make clear contracts with these people? What is your back-up plan if you do not get the support?*
>
> *How can you manage your energy properly? How can you create times for rest and recovery? How can you anticipate and prevent difficulties happening? How can you manage the difficulties if they do happen? How can you keep encouraging yourself on the road to achieving the goals?*

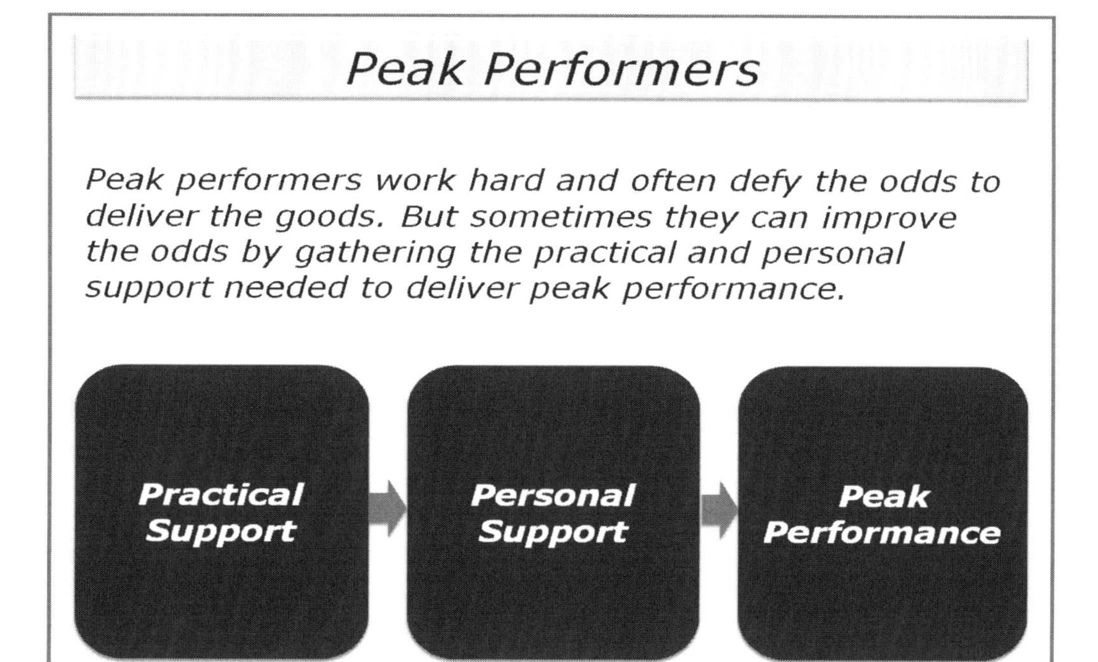

Practical Support

If a person is aiming to achieve certain goals, they will need the tools to do the job. If they are leading a project or taking a new role in an organisation, for example, they will need backing to achieve success. There are many aspects to such practical support, so let's explore some of them.

Imagine that your client has been offered a new role as a manager. They would like to take the role, but clear contracting is crucial. Great workers are happy to be accountable. But they also need the autonomy and authority required to deliver success. Let's explore how to make this happen.

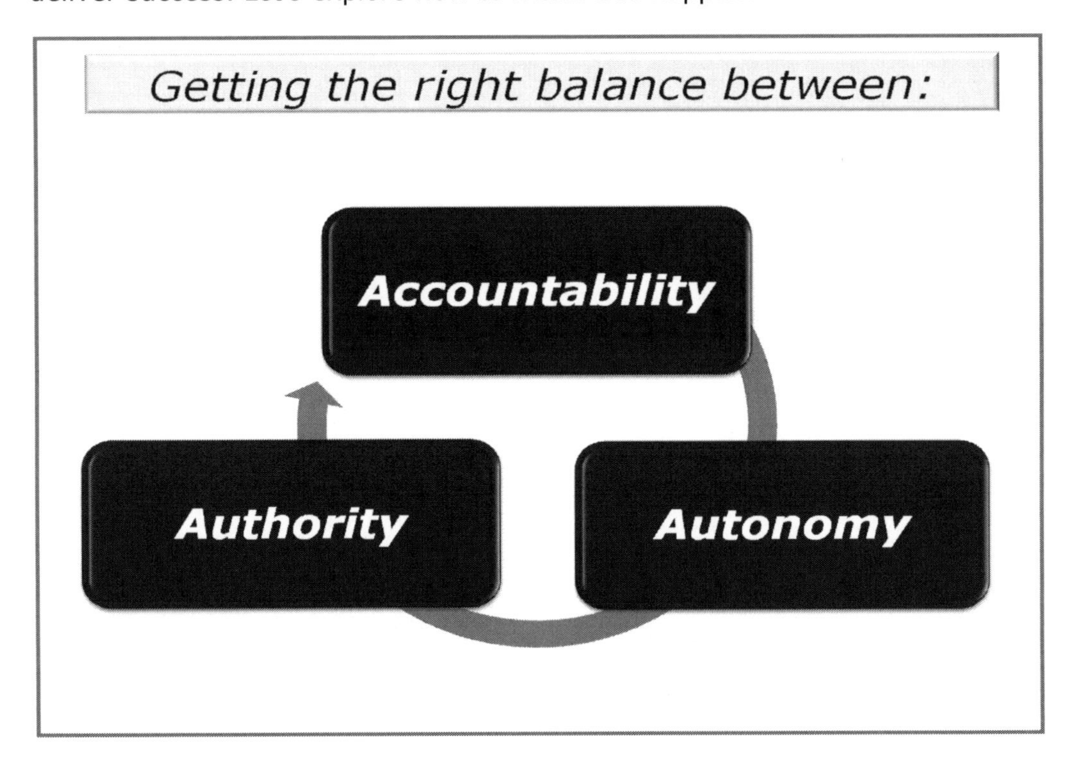

Accountability

You may have already helped the person to clarify the real results they must achieve. As discussed earlier, they need to agree with their sponsors on 'What' must be delivered, 'How' and by 'When'. They can play back their understanding to ensure that everybody agrees on the same picture.

They need to make crystal clear contracts. Their accountability rating for hitting the targets will be 10/10. So they must be absolutely sure about the results on which they will be judged. Invite them to try tackling the exercise on this theme. Looking at the role for which they are applying, they can do two things.

> *Describe what they will be held accountable for delivering.*
>
> *Describe, on a scale 0 – 10, the extent to which they believe they will be held accountable for delivering these results.*

As mentioned earlier, this will probably be 10/10.

Accountability

The specific results I will be held accountable for delivering will be:

*

*

*

The extent to which I will be held accountable for delivering these results will be:

____ / 10

Autonomy

Encourage the client to clarify the autonomy they will have to perform the role. They need to feel they have at least 8/10 in terms of having the freedom to act.

They must operate within parameters, of course, but they need oxygen to breathe. Let's assume they are taking the role of a manager. They can agree with the key sponsors on the autonomy they will have, for example:

To set the team's goals.

To set the team's strategies.

To manage the team's budget.

To decide who to hire and fire.

To do whatever is necessary to achieve the team's goals.

Invite them to complete the exercise on this theme. They are to do the following things.

Describe the kinds of autonomy they would like to have in order to achieve the goals.

Describe, on a scale on 0 – 10, the extent to which they feel they have the autonomy to act.

Describe the specific things they can do to maintain or improve this rating.

Autonomy

The specific kinds of autonomy I would like to have in order to achieve the goals are:

*

*

*

The extent to which I feel I have the autonomy required to achieve the goals is:

____ / 10

The specific things I can do to maintain or improve this sense of autonomy are:

*

*

*

Authority

Invite the client to clarify the authority they will have to perform the role. It is good if it feels like they have at least 8/10 in terms of having the power to act. Autonomy and authority are intertwined, of course, but they need both to operate successfully. One manager explained:

> *"Several years ago I took a high profile European job with a stretching brief but no mandate. The company told me to implement a customer service programme across the region, but we were in the midst of matrix madness. 'Dotted lines' abounded everywhere and nobody took responsibility.*
>
> *"Lacking direct power, I was supposed to influence the different countries into improving their customer service. My time was spent circling in the holding position above airports, attending meaningless meetings and eventually becoming dispirited.*
>
> *"Learning from the tough experience, I got a clear brief and mandate before taking my present job."*

Invite the person to tackle the exercise on this theme. They are to do the following things.

Describe the kinds of authority they would like to have in order to achieve the goals.

Describe, on a scale on to 10, the extent to which they feel they have the authority to act.

Describe the specific things they can do to maintain or improve this rating.

Authority

The specific kinds of authority I would like to have in order to achieve the goals are:

*

*

*

The extent to which I feel I have the authority required to achieve the goals is:

____ / 10

The specific things I can do to maintain or improve this sense of authority are:

*

*

*

Practical support comes in many forms. Getting the right balance of accountability, autonomy and authority can enable the person to perform superb work and deliver success. Let's move on to another aspect of getting practical support – balancing the great work and grunt work.

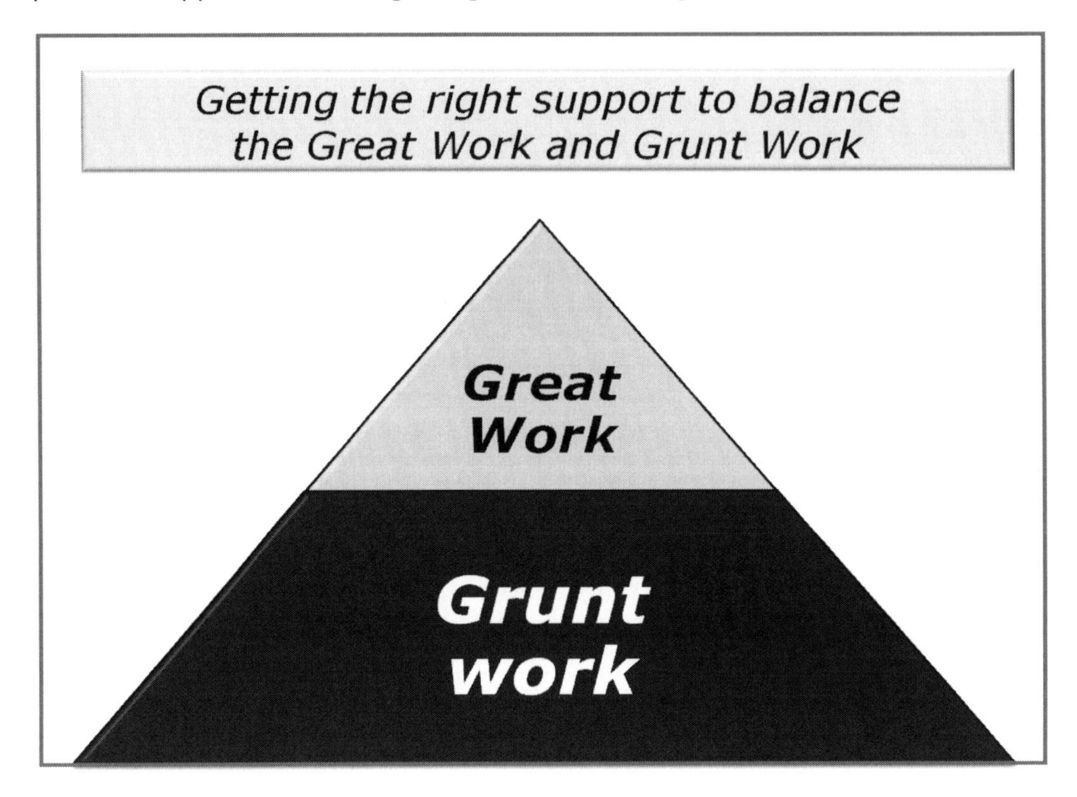

Peak performers don't mind doing the grunt work – sometimes they actually relish it. But they also need to get the support that will release them to do the great work.

Superb organisations recognise the importance of putting in place the right infrastructure. They do this on a systematic basis to ensure that people can use their top talents to get the best results.

Other organisations have a different approach towards infrastructure. Sometimes they decide to 'cut heads' in order to save costs. Certainly it is important to become more efficient. But unless the implications are thought through, it can result in more experts being driven down into grunt work.

One company, for example, decided to 'displace' the four senior Executive Assistants because each was earning over £50k a year. The decision makers believed they could save money by hiring 'temps' at £20k a year.

But the EA's were the people who knew the company inside out. They knew how to save on travel, get the best conference deals and 'manage' the bosses.

"It was the worst decision we ever made," one leader admitted later. "It took us a year to recover. We now employ one of the previous Executive Assistants on a contract basis and are paying them more than when they were employed full time."

Sometimes getting practical support means working with people who can complement one's strengths. This can lead to producing better results. One person said:

"My talents lie in providing leadership for my team and selling to customers. But I used to get bogged down in managing the daily tasks of the 16 people in my team. Looking back, I realised I had always worked best when having a good Co-ordinator who kept the entire team on track. So I made a business case for getting somebody to fill that role. It meant increasing my own sales targets, but that was okay.

"I hired a person I had worked with before who acted like my Operating Managing. That was liberating, but then I had to discipline myself to focus on what I did best.

"Previously I got fed up with bosses who kept saying, 'work smarter, not harder', whilst inundating us with emails requesting pointless information. It got to the point where I almost quit, but then I got the Co-ordinator to manage the daily tasks. Now I am delivering better results for the company."

Invite the person to tackle the exercise on this theme. They are to do the following things.

> *Describe the specific kinds of support and infrastructure they would like in order to do the grunt work.*
>
> *Describe the benefits of providing this support in terms of doing the grunt work and being able to deliver the great work.*

Grunt Work and Great Work

The specific kinds of practical support and infrastructure I would like in order to do some of the Grunt Work are:

*

*

*

The benefits of providing this support in terms of being able to do the Grunt Work and deliver the Great Work would be:

*

*

*

People who go freelance need to pay particular attention to creating the right infrastructure. Frequently it pays for them to spend extra days doing what they do best – such as earning money working with clients – rather than getting bogged down in work for which they have little talent.

Certainly they may need to do both for a while. They may, for example, do their own accounts and bookkeeping for several years. This is recommended to people who start their own business and want to get a feel for the cash flow. But they may then decide to focus on their strengths and earn enough fees to pay for such professional services. This can give them positive energy and provide the springboard for their future business.

You can invite the client to clarify their views on this theme. Looking back at the previous exercise, they can do the following things.

Describe the specific kinds of practical support they would like to get to reach their goals.

Describe the specific things they can do to do their best to get this practical support.

Describe the specific things they can do to find creative solutions if they do not get this practical support.

Practical Support

The specific kinds of practical support I would like in order to be able to reach the goals are:

*

*

*

The specific things I can do to do my best to get these kinds of practical support are:

*

*

*

The specific things I can do to find creative solutions if I do not get these kinds of practical support are:

*

*

*

Personal Support

There are many things a person can do to get encouragement. One approach is to manage their energy properly by getting the right balance between revitalisation, rehearsal and results (see diagram opposite). Let's explore these areas.

Revitalisation

Peak performers keep revitalising themselves to do good work. They know that producing results sometimes calls for being both a marathon runner and a sprinter. They need to maintain their physical and psychological energy for the long run, but also be able to rise to the occasion when it matters. Here are some characteristics of people who do this properly.

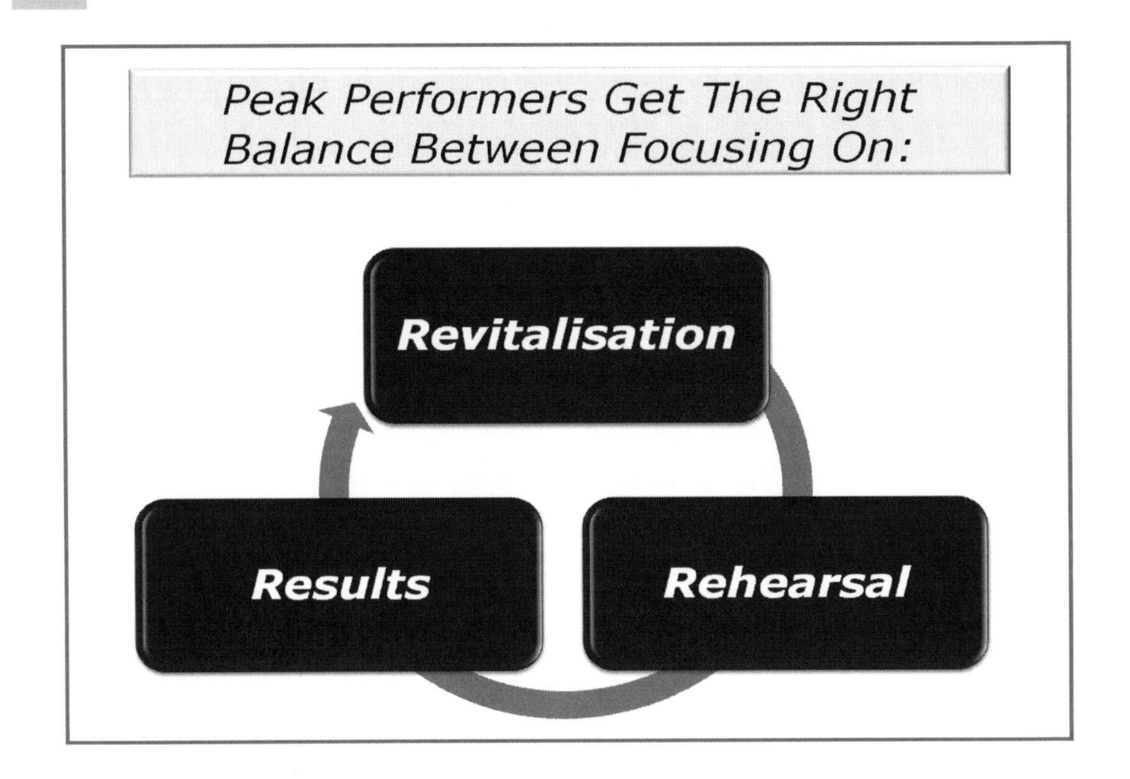

Get enough rest

Sleep is vital. This enables people to revitalise their bodies and unconsciously get over 'yesterday'. They then awake ready to take on new challenges. Failure to get enough sleep means they are constantly playing catch up and may not be fully present in a situation.

Eat properly

Peak performers eat the right food and take care of their bodies. So they may, for example, eat a good breakfast and then eat something nourishing every couple of hours. They tend to 'graze' on food that releases energy slowly, rather than wait for many hours and then binge on a meal. Different people will respond best to different diets. But peak performers stick to the diet that will enable them to do their best work.

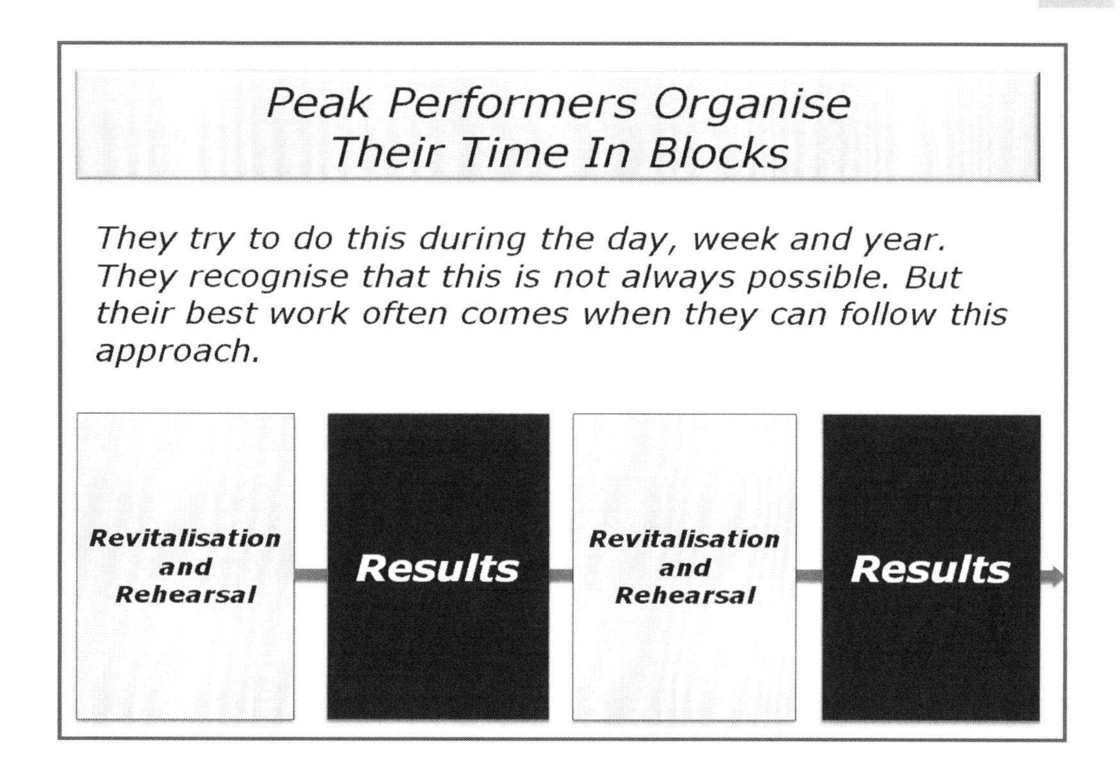

Organise time in blocks

Great workers often organise their time in blocks. This enables them to rest properly, rehearse and then be fully present to deliver the goods. It also enables them to become fully engaged and flow, focus and finish.

They try to take this approach during the day, the week and the year. During a day, for example, it can mean building in time to reflect and rehearse between meetings. This sounds difficult, but it is a good way to be effective.

"Nowadays I only have so much energy, so I have learned how to channel it properly," said one leader.

"Looking at the year ahead, I anticipate the busiest periods of business activity. Bearing these in mind, I create time to both rest and recover. If possible, I plan two long weekends – Friday to Monday – before and after these hectic periods. My partner and I love sunshine. So we get away to warm our bones in November and February."

"Nowadays I also break-down my day into blocks and build in time for recovery. I schedule 45 minute meetings, for example, rather ones that last an hour. I have re-learned to eat properly. Now I have a healthy snack every 90 minutes. I also walk outside to refresh my brain and get oxygen. Previously I hardly ever left my desk. Starving myself between breakfast and lunch, I then ate stodgy food. Now I seem more able to channel my energy."

Make good use of prime times

Great workers make good use of the times of the day when they have most energy or feel most creative. It is important to protect and capitalise on these times.

"I began by identifying my peaks and troughs during the day," said one marketing manager. "My best time is between 8.00 and 11.30 in the morning. I dip during the afternoon, but then come alive again at 9.00 pm.

"Previously I used to berate myself for having low energy during those downtimes. But then I learned to follow these natural rhythms."

Energy is life. Sometimes we have lots of energy, sometimes we feel drained. Sometimes we need to recover to become revitalised. Some people are at their best in the morning, some in the afternoon, some in the evening, some at a combination of these times.

"I became very protective of those times," said the marketing manager. "But I faced a dilemma. My desk is located in an open plan office, but I find it difficult to do creative work in the midst of such activity.

"So now I get into the office at 7.30 am and leave a note about my whereabouts in case of emergency. Then I spend the first hour by myself doing creative work in a 'cave'. Sometimes I am interrupted by urgent requests, but frequently it is my most productive part of the day."

"I have also asked my team members to let everybody know their prime times. Whilst we must all aim to be professional at all times, it is good to know when individual people are at their best."

Spend time with Encouragers

Encouragement gives us energy. Discouragement can sap our energy and dilute our ability to do good work. It is vital, of course, to be an Encourager for other people.

There are many models for looking at encouragement. One of this is based on Virginia Satir's work with the Self-Confidence Pot. A great family therapist, Virginia invited people to see their self-confidence as a pot. Sometimes they would have lots of confidence in the pot, other times they would have little.

Sometimes this was related to whether they were surrounded by Pot Fillers or Pot Drillers. Virginia introduced this idea in the 1950s. It was later used by many other people who talked about Energy Givers and Energy Drains. But it is worth going back to her original work.

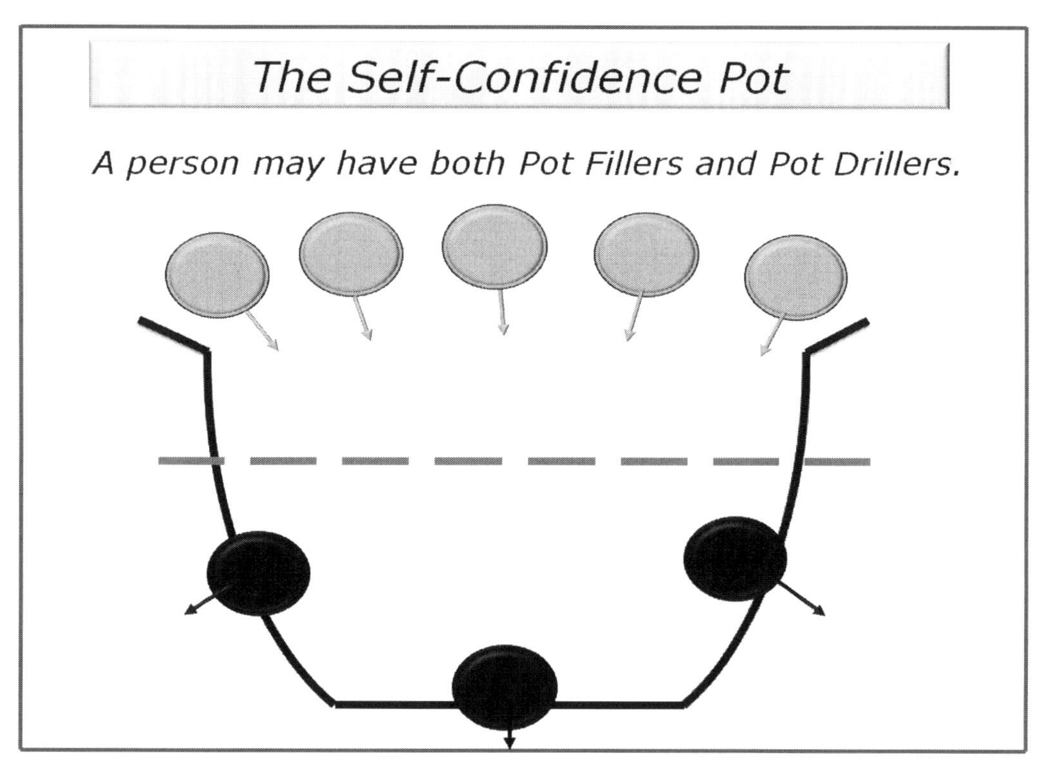

Imagine you are working with a client who wants to improve their level of self-confidence. The best way they can do this is to do stimulating work and achieve success. This normally increases their self-confidence. But it can be that they still feel low energy. If so, it can be useful for them to clarify the kinds of people they are meeting in their life and work.

You can invite them to explore this by tackling the exercise regarding the self-confidence pot. This asks them to go through the following steps.

Clarifying Their Level of Self Confidence

The person is to start by drawing an imaginary pot. Looking at the pot, they are to draw a line that corresponds to how high they feel their self-confidence is today.

If they have high confidence, they can draw it high up the pot. If their confidence is low, they can draw it at a lower point in the pot. The next step explores why it may be at this level.

A person can draw a line showing how high their self confidence is at the moment. If they have high confidence, it will be high in the pot. If low confidence, then it will be lower.

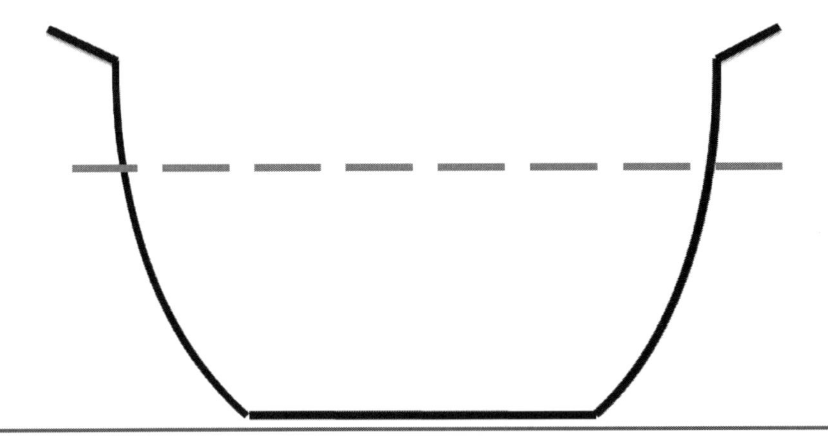

Clarifying Their Pot Fillers and Pot Drillers

The person can write the names of their pot fillers. These are the people who give them encouragement and energy. They look forward to seeing these people and feel more alive after meeting them. They can also describe the things they do to give themselves energy, such as listening to music, reading, gardening or whatever.

If a person has lots of things that give them positive energy, then their pot will be overflowing and they will be more able to pass-on encouragement to other people. But there may be complications, which brings us to the next part of the exercise.

They can write the names of the pot drillers. These are people who sap energy. They leave them feeling drained and discouraged. The more significant they are in the person's life, the nearer they will be to the base. The person may also do things to drill holes in their own pot.

One key point is worth remembering. Whilst we may have people who discourage us, we may also 'allow' them to have this effect. If a person is being negative, for example, sometimes we may have the option of going out of the room, giving them a positive alternative or doing other things to stop their energy affecting us. This is not always the case, but there are options we can apply for dealing with the negative energy.

Some people may be both pot fillers and pot drillers. They may have a 'pleasing–hurting' pattern. Sometimes they are positive then, without warning, they lash out. If this is this case, the client can go back to each of their lists. They can clarify the specific things these people do to encourage or drain them.

Clarifying How They Can Raise Their Level of Self-Confidence

"It is my responsibility to take charge of my future," said one person. "I need to spend more time doing the things that give me positive energy. Sometimes I allow some people to have a negative influence on me. I am going to control what I can in those situations."

How can a person continue to raise their confidence and also encourage other people? Here are some suggestions they may wish to consider.

Spend more time with people who give them energy.

They can spend more time with their encouragers and, if possible, to work with colleagues they find stimulating. People often find that, as they get older, they spend more time with personal and professional soul mates.

The client can also encourage themselves. They can do more of the things they love such as listening to music, skiing, visiting the theatre or whatever. Pursuing these activities will put more energy into their pot.

Spend less time – or no time – with people who drain energy.

Radical changes are difficult to make overnight but, unless the holes are filled, encouragement will simply flow out of the bottom. A person can do two things with the stoppers.

Stop seeing people who drain energy.

Why take such a drastic step? Energy is life. We need pure energy, rather than poisonous energy. Radical changes are difficult to make overnight but, unless the holes are filled, encouragement will ebb away.

Start making clear contracts with the people who both encourage and stop them.

They can start by rewarding the positive. This means giving clear messages about the specific things they do like the other person doing. They can explain how they would like to build on these parts of the relationship.

They can give the person positive alternatives to the possible negative behaviour by saying: "In the future, is it possible for you to ...?" or "I would prefer it if you..."

They can present suggestions to the other person, rather than label them as 'bad'. It is unlikely that a negative person, for example, will respond immediately. Everybody needs time to lick their wounds. But is it important not to argue or fall into the blame game.

What if the negative person refuses to respond? Then it will be time to make a decision. It is important to give, but not become a victim. There is no point in staying around to have their pot drilled by people who choose to be miserable or 'observer critics'.

Be an encourager for other people.

The client can encourage their encouragers. They may find they get even more positive energy and can keep building the relationships.

Finally, when in doubt, the person can ask: "Does this activity give me energy?" If not, they can switch to spending time with the people – and on the activities – that provide stimulation. This may seem tough. But it is much tougher to stay with negative people.

So far we have covered many ideas that a person can use to revitalise themselves. These have included focusing on:

The sleep they can get.

The food they can eat.

The way they can organise their time in blocks.

The way they can capitalise on their prime times.

The way they can spend more time with Encouragers.

If appropriate, you can invite the client to clarify the steps they can take to keep revitalising themselves. They can do this by completing the following exercise. It will be then time to move on to explore further ways they can encourage themselves and do great work.

Revitalisation

The specific things I can do to keep revitalising myself are:

*

*

*

Rehearsal

Great workers continually rehearse what they are going to do to achieve success. This is a superb way of supporting themselves. Such people practise implementing their strategies and finding solutions to challenges. They are then able to be fully present when going into the actual situation.

As mentioned earlier, Charles Garfield introduced this concept to a wider audience in his book *Peak Performers.* The National Business Association produced a summary of his views on mental rehearsal in one of their newsletters.

"Peak performers practise mental rehearsal. They rehearse, in their mind's eye, any incident or event that is important to them. Mental rehearsal is a core capability of peak performers ... Business executives can benefit by rehearsing specific events in the mind's eye, including all those possible outcomes and possible surprises that can materialize. This mental practice can build familiarity and boost confidence and self-esteem."

Here is another description from Scott Williams, Professor of Management at Wright State University and Executive Director of the Center for Innovation Management:

> *"Mental rehearsal involves imagined, mental practice of performing a task as opposed to actual practice. That is, when engaging in mental rehearsal, one imagines performing without having to actually do anything. Many studies have found mental rehearsal to be successful at improving task performance and reducing stress.*
>
> *"A limitation, of course, is that one also has to have a certain degree of knowledge and skill for performing the activity in order to be successful ..."*

There are many models for applying mental rehearsal. Here is one approach. If appropriate, you can invite the client to choose a specific scenario they want to rehearse and then go through the following steps.

Mental Rehearsal

Here are five steps for mentally rehearsing achieving success.

1) Success.

You can start by visualising the picture of success.

2) Strategies.

You can rehearse pursuing the key strategies for achieving success.

3) Solutions.

You can rehearse solutions for overcoming potential challenges on the road to achieving success.

4) Skills.

You can rehearse the specific skills required for achieving success.

5) Success.

You can again rehearse achieving the picture of success.

Different people do, of course, rehearse different scenarios. They may choose to rehearse, for example:

Making a presentation to a client.

Meeting somebody to talk about a difficult matter.

Overcoming potential setbacks.

Building on successes.

Pursuing their principles when performing under pressure.

If appropriate, you can invite a client to practise the art of mental rehearsal. The person can do this either alone or with your help. They can support themselves in this way by completing the following exercise.

Rehearsal

The specific things I can do to, where appropriate, keep practicing mental rehearsal are:

*

*

*

Results

Great workers keep following good habits. They keep repeating what they do right to consistently get to 7/10. Such people then work to reach 10/10. Sometimes people can benefit, however, by reminding themselves of the habits they are following to do good work. These can provide the springboard for doing great work in the future.

Imagine the person you are working with wants to keep topping up the 'half full' part of their glass. How to help them to build confidence and yet also keep developing?

One approach is to invite them to keep a journal called *My Right Book.* I have used this tool when working with people who wanted to be more positive, improve as professionals or to encourage other people. The journal invites them to focus on:

The specific things they have done right during a certain time period and how they can follow these principles more in the future.

The specific things they can do even better in the future and how.

It is good to encourage people to focus on the small things they have done well. They can then continue to repeat these patterns. They can also become better at self-evaluation and more able to improve their performance.

Imagine you want to use this exercise with a client. The following instructions relate to them keeping a daily journal. But they can also focus on a different time period or simply look at their performance in a particular situation.

My Right Book

The Things I Did Right

The specific things I did right today were:

1)

For example:

2)

For example:

3)

For example:

The specific things I can do to follow these principles more in the future are:

1)

For example:

2)

For example:

3)

For example:

The Things I Can Do Better

The specific things I can do better in the future – and how - are:

1)

For example:

2)

For example:

3)

For example:

Focusing On The Results Rather Than The Running Commentary

Great workers focus on the specific results to achieve and cut out all irrelevant 'noise'. This sounds easy in theory, but it can be harder in practice.

Observers, critics, bosses, the press, bloggers and many others want to provide a running commentary. Sometimes this can be helpful. But people can get diverted by those with other agendas, especially if these are provocative. So let's explore how a person can focus on the results to achieve, rather than get distracted.

Clarifying the results to achieve

J.K. Rowling focused on her specific vision, even when experiencing severe difficulties during her twenties. Recalling her early years of writing, she said:

"I had a daughter I adored, a typewriter and a big idea."

She aimed to produce a seven-volume epic for young readers that chronicled the adventures of Harry Potter. She was clear on the road map, the milestones and the feelings each book should evoke.

"I just wrote the sort of thing I liked reading when I was younger (and still enjoy now!)," she explained.

Certainly there were lots of ups and downs along the way, but she pursued her daily disciplines to reach the goal. J.K. Rowling chose to focus on the things that were vital in her life.

Clarifying the potential running commentaries

Peak performers are dreamers who do and deliver. They are, by definition, extremists: they focus on a few things and do them extremely well. Such people choose to be creators rather than complainers; doers rather than talkers.

But doing great work creates waves. Some people will appreciate their efforts, but others will criticise them, especially if their work is in the public eye – such as in sports, the arts, politics or other fields. Great workers learn to focus on the results, however, rather than get distracted by other people's constant running commentaries.

"Professional feedback is vital for me, because I want a reality check," said one pioneer. "But I want it from people I respect.

"The people I listen to are those who share the same values and vision. They give me honest feedback and suggestions about how to get results. I have little time for observer critics, complainers or those with other agendas.

"In the old days, for example, I saw talented people being criticised by moaners in organisations who used 360 degree feedback to vent their frustration. Great workers will be respected by some people, but not be liked by everybody.

"Certainly they should listen to constructive suggestions. But they shouldn't get dragged down by people who have settled for mediocrity."

Imagine the client you are working with wants to focus on the results to achieve and deal with any other noise. Who are the people who might give 'running commentaries'? What might be their agenda? What might they be saying? Will they be constructive, critical or a combination of both? What might be the other kinds of commentaries, 'noises' or diversions?

Clarifying how to focus on the results rather than the running commentary

Peak performers seem to exist in their own space – their own zone, tunnel or bubble. They keep their eyes on the prize. Concentrating on the concrete results to achieve, they cut off other distractions.

Golfers, tennis players and other athletes, for example, often have physical rituals they use to 'brush off' criticisms, heckling, mistakes and other disruptions. Peak performers stay calm in their own space, rather than get caught in other people's agendas.

The Dalai Lama, for example, stays true to his values, even when provoked. Like Mahatma Gandhi, his life is his message. Explaining his philosophy, he says things like:

"Be kind whenever possible. It is always possible ... I find hope in the darkest of days, and focus in the brightest ... My religion is very simple. My religion is kindness ... Our prime purpose in this life is to help others. And if you can't help them, at least don't hurt them."

Imagine your client wants to focus on the results rather than the running commentary. If appropriate, you can invite them to do the following exercise.

Results Rather Than Running Commentary

The specific things I can do to focus on the results - rather than the running commentary - are:

*

*

*

Peak performers love to work hard, which is part of what makes them special. At the same time they sometimes need to create or get personal support.

You can invite the client to sum up what they have decided to do on this theme. Looking back at the topics we have covered, they can do the following things.

Describe the specific kinds of personal support they would like to create or get to reach their goals.

Describe the specific things they can do to do their best to get this personal support.

Describe the specific things they can do to find creative solutions if they do not get this personal support.

Personal Support

The specific kinds of personal support I would like to create or to get in order to be able to reach the goals are:

*

*

*

The specific things I can do to find creative solutions if I do not get these kinds of personal support are:

*

*

*

The specific things I can do to do my best to get these kinds of personal support are:

*

*

*

Let's assume the person has clarified how to get the required support. It is then time to get the show on the road and perform superb work. This takes us to the next step.

Superb Work

Great workers translate their strategies into action and get some early successes. They perform superb work and keep their sponsors informed. They provide great service and help their internal and external customers to achieve success.

Imagine your client wants to go through these steps on the way towards achieving their goals. Let's explore how to make this happen.

Superb Work

Peak performers love to sweat. T.E. Lawrence described the 'dreamers of the day' who were likely to follow their dreams. He wrote:

> *"All men dream; but not equally. Those who dream by night in the dusty recesses of their minds wake in the day to find that it was vanity; but the dreamers of the day are dangerous men, for they may act out their dreams with open eyes, to make it possible."*

Great workers follow certain daily disciplines. They do the right things in the right way every day. Such people have a Gold Medal Mentality. Whatever their chosen field, they go beyond aiming to get a Bronze or Silver. They strive to deliver their equivalent of a Gold.

Getting Some Early Successes

Let's assume your client knows their action plan for achieving their goal. They can start their campaign by getting some early wins. This can create positive momentum and a winning feeling.

Bearing this in mind, it can be useful to invite the person to tackle the following exercise. Ask them to describe the specific things they can do to get some early wins. This can generate the energy to go to the next stage.

The specific things I can do to get some early successes are:

* *To*

* *To*

* *To*

Being Professional

Great workers take a pride in being professional. They always do the basics and then add the brilliance. There are many models for performing fine work. One approach is described by Peter Vidmar, who won a Gold Medal in gymnastics at the 1984 Los Angeles Olympics.

Looking back at how his event was scored in those days, he describes the steps gymnasts took to get a Perfect 10. This was first achieved by Nadia Comaneci in Montreal.

First they must achieve the Olympic standard of technical competence. This often took years of dedication and gave them the 9.4. They could then add 0.2 by taking a risk; 0.2 by demonstrating originality – something that had never been done before; and 0.2 by showing virtuosity – flair. Such a brilliant performance would produce the Perfect 10 and, hopefully, the Olympic Gold.

Peter is a class act who now makes his living as an inspiring speaker. Many people leave his sessions fired up. He reports that one reaction is them saying:

> *"We now know how to do great work. We need to be original, take risks and demonstrate virtuosity."*

They only forget one thing. Peter's most important message is that people must first achieve the 9.4. That is the first step towards winning an Olympic Gold.

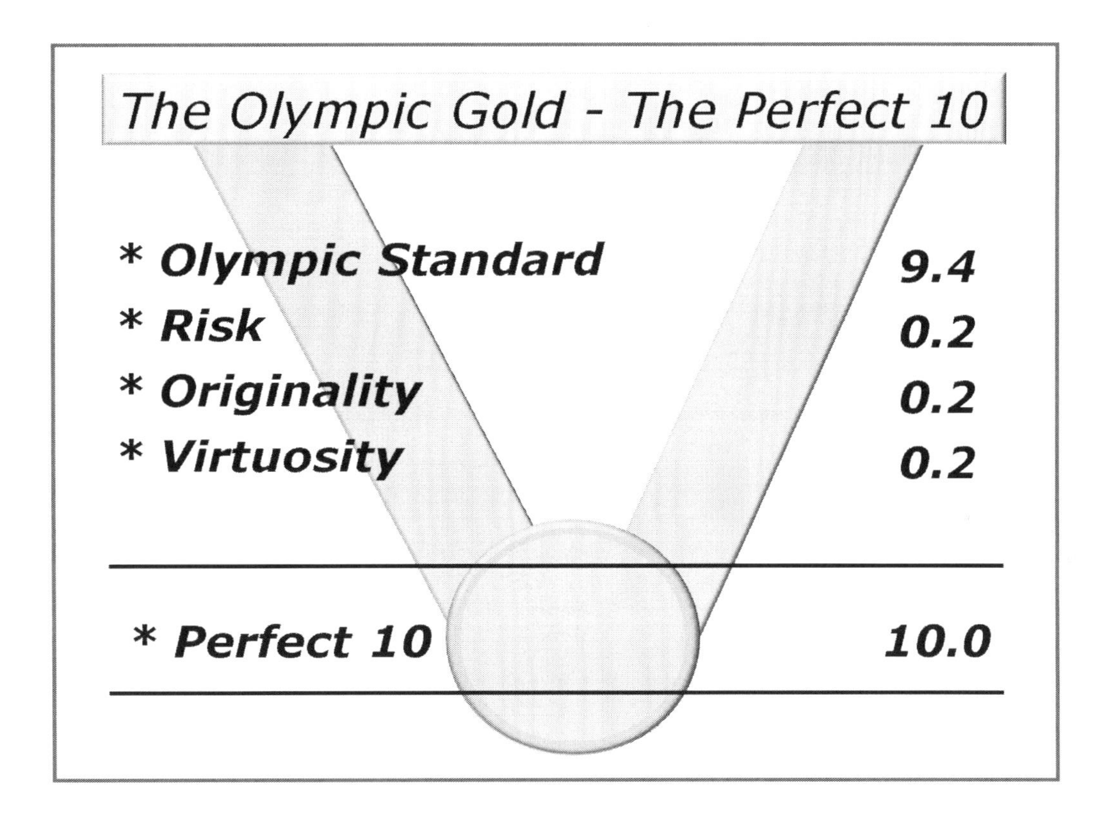

Great workers adopt a similar approach. Many of them follow certain ethics in their daily work. They keep pursuing these on the journey towards reaching their goals. One person summarised their approach in the following way.

"Many years ago I created my Professional Credo. This is something I aim to follow each day. Without going into detail, here is the framework I use.

My Professional Credo

Dos. The specific things I can do to be professional in my work are:

Do

Do

Do

Do

Do

Don'ts. The specific things I must not do if I am to be professional in my work are:

Don't

Don't

Don't

Don't

Don't

Different people have different approaches to developing their disciplines. Imagine that you are working with a client who wants to focus on their daily actions. You can invite them to tackle the following exercise on how they can perform fine work on the road to reaching their goal.

The specific things I can do to translate the strategies into action and perform superb work are:

1) To

For example:

** To*

** To*

** To*

2) To

For example:

** To*

** To*

** To*

3) To

For example:

** To*

** To*

** To*

Managing Sponsors

Ten years ago I worked with a young sales person who was new to a big multi-national. Like all new employees, he was on a 3 month probationary period. But there were doubts about offering him a full time role. Why?

He was obviously a great sales person.

He came from a business background, however, where he was used to being a Lone Ranger and never informing his key sponsors – his managers and other stakeholders – what he was doing.

He then pulled the rabbit out of the hat at the last moment and became the hero by beating everybody else's sales figures.

This approach worked in his previous company, but not in the multi-national. His manager asked if he was prepared to get some coaching on how to function in such a company.

The probationer agreed to the deal. He was serious about learning, however, rather than just going through the motions of coaching. The sessions went well. He implemented the ideas, worked hard and now – ten years later – is the Global Sales Director of a huge company.

During the sessions we focused on how to satisfy his key sponsors. Certainly this meant delivering the numbers. But it also meant keeping them appropriately informed. People would then feel reassured and turn their attention to other matters.

Peter Drucker wrote: "The purpose of business is to create and keep a customer." The same rule applies when a person contributes to an organisation. Whether they work as a freelancer or as a full-time employee, their role is to satisfy their sponsors – the people who can hire or fire them.

Some people forget this rule and become institutionalised. They stop keeping their manager informed, stop taking initiatives and wait to be 'managed'. Many of today's businesses, however, want people who are positive, proactive and professional.

Imagine that your client wants to focus on how to manage their sponsors in a professional way. This calls for them taking responsibility, reassuring the sponsors and delivering results. Let's explore these themes.

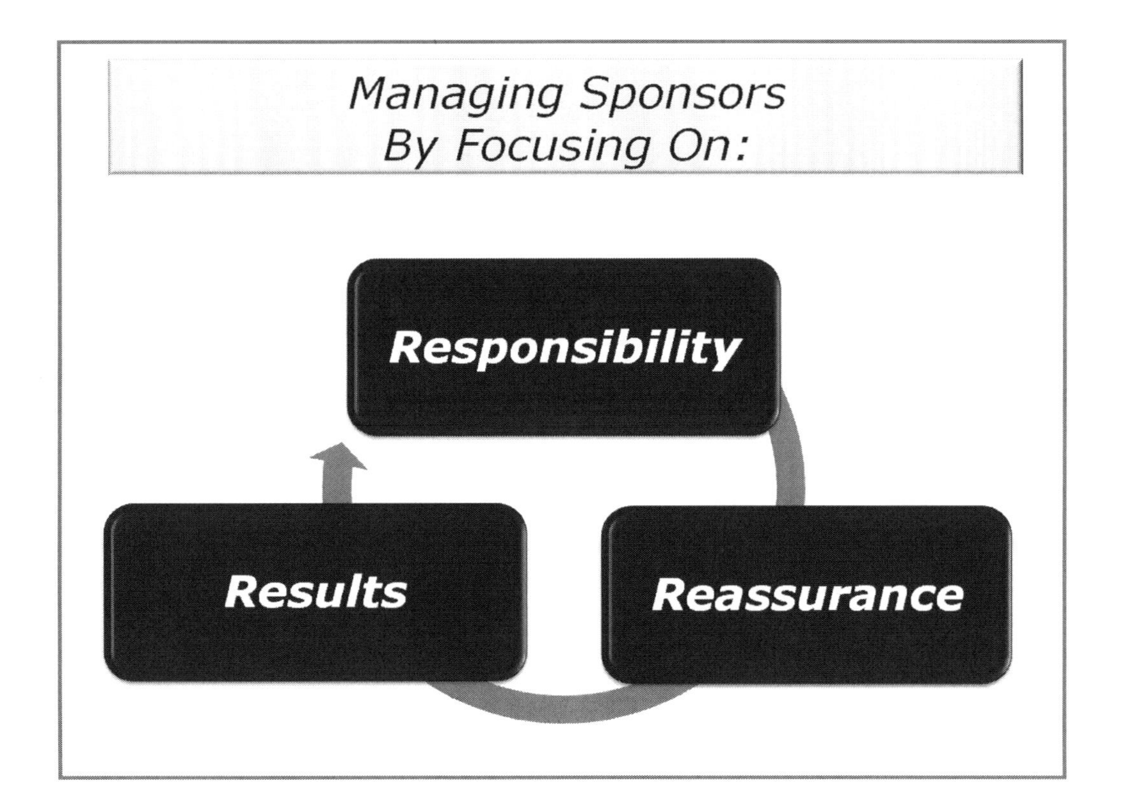

Responsibility

"I want people to step forward," said one leader. "I want them to understand our goals, say how they want to contribute and then deliver on their promises.

"Too many people sit waiting for me to dish out the jobs. That may have worked in the past, but now I want self-managing people who take initiatives. This frees me up to take a more strategic role in shaping the business."

Writing in the 1980s, Peter Drucker predicted the need for people to behave like volunteers in organisations. This calls for three things.

The leaders to provide a compelling vision and the support people need to do the job.

The individuals to opt-in and behave likes volunteers, rather than victims.

The whole team to work together by making clear contracts and doing what is required to deliver the agreed results.

People who take responsibility are more likely to build a good reputation and put good will into the bank. This also leads to the next step.

Reassurance

Sponsors worry. They go to bed at night worrying about hitting the numbers, satisfying their bosses, improving service quality, getting the right people and staying out of trouble. Similarly, their own bosses are under pressure from the banks, stock market or other outside forces.

Great workers show they understand the business from the sponsor's point of view.

They proactively keep sponsors informed about their progress towards achieving the goals. They also show they have thought ahead about the challenges that must be tackled in the forthcoming weeks. They show they are on top of the game.

Sponsors do not like nasty surprises, but honesty is crucial, especially when faced by potential crises. Professional people then present the possible options for dealing with a problem and the consequences of each option. Where appropriate, they also give their recommendations.

Results

"Football is a results business," said one leading football manager. "I can talk a good game with the press, but I must deliver results on the field. Otherwise I will get sacked."

Sponsors will judge a person by their results. So this calls for a supplier or full time employee doing three things.

Being crystal clear on what they must deliver.

Performing superb work, keeping sponsors informed and delivering the goods.

Going that extra mile and producing something special.

People buy people and, in the future, they will remember if somebody gave them great service. Taking these steps will enable a person create and keep customers. If appropriate, you can invite your client to tackle the following exercise. This asks them to do two things.

Describe the specific things they can do to manage their sponsors.

Describe the specific benefits of doing this in a proactive and professional way.

Managing Sponsors

The specific things I can do to manage my sponsors are:

*

*

*

The specific benefits of doing this in a proactive and professional way will be:

*

*

*

Providing Great Service

"My role is simple," explained one service giver. "It is to help people to succeed. That is what you do in the service business – whether you are a coach, teacher, software designer, sales person or whatever. This calls for clarifying the customer's aspirations and focusing on their specific goals. You can then provide services that help them to succeed."

Let's assume that your client knows how to establish clarity, make clear working contracts and deliver concrete results to their sponsors.

Everybody knows what good service givers do right. They make the customer feel special, clarify the customer's goals, perform great work, solve problems, deliver the goods and sometimes add that touch of class. They make it easy to do business with them and afterwards the customer may say:

"You provided great service. I will recommend you to my friends."

Imagine that your client is already doing many of these things with their customers. It can also be useful for them to look at how they continue to develop as service givers.

Improving The Total Service Package

There are many models for improving customer service. One approach that works was developed by Barrie Hopson and Mike Scally. This was described in their book *12 Steps To Success Through Service*.

They describe four elements that make up the total service package. These are the product, people skills, procedures and packaging. Let's explore these factors.

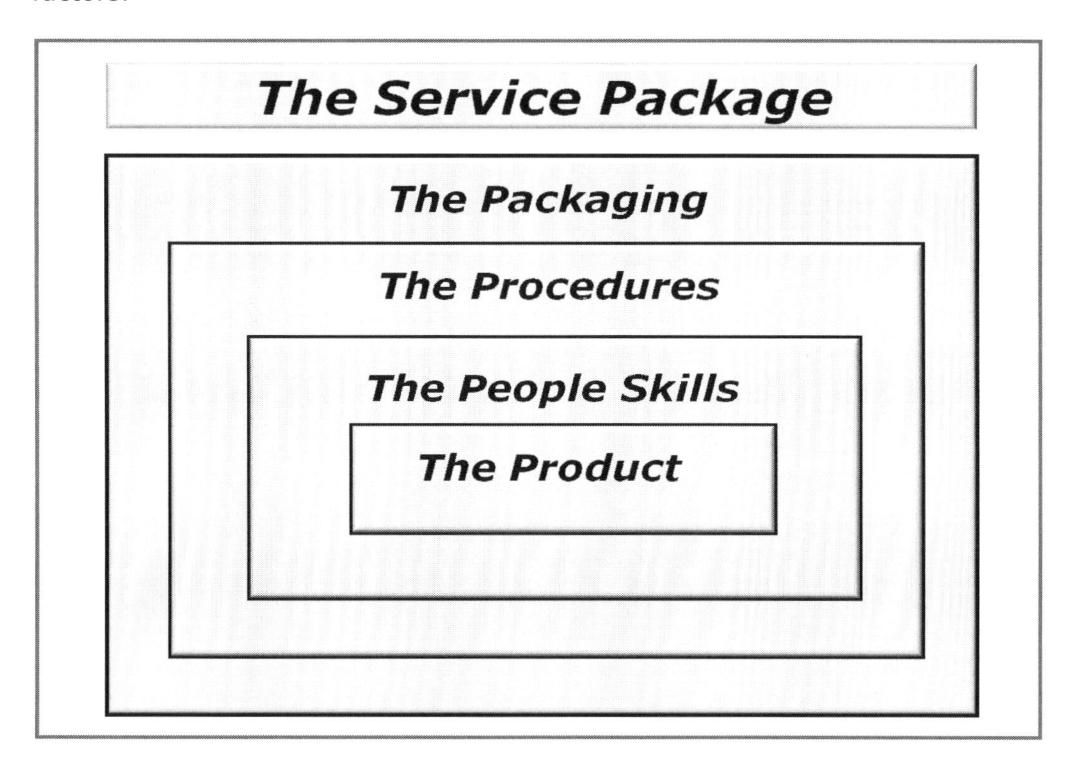

The 'Product'

This is the basic product or service that the person offers to their customer. They may provide mentoring, consultancy, technical solutions, marketing, hospitality or whatever. This product or service must be right – otherwise everything else will be irrelevant.

Invite the person to do two things. First, to rate the quality of the products or services that they offer to their customers. They are to do this on a scale 0 – 10. Second, to describe the specific things they can to do maintain or improve this rating.

> **The Product**
>
> *The rating I would give regarding the quality of the products or services that I offer to customers is: ____ /10*
>
> *The specific things I can do to maintain or improve this rating are:*
>
> *
>
> *
>
> *

The People Skills

These are the people skills the person employs when carrying out their work. These may include making the customer feel welcome, listening, clarifying goals, acting as a trusted advisor, finding creative solutions or whatever. These softer skills are often crucial. Customers report that many bad experiences stem from being treated rudely.

Invite the person to do two things. First, to rate the quality of the people skills they employ when providing the products or services to customers. Second, to describe the specific things they can to do maintain or improve this rating.

The People Skills

The rating I would give regarding the quality of the people skills I employ when providing the products or services to customers is: ____ /10

The specific things I can do to maintain or improve this rating are:

*

*

*

The Procedures

Great service givers make it easy for the customer to do business with them. They design their systems to put the customer first, rather than last.

Good organisations ensure that their people take responsibility for delivering superb customer service and, where appropriate, to act as a 'one stop' shop. They are also good at recovering from mistakes. They apologise, accept the customer's experience is real for them and act to solve the problem. Such organisations do not ship customers from department to department.

Suppliers need to make it easy for customers to reach them and for them to respond quickly. They need to ensure the customer feels as if they are the centre of the world. They must provide successful services and, where appropriate, find solutions that are a win for the customer and a win for themselves.

Invite the person to do two things. First, to rate their procedures in terms of making it easy for the customer to do business with them. Second, to describe the specific things they can to do maintain or improve this rating.

The Procedures

The rating I would give regarding the quality of the procedures – putting the customer first and making it easy for them to do business with me – is: ____ /10

The specific things I can do to maintain or improve this rating are:

*

*

*

The Packaging

This was the way the person presents their products and services to the customers. This may include the way they present their web site, knowledge, solutions or whatever.

Great service givers position what they offer in terms of relevance to the customer. They make this user-friendly and rewarding for the customer.

The 'packaging' embodies their values as service givers that aim to help the customers to succeed.

Invite the person to do two things. First, to rate the packaging of the products or services they offer to customers. Second, to describe the specific things they can do to maintain or improve this rating.

The Packaging

The rating I would give regarding the quality of the packaging of the products or services that I offer to customers is: ____ /10

The specific things I can do to maintain or improve this rating are:

*

*

*

There are many models for improving customer service. The Service Package approach is one that works with individuals and also in organisations. During the past 20 years, for example, I have worked with organisations that have set up teams to constantly improve each of the Four Ps. They implement the ideas and develop the total Service Package.

Soon it will be time to move on to helping the client to find solutions to challenges. Before then, however, you may wish to invite them to focus on how they can continue to deliver great service to customers. Here is the final exercise in this section on superb work.

Great Customer Service

The specific things I can do to keep providing great service to customers are:

*

*

*

The specific benefits of providing this great service to customers will be:

*

*

*

Solutions

Peak performers are resilient. They harness their inner strength, find solutions to challenges and overcome setbacks successfully. Such people often grow from these experiences.

Al Siebert's work shows that resilient people think ahead. They use their personal radar to anticipate and, if possible, prevent potential difficulties. Nevertheless, setbacks are bound to happen. As Al wrote in *The Survivor Personality,* however:

> *"The survivor way of orientating to a crisis is to feel fully and totally responsible for making things work out well."*

Some people welcome tough challenges. One tennis champion said:

> *"I look forward to crises in a game. Why? Both my opponent and I are bound to encounter difficulties during a match. I am good at dealing with such problems. Showing I can overcome setbacks gives me an advantage. The other player may not be as strong when they meet difficulties. So therefore I embrace challenges."*

Imagine that client has already anticipated and prevented certain difficulties happening. Despite this, they are bound to meet setbacks along the road. Let's explore how you can help them to remain strong and find creative solutions to challenges.

Managing Setbacks Successfully

There are many models for understanding reactive change. Most are based on the writings of Elisabeth Kübler-Ross. She is best known for her work on the grief cycle that people may experience when approaching dying.

Building on her ideas, other writers have outlined the stages that people may go through after experiencing a setback. A person may have had an accident, lost a job, suffered a rejection or whatever. Whilst everybody reacts differently, many go through the reactive change curve.

They experience the stages of shock, denial, paralysis, anger and hurt. Healing takes time. But they gather new strength, set new goals, work hard, achieve success and gather self-confidence. People sometimes emerge stronger, wiser and more able to shape their future.

The process is not linear. A person may start climbing the curve, think they are over the worst and then revert back to hurt, anger or healing. Sometimes they may also get flashbacks, perhaps getting upset with themselves for their part in the situation. Many people do, however, recover.

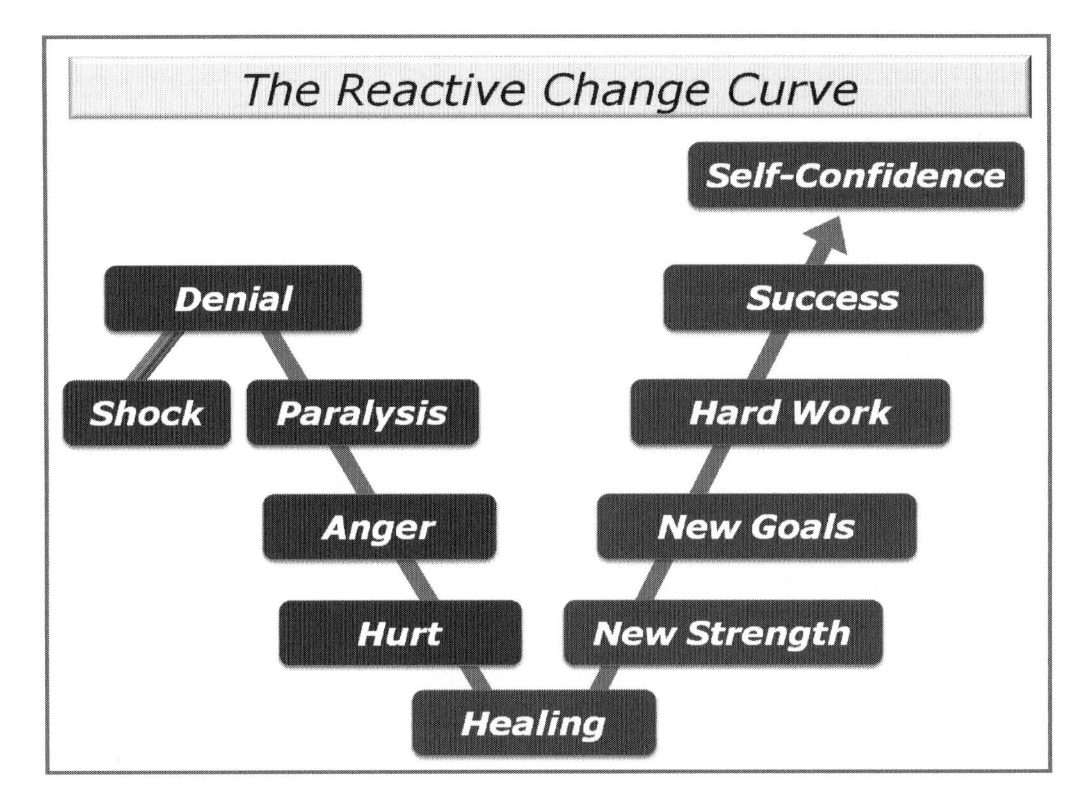

How can you help a person to come through the change curve? Classic counsellors often provide a supportive and non-directive environment in which a person can talk through their experiences. This enables them to work through the curve and take charge of shaping their futures.

Strengths coaches sometimes add another element. They recognise it can be important for a person to work through these stages. But at an appropriate time, however, they may make certain interventions. These are geared to helping a person to focus on their inner strength and successful patterns.

So they may, for example, invite the person to look back at their positive history. They may ask them:

To recall a time when they have overcome a similar challenge successfully.

To clarify what they did right then.

To clarify how they can follow some of these principles to overcome the present challenge successfully.

Even if the person is not facing a tough challenge, you can invite them to do the following exercise. This reinforces the philosophy that they already have great inner resources. They can harness these if they encounter difficulties in the future.

Managing Setbacks

Looking back at my positive history, a time when I managed a setback successfully was:

* *When I*

Here is a fuller description about the situation I managed successfully:

*

*

*

The specific things I did right then to manage the setback successfully were:

*

*

*

The specific things I can do to follow some of these principles to manage setbacks successfully in the future are:

*

*

*

Finding Solutions to Challenges

There are many approaches to creative problem solving. The following pages explore one model. It invites you to help somebody to tackle a challenge by focusing on clarity, creativity and concrete results.

Let's assume that your client faces a particular challenge. They may want to change their career, take greater care of their health, turnaround a team, change an organisation's culture or whatever.

How can you help them to tackle challenge? One approach is to guide them through the Three C Model for creative problem solving. Let's explore these steps.

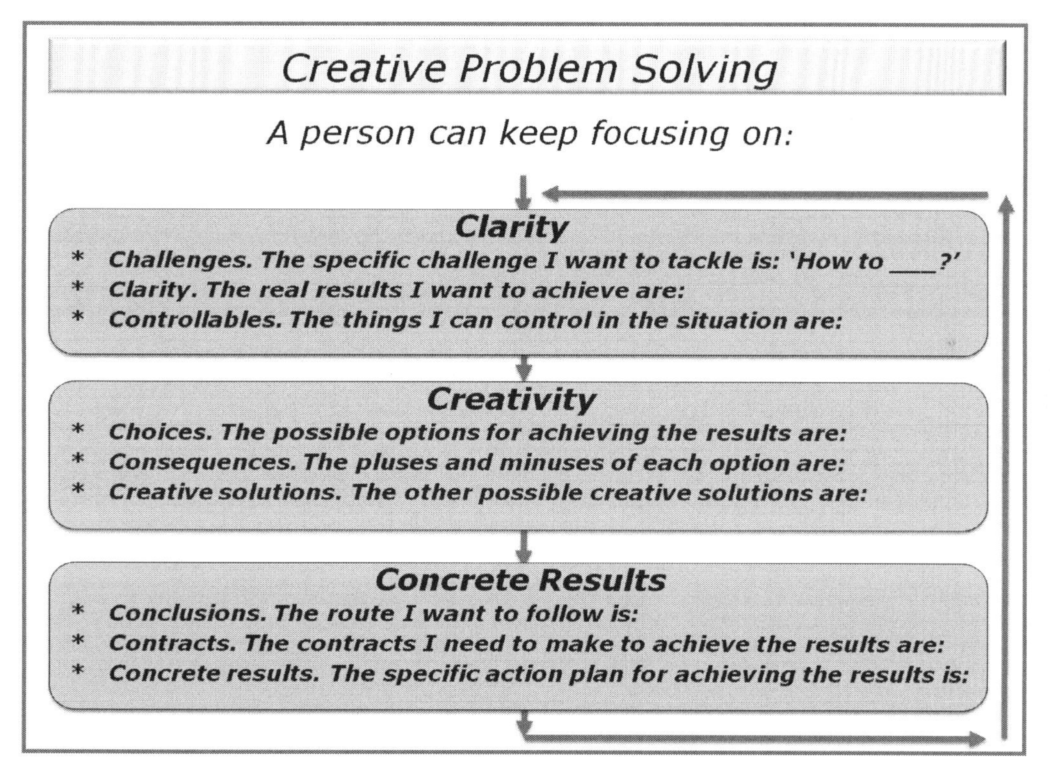

Clarity

Clarity is crucial to creative problem solving. A person is more likely to succeed if they clarify the real results they want to achieve – the 'What' – before embarking on the 'How'. So you can go through the following stages to help a person establish clarity.

Challenges

Invite the person to start by listing the various challenges they face. Then focus on the specific issue they want to tackle. As mentioned earlier, invite the person to frame it in positive terms. For example: "How to stay healthy?" rather than "How to stop smoking?"

It can also be useful to write the challenge in terms of: "How to ____." For example: "How to do fulfilling work?" rather than: "I want to change my career." The "How to ___." phrase often encourages them to use their imagination to begin generating solutions.

If appropriate, you can also invite the person to give more background about the situation. This can help when focusing on their priorities. Bearing this in mind, invite the person to complete the following sentences.

Clarity

Challenges. The specific challenge I want to explore is:

* *How to*

Here is some more information about the situation:

*

*

*

Clarity

Looking at the challenge the person wants to tackle, ask them: "What are the real results you want to achieve?" Sometimes this process takes a little time, but it is a vital step in creative problem solving.

Let's explore one example of how this works in practice. Imagine your client is a leader. One of the key challenges they face is:

> *"How to motivate difficult people in the organisation?"*

Looking beyond this issue, however, what are the real results they want to achieve? After some exploration, they may eventually conclude that the real 'What' is:

> *"How to build a successful organisation."*

The strategies for achieving this goal may be much more extensive – and effective – than those involved in tackling the first issue.

> *"But surely you have to turnaround difficult people in an organisation," somebody may say.*

Not necessarily. Great leaders communicate the story, strategy and road to success. They say:

> *"This is the future culture that is required if we are to achieve success."*

They then invite people: a) To decide if they would like to opt-into the future culture; b) To show how they want to contribute to achieving the picture of success. People can choose whether they want to be part of making it happen. Great leaders keep focusing on the key strategies for enabling the organisation to achieve success.

Let's consider another example. During one session a father asked how to help Tom, his son, to be better at passing school exams. Both of Tom's parents had been good at school and believed in paper qualifications.

Tom had other gifts, however, such as being a 'Trader'. He did a paper-round, plus had a Saturday job in a music store. So was the goal to help Tom to pass exams or to enable him to develop a fulfilling career? The father eventually decided to encourage Tom to build on his strengths and pursue his route as a Trader.

Let's return to the specific challenge the person wants to explore. Invite them to do two things. First, to clarify the real results they want to achieve. If appropriate, brainstorm all these goals. Second, to list these results in order of priority. Invite them to complete the following sentences.

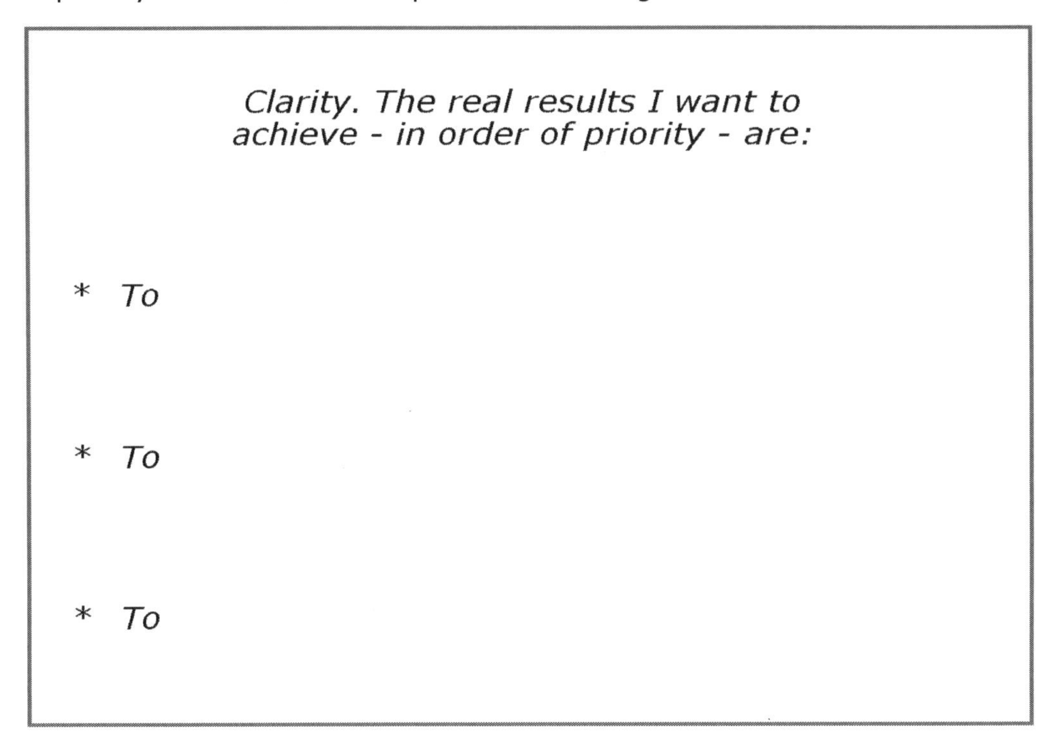

Controllables

Let's assume the person is clear on the results they want to achieve. Before pitching into finding solutions, however, it is good to do a reality check. Peak performers 'control the controllables'. They build on what they can control and manage what they can't control. The same rule applies to your client.

Imagine that they want to build a good relationship with their manager. They can control their own attitude and try to make clear working contracts. But they cannot control their manager's behaviour or what the manager says about them. Bearing this in mind, they can aim to act as a total professional. Things may or may not work out, but they will have done their best.

Returning to the results your client wants to achieve, invite them to describe the things they can control in the situation.

> *Controllables. The things I can control in the situation are:*
>
> *
>
> *
>
> *

So far the person has clarified the challenge, the results to achieve and the controllables. It's now time to move on to the possible creative solutions.

Creativity

Let's return to one of the challenges mentioned earlier. Imagine your client is a leader who has been charged with turning around an organisation. At first the issue seemed to be: "How to motivate difficult people in the organisation?" But they concluded that the real 'What' was: "How to build a successful organisation."

Let's assume they are also crystal clear on what will be happening by a certain date. They have clear targets regarding the profits, 'products' and people. For example, they may say:

"The profits will be: ______. The product quality – including customer satisfaction ratings – will be: _______. The people morale ratings will be: ______."

They will then move onto finding imaginative ways to achieve the goals. This often involves going through the process of exploring the choices, consequences and creative solutions. Let's consider these stages.

Choices

Bearing in mind the goals they want to achieve, explore the possible options they can pursue. If the client is a leader who wants to build a successful organisation, for example, they have a number of possibilities. These include:

a) *To tweak the organisation a little and hope things improve. (Not the best option, but it is still an option.)*

b) *To take a 'command and control' policy, focus on the detail and drive everybody towards the goals.*

c) *To concentrate on the profitable parts of the business and cut everything else.*

d) *To put everybody through a 'change programme' geared to people changing their behaviour and delivering the goods.*

e) *To maintain some parts of the present business, but build prototypes that demonstrate how the business could be successful in the future.*

Looking at the goal they want to achieve, invite the client to outline the possible options they can follow. Once these are out in the open, it will be time to go onto the next stage, considering the implications.

Consequences

Looking at each option in turn, they can consider the respective pluses and minuses.

Great decision makers, for example, often base their decisions on the consequences of each option, rather than the options themselves. They then build on the pluses and minimise the minuses.

Depending on the challenge they face, the client can outline the various options. They can then rate the attractiveness of each option on a scale 0 – 10.

Creativity

Choices and Consequences. The possible options for tackling the challenge – together with the pluses, minuses and attractiveness - are:

a) To

The pluses are:

The minuses are:

The attractiveness of this option is: ______ / 10

b) To

The pluses are:

The minuses are:

The attractiveness of this option is: ______ / 10

c) To

The pluses are:

The minuses are:

The attractiveness of this option is: ______ / 10

Creative Solutions

Looking at the goals the client wants to achieve, are there any other possible creative solutions? You can help them to do this by recapping what has been covered and perhaps asking some of the following questions.

> *"Let's start by re-establishing your goals. What are the real results you want to achieve? How can you do your best to achieve these results?*
>
> *"Let's look at the different options you have outlined. Is it possible to take the best parts from each option and create a new road? If so, how would this look in practice?*
>
> *"Looking at your goals, try to identify what might be the most successful strategies. Ask yourself: 'What are the three key things I can do to give myself the greatest chance of success?'*
>
> *"Let's learn from your positive history. Looking back, have you ever been in a similar situation and managed it successfully? What did you do right then? Is it possible to follow any of these principles to achieve the goals?*
>
> *"Sometimes we can get too close to events. Imagine for a moment that you are a consultant who is hired to give tough but fair advice. What advice would you give yourself to tackle the challenge and reach your goals?*
>
> *"If you are tackling a conflict, keep asking: 'How can we do our best to get a win-win?' At first this may seem difficult, but focus on what people have in common. Most problems are solvable, but sometimes it takes a lot of creativity. Keep going until you find possible solutions.*
>
> *"Let's explore what you can learn from best practice. Are there any other people, teams or organisations that have managed this kind of challenge successfully? What did they do right then? How can you follow these principles in your own way?*
>
> *"Let's conclude by exploring any other options. Looking at the challenge: Is there anything else you can do? Are there any imaginative possibilities? Are there any other creative solutions?"*

Invite the client to keep going until they feel they have explored all the possible options. They can then complete the following sentence.

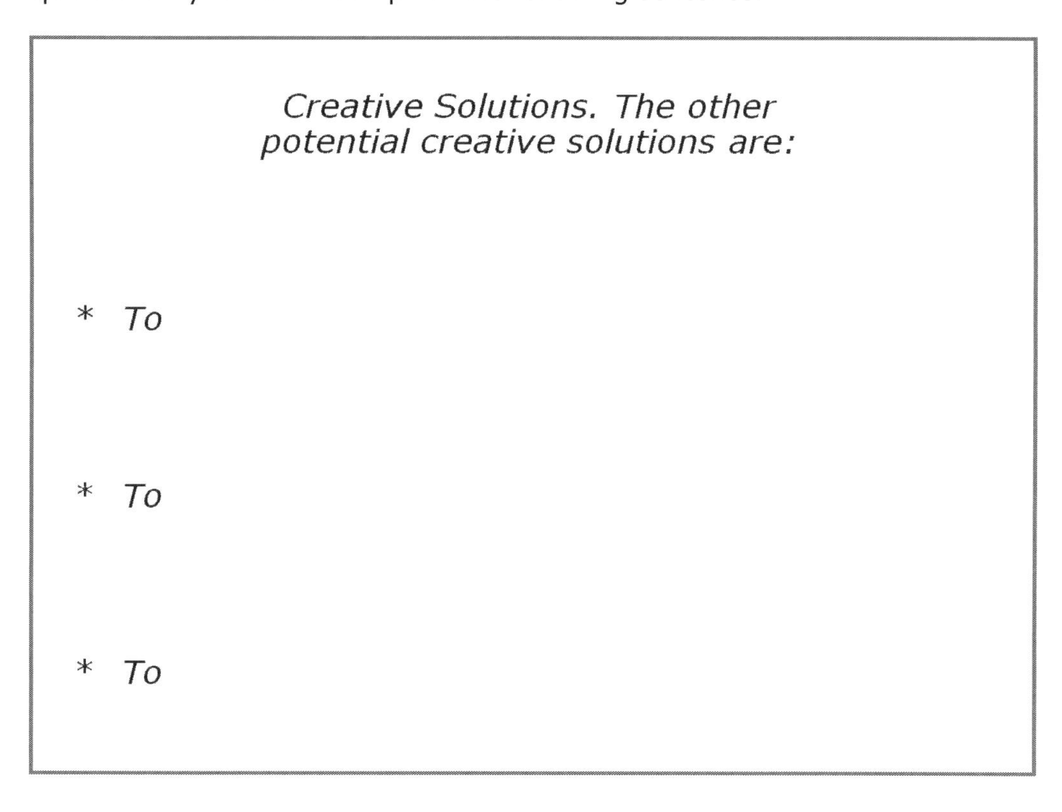

Creative Solutions. The other potential creative solutions are:

* *To*

* *To*

* *To*

Concrete Results

It is then time to translate the ideas in action. They person can do this by going through the following stages.

Conclusions

Looking at the various ways forward, they can settle on the route they want to follow. Sometimes they will choose to pursue one main option; sometimes to pursue multiple options. What will be the pluses and minuses involved? How can they build on the pluses and minimise the minuses? Looking at the results they want to achieve, invite them to complete the following sentence.

Concrete Results

Conclusions. The route – or combination of routes – I want to follow for tackling the challenge and achieving the results is:

* *To*

* *To*

* *To*

Contracting

Looking at the road ahead, invite the person to consider if they need to make any contracts with people.

Their main contract, of course, is with themselves. Looking at the whole package – the pluses and minuses involved – do they want to make the inner commitment to achieving the goals? If so, they may also need to make clear working contracts with other people who can help them to reach the goals. Invite them to complete the following sentence.

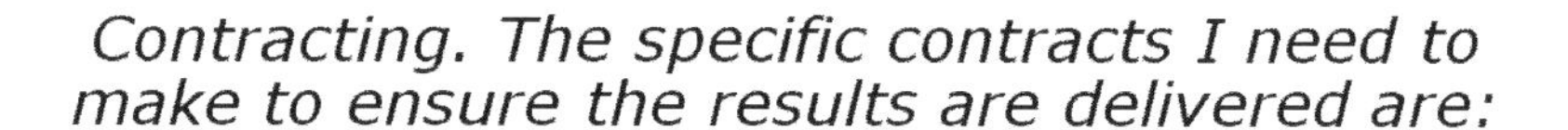

* To

* To

* To

Concrete Results

The person can then make a clear action plan and build in some early successes. This can help to create positive momentum on the route to achieving their goals. Bearing this in mind, invite the person to complete the following step.

Concrete Results. The specific action plan for achieving the results – including getting some early successes - is:

* *To*

* *To*

* *To*

There are many models for tackling challenges. Here we have focused on clarity, creativity and concrete results. You can adapt this approach in your own way, of course, to help the client to achieve their goals.

Spending Time In A Sanctuary To Shape Future Success

Different people behave in different ways when aiming to find solutions. One approach is for them to take the following steps. It is to spend time in a sanctuary, begin shaping their future and then get a success. Let's explore these themes.

Sanctuary

People who suffer a setback often need to spend time in a sanctuary. They need to lick their wounds and perhaps begin to make sense of the experience.

Different people choose different kinds of sanctuaries. They may rest, sleep, write, listen to music, see a counsellor or whatever. People begin to heal and regain their strength.

Shaping

Sanctuaries are great for a while. But then it's important for a person to begin exercising their muscles, otherwise their body can atrophy.

"I had two choices after suffering a particular setback," said one person. "Put simply, I could choose to succeed or sulk. I could dwell on the past or develop the future. So I chose to succeed."

People do not always choose what happens to them, but they do choose their response to these events. They can focus on what they can control. When they feel ready, they can emerge from the sanctuary and begin shaping their future.

Success

It's time to do the work. After deciding on their chosen path, a person will then pursue their action plan. It is good if they can follow certain daily disciplines. One MD explained.

> *"The new owners of our parent company 'displaced' me one Friday. After taking a week off to collect my thoughts, I then made 'getting a job' a full-time job."*
>
> *"I sat down at 8.30 on the Monday to contact people by email and focused on those in my network. These were the people who knew what I offered."*
>
> *"Writing customised letters – rather than sending out a conventional CV – I outlined 3 things I could deliver to help their business to be successful. I also said I would be visiting their part of the country within the next month, even if I wasn't."*
>
> *"I asked if it would be useful to drop in for a coffee. Within 6 weeks I had two offers, both at similar salaries to my previous job."*

Sometimes a person may hit a wall. They can then retire for a short time to their sanctuary and emerge even stronger. This takes us to the next stage: the person working hard to achieve their goals.

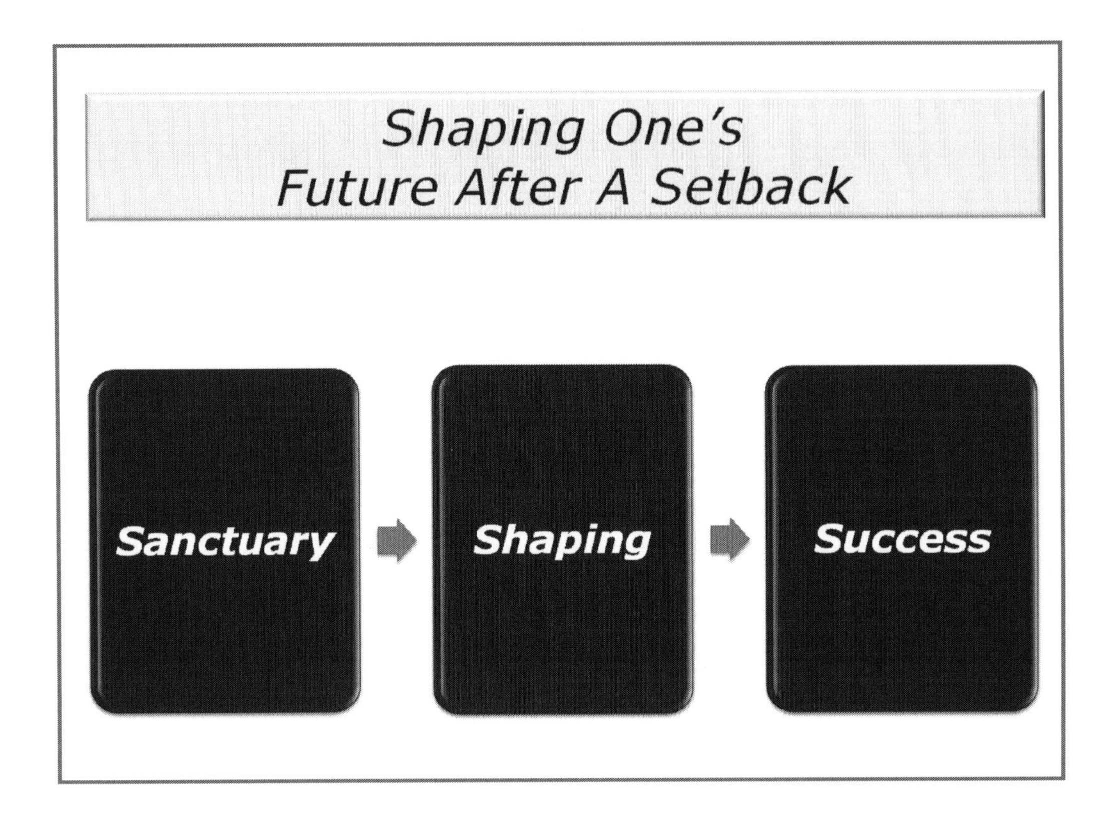

Success

Peak performers are good finishers. They deliver on their promises and satisfy their sponsors. They always do the basics and then add the brilliance. Sometimes they reach their goals by adding that touch of class.

Finishing is another name for beginning. After completing their project, a person may take time to review their learning, then revitalise their body and soul. After a while, however, they may focus on their next satisfying project. They will then continue along the peak performer's path.

Imagine your client is looking at how to finish a specific piece of work. You may want to help them to explore the following steps.

Being A Good Finisher

Finishing is a key skill in life. "Flow, focus, finish and, as a by-product, find fulfilment," is the motto. Sounds easy in theory, but how does it work in practice?

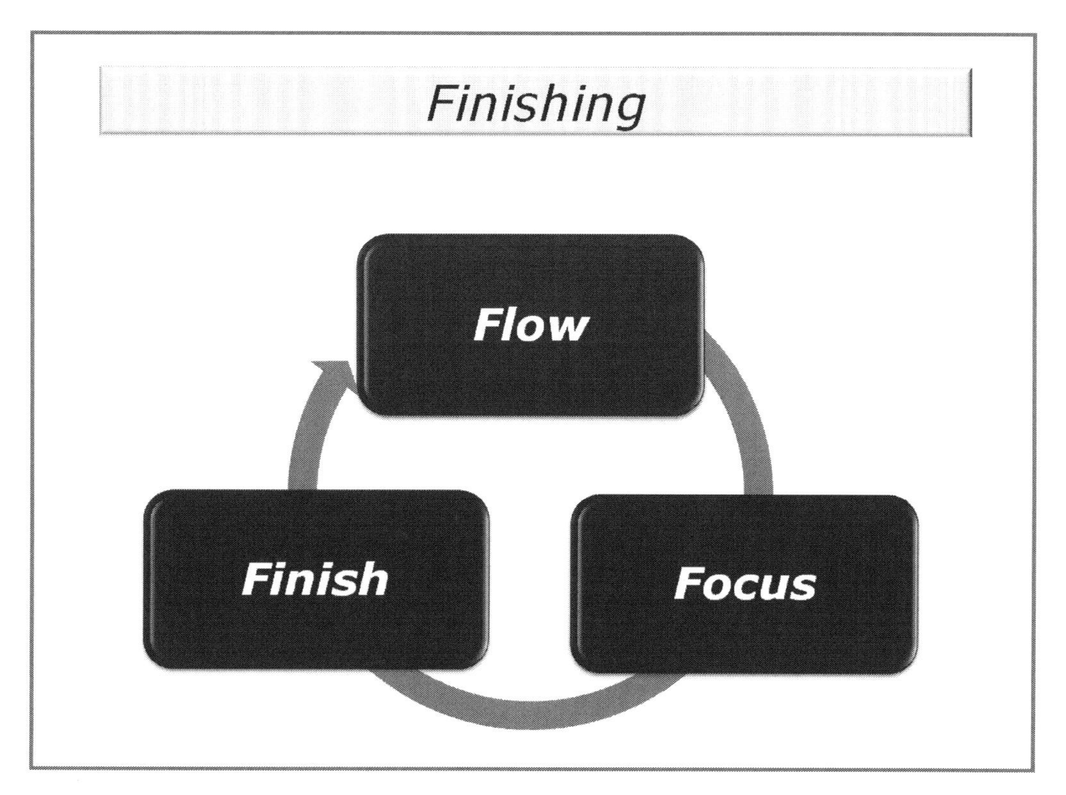

Everybody has a successful pattern of finishing, though sometimes they beat themselves up about the things they don't finish. So how can a person find their pattern?

One approach is to look back on their life and describe something they have finished successfully. What did they do right then? It is important for them to be specific. One person said, for example:

"Five years ago I finally completed work on refurbishing the 'Granny annexe' at our house, something I had delayed for years. I followed certain steps to make this happen.

"First, I decided whether or not I wanted to do it. Certainly I could have hired a local builder – which would have freed up time – but I chose to finish it myself.

"Second, I set aside time to do the job, booking long weekends over a period of 12 months. I ring-fenced this time, rather than allowing it to become cluttered by other events.

"Third, I established a working ritual, starting on Friday morning, working all day and most of Saturday, then allocating the rest of the weekend to the family.

"Fourth, I made it as pleasurable as possible, playing my favourite music, listening to the radio and having frequent coffee breaks.

"Fifth, I followed the discipline and kept working until it was finished. Now my teenage kids have moved into that part of the house. Granny may need to wait for a while, but she is happy where she lives at the moment."

If it is appropriate, you can invite your client to tackle the exercise on this theme. This invites them to do the following things.

Describe three projects they have finished in their life or work. They may, for example, have written a book, launched a web site, passed an exam, ended a difficult relationship or whatever.

Describe some of the specific things they did to right to finish these projects.

Describe how they can follow some of these principles – plus maybe add other elements – to finish present or future projects successfully.

This final point is interesting. Whilst it is important for a person to build on their successful patterns, there may be other strategies and skills they can add to become an even better finisher.

Finishing

My Successful Pattern

Three 'projects' that I have finished successfully in my life or work have been:

1)

2)

3)

Looking at these projects, some of the specific things I did right to finish them successfully were:

*

*

*

*

*

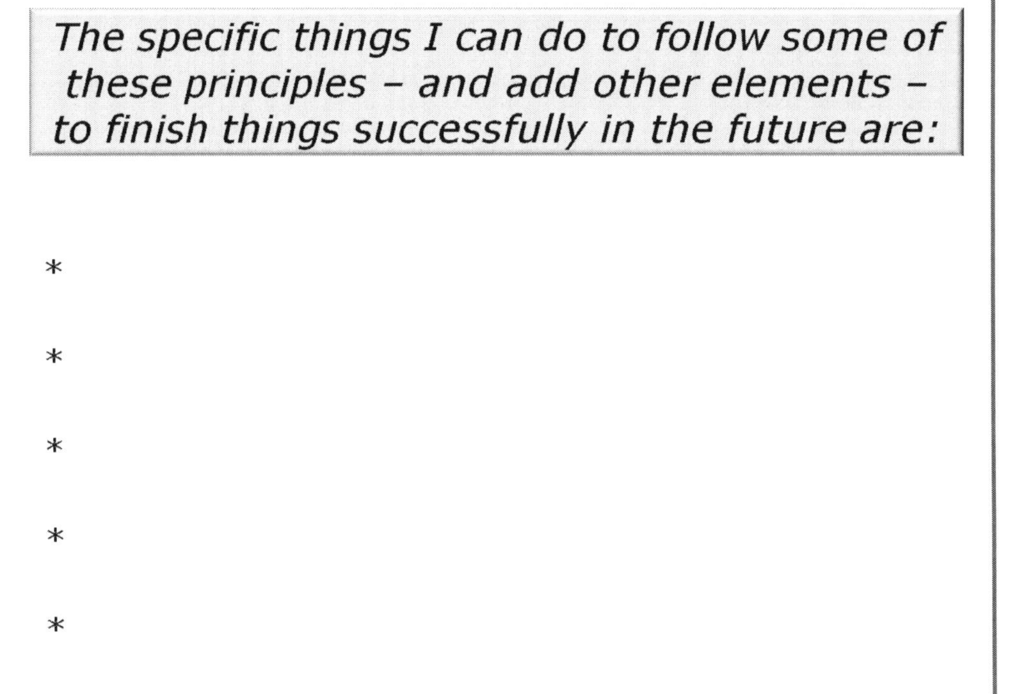

The specific things I can do to follow some of these principles – and add other elements – to finish things successfully in the future are:

*

*

*

*

*

Becoming A Class Act

"They are a class act," is a phrase used to describe somebody who consistently performs brilliantly. They do whatever is required to reach the goal and sometimes achieve it by adding that touch of class.

The footballer scores with a breathtaking volley; the singer produces a memorable encore; the 'victor' behaves generously; the 'loser' makes a gracious speech; the soldier behaves courageously in the heat of battle. Such people demonstrate grace under pressure.

Nelson Mandela turned away from violence and personally thanked his warders when leaving Robben Island. His warmth and double-handed handshake became his trademark. I witnessed this once when he arrived at a hotel. He went out of his way to make individuals feel special. People who met him nursed the memory for life.

Lady Marie Stubbs set the tone when taking over the school where Philip Lawrence was murdered. On her first day at St George's, Westminster, she shook hands with every pupil. Tackling the challenge head-on, she worked with the staff and students to turn around the school.

Severiano Ballesteros was seen as a class act on the golfing arena. He dashing style excited spectators and won many tournaments. Seve also showed class, however, after being treated for a brain tumour.

Knowing that his days were numbered, he reached out to worldwide audiences to raise money for cancer research. People should not feel sorry for him, he said, because he had been lucky enough to enjoy a wonderful life.

Sometimes a person is a class act in one area – the activity in which they feel at ease and excel – but maybe not in others. Nevertheless, they can aim to follow such principles and apply them to the project they are tackling. Sometimes they make things memorable by adding that touch of class.

If it is appropriate, you can invite your client to tackle the exercise on this theme. This invites them to do the following things.

Describe a person they admire who they believe has been – or is – a class act.

Describe the specific things the person did – or does – to be a class act.

Describe the specific things they can do to try to be a class act in their own way – or simply add a touch of class – in their work.

Becoming A Class Act

A Class Act

The person who I believe has behaved – or does behave - like a class act is:

*

The specific things they did – or do – to behave like a class act are:

*

*

*

Becoming A Class Act

The specific things I can do to try to behave like a class act – or simply aim to add that touch of class - are:

*

*

*

Bearing in mind these two themes – finishing and adding a touch of class – invite the person to complete this section by doing the following exercise. Start by focusing on the project they are tackling or the piece of work they aim to deliver. Then invite them to do the following things.

Describe the specific things they can do to finish the project successfully.

Describe the specific things they can do to – if appropriate – add that touch of class.

Finishing Successfully

The specific things I can do to make sure I finish the project – or other piece of work I am doing - properly are:

1) To

For example:

2) To

For example:

3) To

For example:

The specific things I can then do to – if appropriate – add that touch of class are:

1) To

For example:

2) To

For example:

3) To

For example:

Following The Satisfying Work Curve

Let's assume that your client has delivered their piece of work successfully. Reviewing what they have learned, they may well reflect on:

> *The specific things they did well and how they can follow these principles more in the future.*
>
> *The specific things they can do better in the future and how.*

It will be time for rest and revitalisation. They can then find or create the next stimulating project. At some point, however, they may want to take a wider view of their possibilities.

There are many models for looking at how a person can develop their career. One approach is to explore the satisfying work curve. People sometimes go through several stages when doing certain kinds of work.

Stage One is their Seed Corn.

They plant lots of seeds and explore many possibilities. Some seeds grow and, for example, some potential customers show interest. So the person puts extra effort into pursuing these opportunities.

Stage Two is their Satisfying Work.

They focus on these fulfilling activities and sometimes begin searching for funding. There is a sense of adventure and they discover new things. This can be one of the most satisfying stages in the work cycle.

Stage Three is their Salary Earner.

They translate the satisfying work into money-earning activities. This pays the bills and can also be fulfilling because they see a response. After awhile, however, they may want to move on.

Stage Four is their Spent Force.

The cash is still coming in, but performing the activities no longer generates energy. That does not matter, providing they have been continuing the development cycle and nurturing their next crop of seed corn.

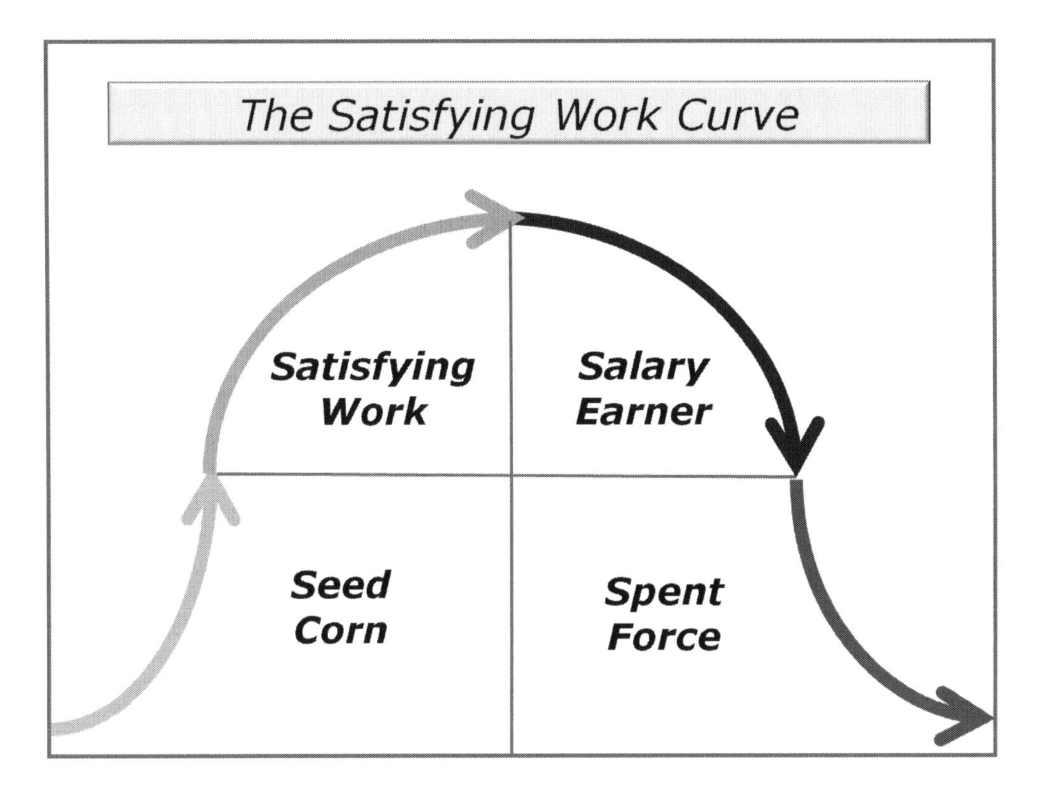

If appropriate, you can invite a person to clarify where they are on the curve. They may, of course, be at different stages with different projects or activities.

It can be useful to encourage them to focus on the stimulating activities where they can use their strengths. They can then plant seeds and continue along the satisfying work curve. Some people neglect this activity, however, and do not react until they reach their spent force.

Bearing this in mind, you can invite them to tackle the following exercise. This explores how they can plant seed corn and continue to develop their careers.

My Seed Corn

The specific things I can do to keep pursuing the activities I find stimulating and planting seed corn are:

1) To

2) To

3) To

The specific things I can do to translate some of these activities into satisfying work and maybe even into a salary earner are:

1) To

2) To

3) To

The Peak Performer's Path

There are many models for doing fulfilling work. We have looked at how a person can build on their strengths, find sponsors and deliver success. But there are, of course, other approaches.

You will have your own model for helping people to do satisfying work. If appropriate, however, you can conclude the sessions by inviting the person to look at the peak performer's path. This provides another perspective on how they can do their best.

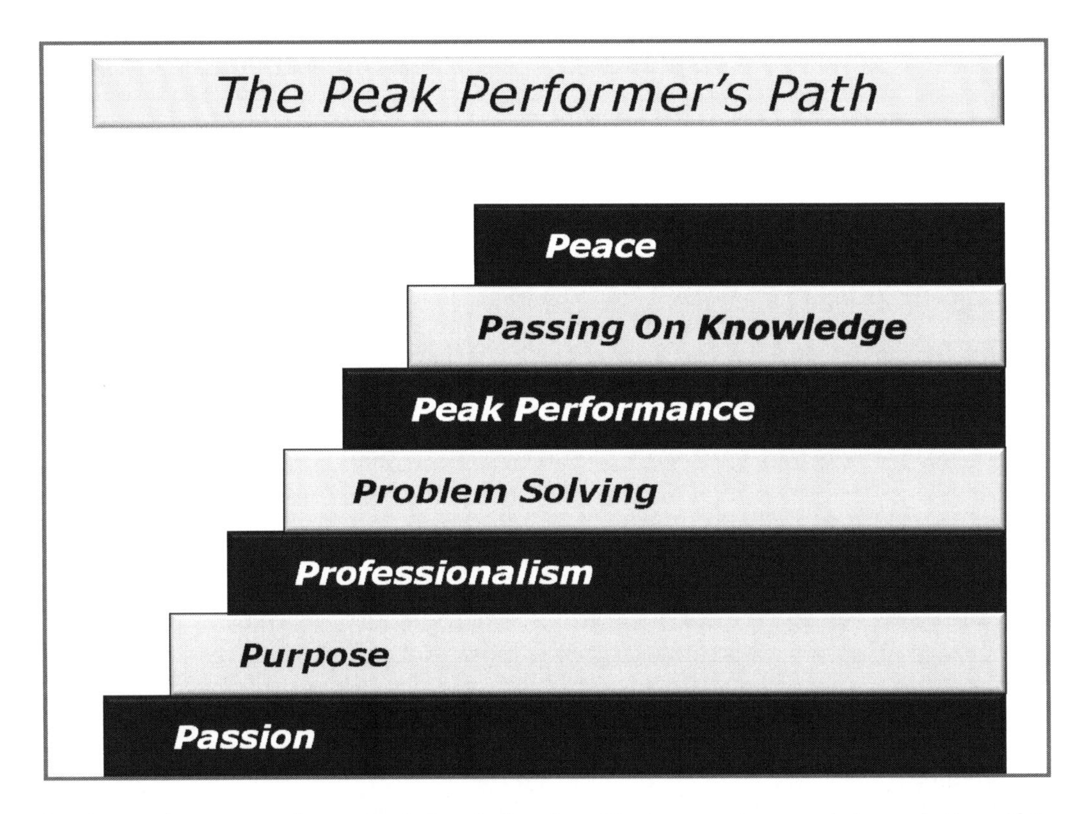

Peak performers often start by following their passion and translating this into a clear purpose. They may aim to write a book, find a medical cure, become the best kind of athlete they can be or whatever. They aim to be super professional, solve problems and achieve peak performance.

Some people stop at this stage, but others go on. They pass on their knowledge to help others to succeed. Providing they have done their best, they may feel a sense of peace. People then rest for a while, before embarking again on pursuing the peak performer's path.

If it is appropriate, you can invite the client to tackle an exercise on this theme. This invites them to do the following things.

Describe a time when they followed some or all stages of the performers path.

Describe the specific things they did right then.

Describe the specific things they can do to follow some of these principles in the future.

The Peak Performer's Path

The specific time when I followed some or all of the stages in the peak performer's path was:

* *When I*

Here is some more background about the situation:

*

*

*

The specific things I did right then were:

*

*

*

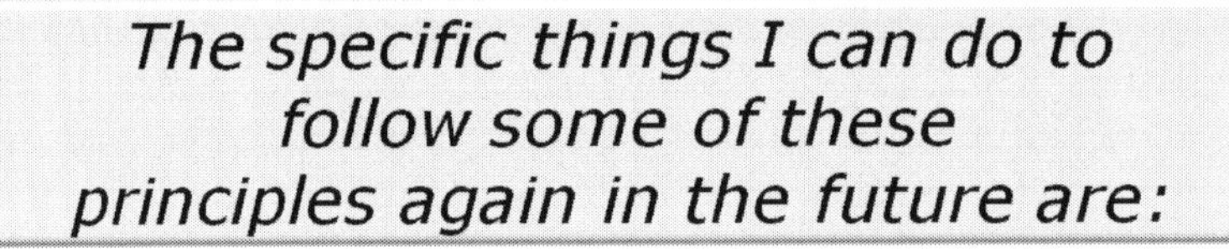

*

*

*

Conclusion

There are many ways to conclude a coaching session. One approach is to the person's goals and say something like:

> *"Let's return to the topics you wanted to explore in the session. These were:*
>
> *
>
> *
>
> *
>
> *"Looking at the things we have covered, have you got some ideas and tools you can use to achieve those goals? If so, are there any specific ways that you can apply these?"*

Another approach is to invite the person to describe their 'take aways' from the session. This can also include any things they have learned or, more probably, relearned. The person can also focus on how they can use these ideas to achieve their goals. So you may ask them to consider the following topics.

My specific 'take aways' from the session – including the things I have learned or relearned - are:

*

*

*

The specific things I can do to apply some of these ideas are:

*

*

*

There are many models for coaching. The strengths approach enables people to build on their strengths and achieve ongoing success. Different people will, of course, apply these ideas in their own ways.

Strengths coaching can be applied in many situations. So let's explore how it can help people to build teams and organisations that achieve their picture of success.

The Art of Helping People to Build Super Teams

This section focuses on helping people to build super teams that achieve their picture of success

There are many models for building great teams. The super teams approach is one that has a track record of helping teams and organisations to achieve their goals. Here is a brief overview of the approach.

Super teams often start by building on their strengths and clarifying their picture of success. They then translate this into a compelling story, strategy and road to success. Everybody knows what mountain they are climbing, why they are climbing it and how they will reach the summit. They also know who will be delivering what and by when.

Such teams are made up of people who want to be positive, professional and peak performers. They choose to opt in and make clear contracts about their best contribution towards delivering the goals. Super teams co-ordinate people's strengths to perform superb work. They overcome setbacks and find creative solutions to challenges. People do whatever is required to achieve the picture of success.

Super Teams

Super teams often start by building on their strengths and clarifying their picture of success. They then translate this into a clear story, strategy and road to success.

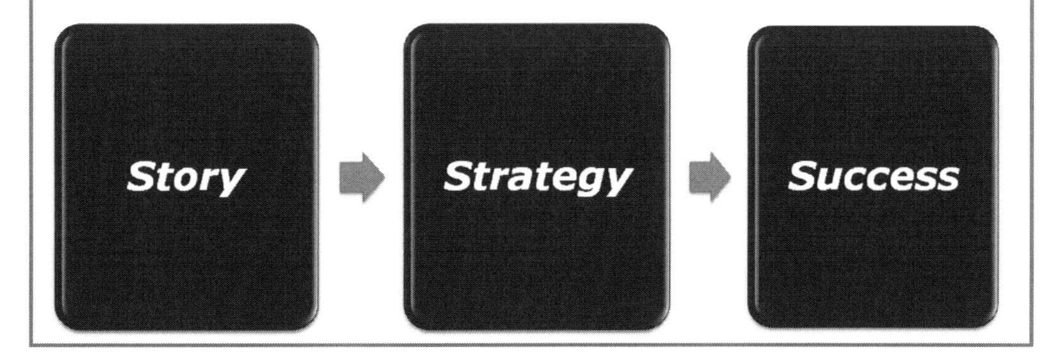

The super teams approach is based on what works and has been used successfully by both small companies and large organisations. They have, of course, adapted the ideas in their own ways. The following pages describe how the approach can be implemented. Whilst the chapter refers to working with a team, the ideas can be applied to whole organisations.

Imagine you have been asked to work with a team. A common approach is to start by working with the leaders and then expand the work to involve the whole team. Here are some of the steps you can take to help the team to reach its goals.

Setting The Scene

This involves creating an encouraging environment and clarifying the team's picture of success. It also involves making clear working contracts.

Strengths

This involves focusing on the team's strengths, successful style and perfect customers.

Specific Goals

This involves focusing on the team's specific goals on the road to achieving its overall picture of success.

Strategies

This involves focusing on the key strategies the team can follow to give itself the greatest chance of success.

Support

This involves focusing on getting the right support – including the right people – required to achieve the team's goals.

Superb Work

This involves focusing on how the team can do superb work and provide great service to its customers.

Solutions

This involves focusing on how the team can find creative solutions to challenges on the road to achieving its goals.

Success

This involves focusing on how people in the team can do whatever is required to achieve the picture of success. It also looks at how to build a second-generation super team.

As mentioned in the previous chapter, you can use the Seven Step model as a framework, rather than as a straitjacket. You can focus on the step that is most useful to the team at any given time. Let's imagine, however, that you will meet with the leaders and start from the beginning. Here are some tools you can use to help the team to achieve ongoing success.

Strengths Coaching With Teams

Start by setting the scene and clarifying people's picture of success. You can then help the team or organisation to take the following steps towards achieving their goals. They can focus on their:

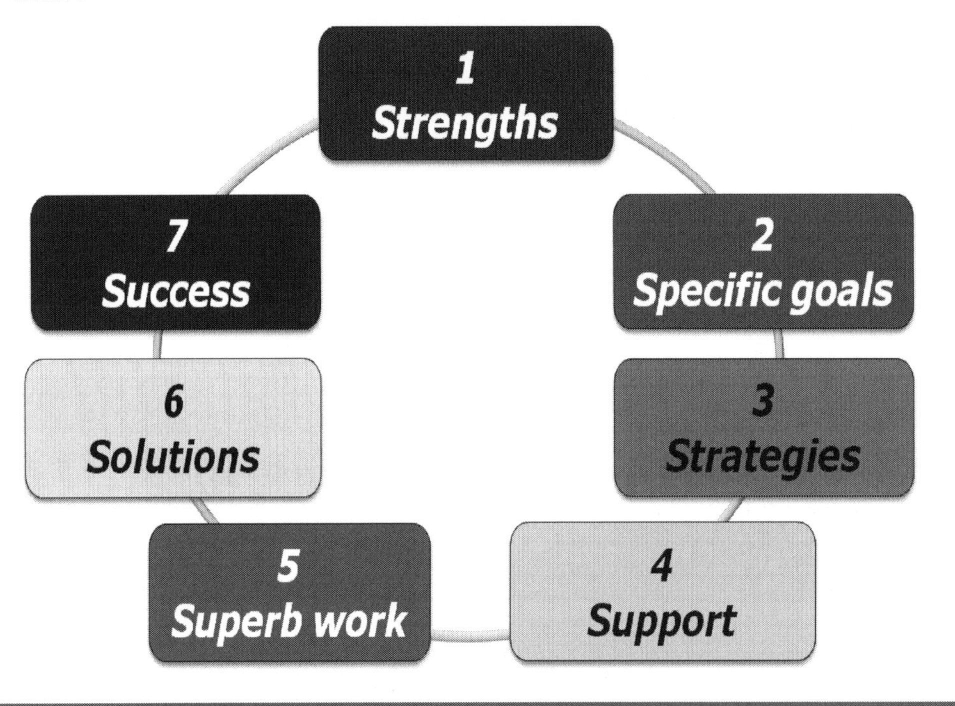

Setting the Scene

–

Clarifying the

Picture of Success

Imagine that you have been invited to help a team to achieve its goals. You will start by meeting with the leader and, for example, key members of the leadership team.

You will already have done lots of research about the leaders, the team and their overall goals. So, when meeting them, the process you will aim:

To show you understand the leaders' agenda, the challenges they face and their picture of success.

To show how the super teams approach can be used to help the team to achieve its picture of success.

To clarify what they see as the team's picture of success.

Good coaches bring the ideas to life by giving lots of specific examples. They keep moving between the concept and the concrete. This shows they understand the leader's world and the challenges they face.

Let's assume that you have outlined the model, brought it to life and the leaders want to go ahead. The next step will be to clarify the team's goals. You can position this by saying something along the following lines. It will be important, of course, to cover this in your own way.

"Great teams often have a clear story, strategy and road to success. Everybody knows what mountain they are climbing, why they are climbing it and when they will reach the summit.

"So it will be good to ensure that your people continue to understand the following things. As we know, good leaders keep communicating:

The 'What': *The picture of success.*

The 'Why': *The benefits of achieving the goal.*

The 'How': *The key strategies the team can follow to give itself the greatest chance of success.*

The 'Who': *The spirit everybody will need to demonstrate and the responsibilities of various people in working towards achieving the goal.*

The 'When': *The specific road map towards achieving the picture of success.*

"Bearing this in mind, I wonder if we can start by clarifying your overall goal."

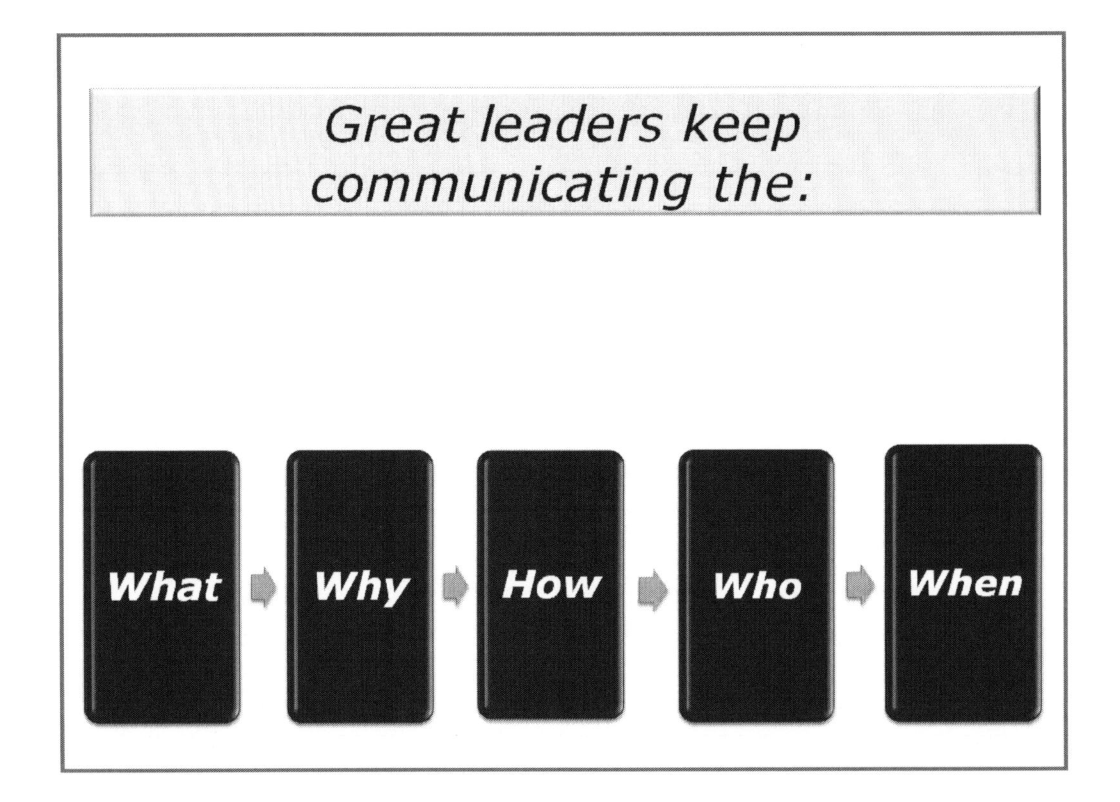

Clarifying The Picture of Success

Let's assume that the leaders are clear on the team's overall purpose. Such a purpose is often articulated in terms of the direction the team aims to pursue. This purpose may be expressed in different ways, however, at different times during the team's life.

Different teams from different fields will articulate their purpose in different ways. They may aim, for example:

> *To provide pioneering breakthroughs in medicine that benefit patients.*
>
> *To build a financially sound sports organisation that nurtures talent and wins trophies.*
>
> *To provide outstanding services in the area of ____ that help our customers and our company to achieve ongoing success.*

Looking at the corporate world, David Maister, author of *The Trusted Advisor,* says that every company in the world has roughly the same purpose. Companies always say something about providing great profits for their owners, great products for their customers and great careers for their people. They translate this into specific goals. So what makes the difference? David argues that:

> *Great companies do what they say they are going to do. Most companies don't do what they saying they are going to do.*

Great companies set their goals and think through the implications. They are serious about doing what is required to achieve success. They then keep doing the right things to pursue their short, medium and, most of all, their long-term goals.

Many companies set grand sounding goals, but do not properly think through the implications. Such companies say they are serious, but they do not really focus on what is required to achieve success. They then revert to short-termism and fire fighting.

Let's assume the leaders you are working with are clear on their team's purpose. The picture of success is a 'photograph' of how the purpose may be expressed by achieving certain goals by a specific date. Here are some examples.

A football club's purpose may be to create a long lasting dynasty. The way this may be expressed is by achieving a certain number of trophies by the end of a particular season. That will be the picture of success.

A probation service's purpose may be to help offenders to live without committing crimes. The way this may be expressed is by a certain percentage of former offenders living within the law and enjoying fruitful lives by a certain date. That will be the picture of success.

A company's purpose may be to create a pioneering and profitable business. The way this may be expressed is by it achieving a certain level of profitability, product quality – plus customer satisfaction ratings – and internal people morale by a certain date. That will be the picture of success.

Choosing A Template

Every team will have a different end goal and will use a different template to chunk this down into sub-goals. If you are working with a hospital, for example, the framework may relate to health care, patient feedback and meeting the budget. If you are working with a football club, the framework may relate to their aims regarding the football, fans and finances.

Many leaders in companies focus on the 3 Ps when clarifying their key goals. They focus on the Profits, Products – including Customer Satisfaction – and People. For example:

Profits: *The profitability they want to deliver.*

Products: *The product quality and customer satisfaction they want to deliver.*

People: *The culture, internal morale and development opportunities they want to deliver.*

These headlines provide useful pointers, but people work best by aiming to achieving specific goals. So let's consider this step.

Setting Specific Goals

How to help people to agree on the goals? Imagine you are working with a business team. You may wish to go through the following process.

Start by inviting the leaders to pick a suitable date in the future. Sometimes this is driven by events, such as if the team must deliver something by a certain deadline.

If you are working with a team in a different field, the deadline may be driven by the need to stage a play, launch a product, compete in a competition or whatever.

If you are working with a team in business, however, it may be useful to choose a date that ties in with the end of their financial year. This could be in 12 months, 18 months, 2 years or whatever.

Once agreed upon the date, you can then invite the leaders to do the following things.

To brainstorm a one line goal that embodies what they believe the team should achieve by that date.

To brainstorm what the team needs to have achieved by then under each of the headings of profits, products and people.

To agree on the one liner and also what must have been delivered by the end date under each of the three headings - profits, products and people.

(Some of these deliverables may, of course, need to be delivered some time before that end date.)

The leaders may end up with a long list of items to achieve. Certainly it is possible to include all these elements. For the moment, however, it can be useful to break these down into three bullet points under each of the headings of Profits, Products and People. These can be revisited and, if necessary, expanded in the final version.

So the initial picture of success may look something like the following.

The 'What' - The Picture of Success

The specific goal we want to achieve by __________ is:

* *To*

The specific things that will be happening then that will show we have reached the goal will be:

Profits

*

*

*

Products

*

*

*

People

*

*

*

Here is an initial draft produced by one organisation in the technology sector. They aimed:

> *"To be a pioneering and profitable technology company that people enjoy working with each day."*

They translated this purpose into targets for the next financial year. Building on this draft, they went on to refine and deliver their specific goals.

The Picture of Success

The specific goal we want to achieve by the end of the next financial year is:

To be recognised – by our corporate backers, customers and colleagues – as one of the top three technology companies in our chosen field.

The specific things that will be happening that will show we have achieved this goal will be:

Profits

* *To have achieved the financial targets – a profit of £10 million.*
* *To have introduced three new products that have achieved a profit of £1 million.*
* *To have redistributed our overheads and invested £1 million in the growing parts of our business*

Products

* *To have achieved a customer satisfaction rating of 90%+ of our customers being extremely satisfied with our work.*
* *To have produced 10 success stories that describe our work with clients and to have won a specific award for outstanding customer service.*

* *To have developed 2 new products and piloted these successfully with pace-setting customers.*

People

* *To have achieved an employee morale rating of 85%+ of our people enjoying coming to work each day.*
* *To have maintained a culture where people take responsibility, encourage each other and feel in charge of shaping their future careers.*
* *To be rated as one of the top 3 places to work in our industry.*

Different teams in different fields will, of course, have different templates. These will reflect the specific results they must deliver.

Let's assume that the leaders have clarified the goals. It is then possible to move on to the story and road map. Some coaches immediately move to these stages with the team. Another approach is to say something like the following.

"We now have two options. We can immediately translate these goals into a story, strategy and road to success. These can be communicated to your people and we can get the show on the road.

"Another option is to double-check that you are choosing to build on your strengths and set yourselves up for success. This will involve looking at how it is possible:

To focus on your specific strengths.

To focus on the specific customers with whom you work best.

To focus on the specific place in the market where you are most likely to achieve success.

"Taking these steps will probably confirm your goals. But it can be worth doing, just to double check that you have chosen the right picture of success.

"Looking at these two options, which would you like to pursue? Going straight into the story or double-checking that you are really playing to your strengths?"

During the past few years I have found that more teams are opting for the second route – making sure they are building on solid foundations. This has resulted in a much more rooted picture of success.

Good coaches outline the possible ways forward, however, together with the consequences. They then respect the customer's chosen route and do whatever they can to help them to achieve their goals.

Let's assume that the leaders you are working with opt to revisit their strengths and check they are on the right track. You can then explore the following step.

Strengths

Super teams build on their strengths and follow their successful style of working. They clarify their perfect customers and how they can help these people to succeed. They focus on the specific activities in which they can deliver peak performance.

Some teams employ approaches such as Appreciative Inquiry. As described earlier, this enables people:

To clarify when they have performed brilliantly.

To clarify the principles they followed to perform brilliantly.

To clarify how they can follow these principles – plus add other elements – to perform brilliantly in the future.

Such teams follow an organic approach. This is a common method in sports psychology and other fields that call for superb teamwork. People revisit their best performances and focus on the specific things they did right. They can then follow these patterns – and perhaps add other skills – to continue performing great work. This provides the natural foundation for their story, strategy and road to success.

So how can you find a team's strengths – where it delivers As, rather than Bs or Cs? Here are some exercises that you can use to help the team to focus on what it does best.

Clarifying a team's strengths – Learning from its positive history

One approach is to explore the team's positive history. The team's talents can be found in a combination of 'What' it delivered, 'How' it was delivered and to 'Whom'.

You can ask people to tackle the following exercise on this theme. Building on the approach described in Appreciative Inquiry, this invites them to do the following things.

Describe the specific times when the team has performed brilliantly.

Describe the specific things that people did right to perform great work..

The Super Team
Learning From Its Positive History

The specific times when the team performed brilliantly were:

1)When

The specific things that people did right then to perform brilliantly were:

* *They*
* *They*
* *They*

2) When

The specific things that people did right then to perform brilliantly were:

* *They*
* *They*
* *They*

3) When

The specific things that people did right then to perform brilliantly were:

* *They*

* *They*

* *They*

This exercise provides real life examples of when people have performed superbly. These can provide material for the next exercise.

Clarifying where a team delivers As, rather than Bs or Cs.

Bearing in mind the answers from the previous exercise, invite people to go through the following steps.

> *Describe the specific activities where the team has a proven record of delivering As, rather than Bs or Cs.*

It is good for people to give concrete examples of when this has happened in the past. They can describe the specific kinds of projects, products, services, tasks or other activities when the team has shown it is capable of delivering great work.

The key is to focus on where the team has delivered outstanding results for customers. The team's strengths go beyond 'What' it delivers. They are often contained in 'How' it delivers these things.

The Super Team's Strengths

The specific activities – the projects, services, products, tasks or other activities - where the team consistently delivers As, rather than Bs or Cs, are:

1)

The specific examples of when it has demonstrated this strength in the past have been:

*

*

*

2)

The specific examples of when it has demonstrated this strength in the past have been:

*

*

*

3)

The specific examples of when it has demonstrated this strength in the past have been:

*

*

*

So far this exercise has looked at where the team has a proven record of delivering fine work. If appropriate, you can invite people to also include the following step.

Describe the specific activities where the team may have the potential to deliver As, rather than Bs or Cs.

Describe the reasons why they believe the team has the ability to deliver As in this particular activity.

The Super Team's Potential Strengths

The specific activities where the team may have the potential to deliver As are:

1)

The specific examples of when it has demonstrated this strength in the past have been:

*

*

*

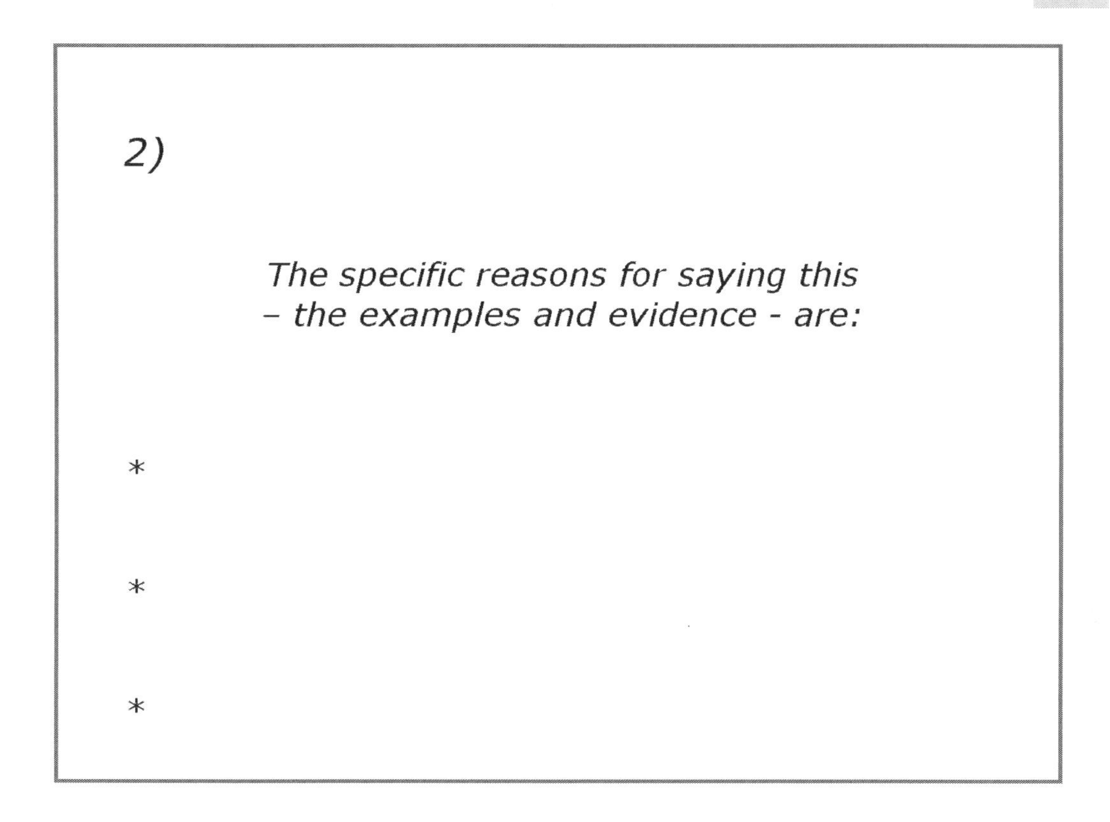

Clarifying the team's perfect customers and how it can help them to achieve success

Peak performing teams often work best with certain kinds of customers. Whilst it may not be possible to work with these people all the time, it can be useful to identify and reach out to these types of customers.

So who are the team's perfect customers? This may main focusing on those with certainly 'personality types'. For example, the team may work best with pacesetters, established companies or those in a certain sector.

Getting the right match means that the team and the customer start off at 7/10. They often have shared values. This helps them clarify a shared vision, work well together and deliver visible results.

How to clarify the preferred kind of customer? One approach is to recall when the team has done great work. What were the personality styles of the key people with whom they worked? How would they describe the customer's culture? How did the team and customer work well together to get positive results?

Bearing these answers in mind – plus adding other qualities that may be important – invite the team to do the following things.

Describe the team's perfect customers.

Describe the specific goals these customers want to achieve in their work and the challenges they face.

The Super Team's Perfect Customers

The specific kinds of customers with whom the team works best are:

The type of customer or the customer's name is:

1)

The specific goals they want to achieve are:

*
*
*

The specific challenges they face are:

*
*
*

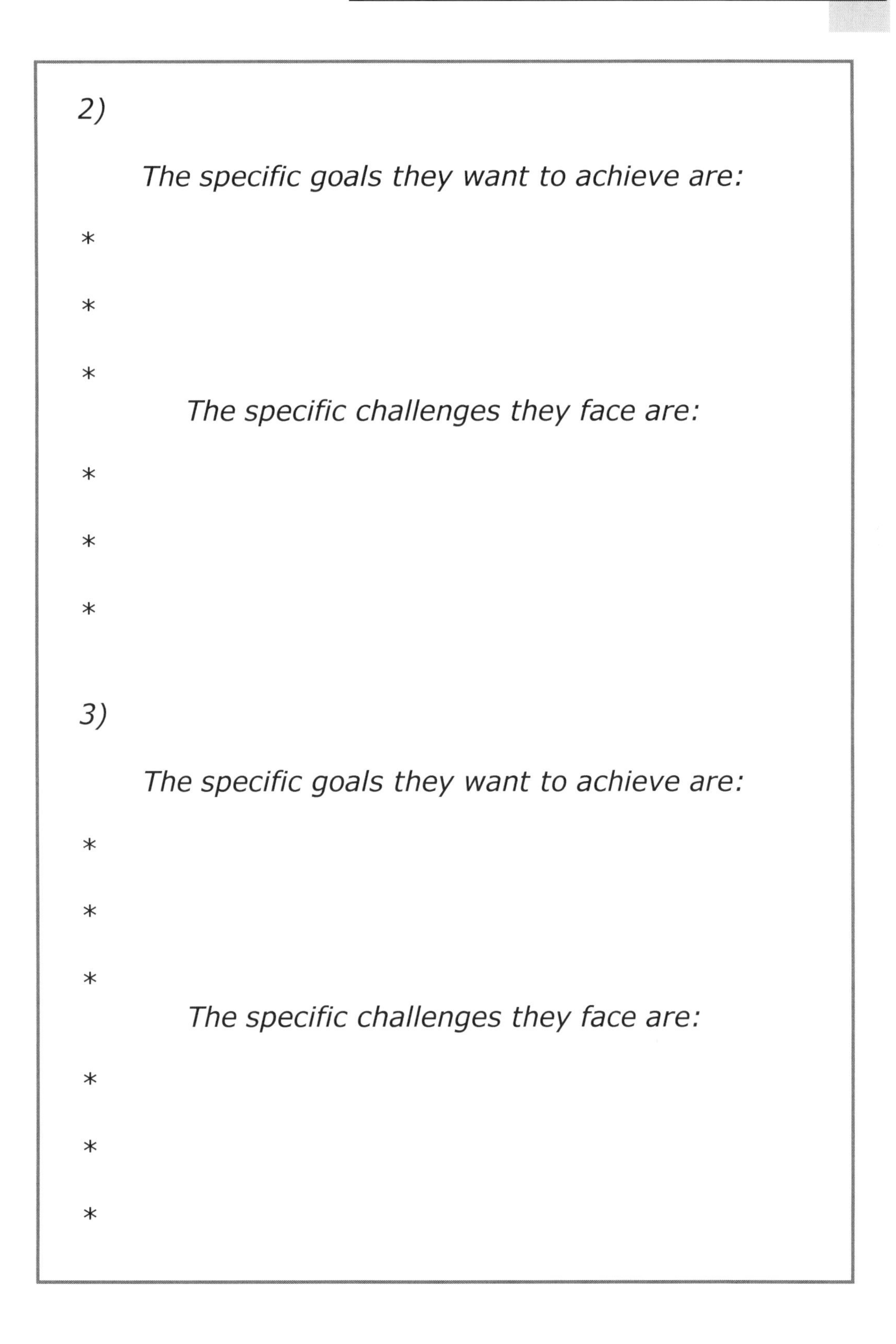

2)

The specific goals they want to achieve are:

*

*

*

The specific challenges they face are:

*

*

*

3)

The specific goals they want to achieve are:

*

*

*

The specific challenges they face are:

*

*

*

We are now coming to the key point. Good service givers help their customers to achieve success. Bearing in mind their answers so far, invite the team to focus on the following themes. They are to:

Describe the specific things the team can deliver to help its customers to achieve success.

Describe the specific benefits to the customers of delivering these things.

The Super Team's Specific Contribution

The specific things the team can deliver to help the customers to achieve success are:

1) To

For example:

*

*

*

2) To

For example:

*

*

*

3) To

For example:

*

*

*

Let's assume that you have clarified the team's strengths, successful style and how it can help its customers to succeed.

Building on the work done earlier, these elements can be fed into the next stage. This focuses on the team setting specific goals on the route to achieving its overall picture of success.

Specific Goals

Let's assume that the leaders you are working with have done two things. First, they have created an initial picture of success. Second, they have clarified the team's strengths.

Sometimes identifying the strengths can lead to changing the team's original aim. But more often it tends to solidify the target. The leaders see they are on the right track. They are also able to give specific examples of how they have followed similar principles in the past. This enables them to have an even greater belief in the future picture of success.

The next step is to be clearer on the specific goals. This often means translating the aims into a compelling story, strategy and road to success. This chapter looks at how to help a team to make this happen.

The team's goals and strategy are often intertwined. So we will begin by focusing on how to combine these together. The next chapter will focus on translating the strategy into a specific road map.

Creating The Team's Story

Imagine the leaders have a clear picture of success. There are two options they can now pursue to communicate the aims and involve key people in getting a sense of ownership of the story. You can help the leaders to pursue either of the following two options for communicating and clarifying the team's goals.

(Bear in mind that, for the moment, this is an 'internal story'. It is geared to giving people in the team an overview of the future direction. This can later be expressed as an external story that resonates with different audiences.)

Option A

The leaders can communicate the story and strategy. They can then give key people the chance to add their responses and additions.

The leaders can gather key people and communicate the 'What, Why, How, Who and When'. (See later illustrations.) They can give their rationale for choosing the particular direction by saying something like the following.

"Welcome to the session. Today we would like to look at how the team can continue to achieve ongoing success.

"Bearing in mind the various challenges we face, there are many different routes the team can take towards achieving its goals. Here is an overview of some of the possible routes we could take in the future.

"Option A would be to: ______. The pluses and minuses of this route would be: ______.

"Option B would be to: ______. The pluses and minuses of this route would be: ______.

"Option C would be to: ______. The pluses and minuses of this route would be: ______.

"Option D would be to: ______. The pluses and minuses of this route would be: ______.

"Option E would be to: ______. The pluses and minuses of this route would be: ______.

"Bearing these options in mind, we have chosen to take the following route ______. The reasons we have chosen this route are because: ______.

"There are, of course, pluses and minuses involved in pursuing this route. The specific things we can do to build on the pluses and minimise the minuses are: ______.

"We have therefore put together the following story, strategy and road to success. For the moment we are going to describe the story and strategy.

"Later we will describe the potential road map. We will then want your input regarding the action plan. So here is our story and overall strategy."

The Team's Story

The 'What, Why, How, Who and When'

Introduction

The purpose of our team – the specific thing we are here to do - is:

* *To*

The 'What' – The Picture of Success

The goal we want to achieve by ___ is:

* *To*

The specific things that will be happening then that will show we have reached the goal will be:

Profits

*

*

*

Products

*

*

*

People

*

*

*

The 'Why'

The benefits of reaching the goals will be:

For the company

*

*

*

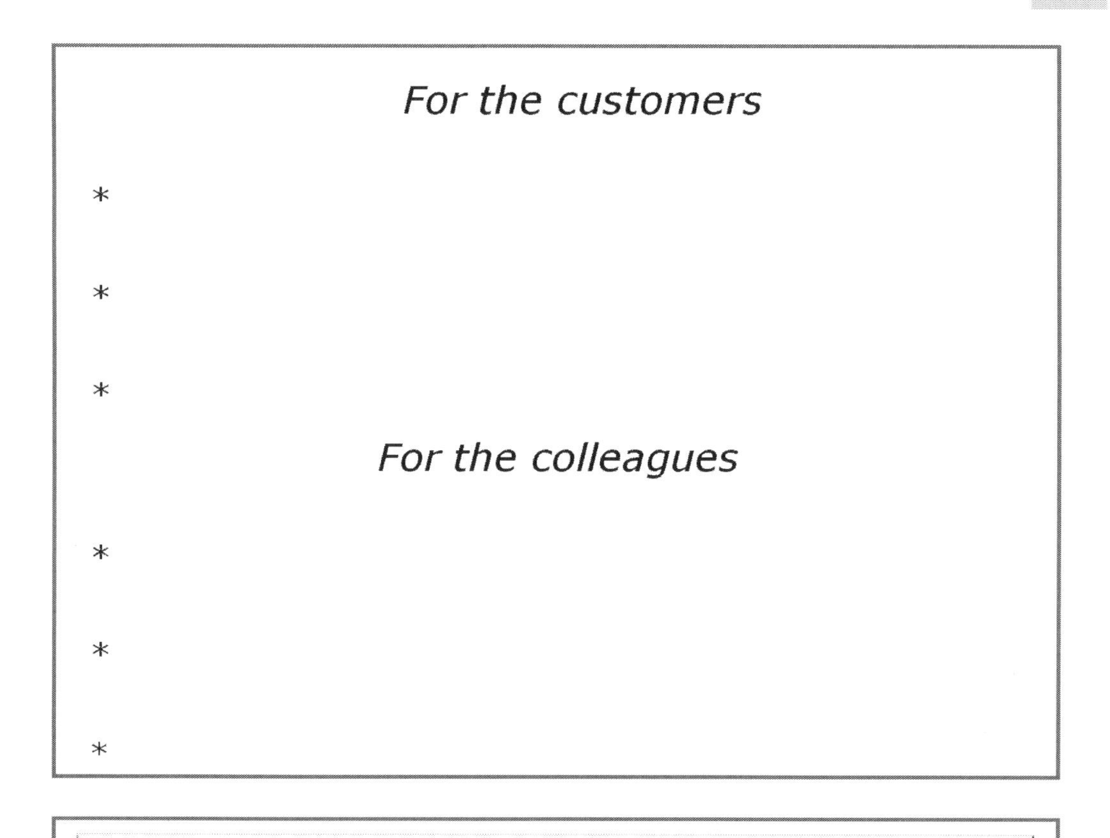

The 'How'

The key strategies we can follow to give ourselves the greatest chance of success are:

Profits

* *To*

* *To*

* *To*

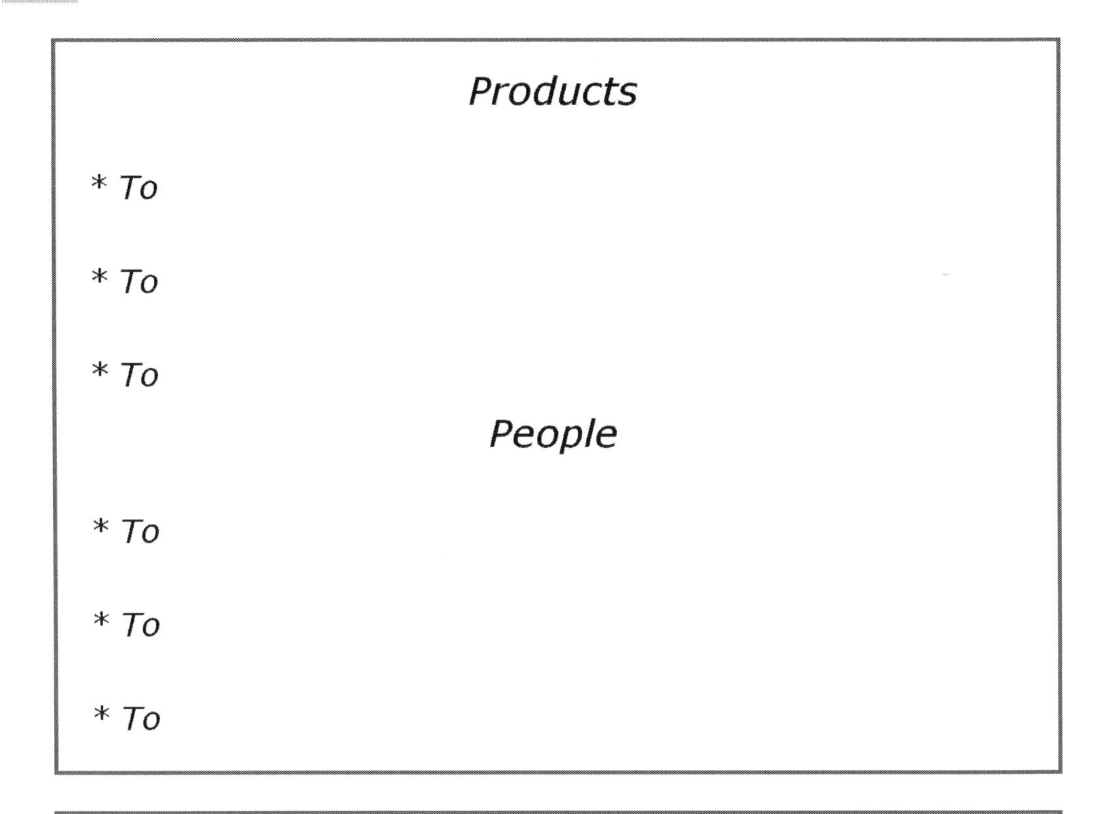

The 'Who'

The leadership team's responsibilities in working to achieve the goals are:

** To*

** To*

** To*

The manager's responsibilities in working to achieve the goals are:

** To*

** To*

** To*

The colleagues' responsibilities in work to achieve the goals are:

** To*

** To*

** To*

When going through the slides, the leaders may underline the respective responsibilities. They do this to make 'The Deal' clear. So they may say something like the following.

"Looking at the story, here is an overview of the various roles people will play in making it happen.

The leadership team's responsibilities include, for example:

To act as good models and keep people's eyes on the picture of success.

To ensure the right people are in the right places to get the right results.

To provide people with the support required to achieve the goals.

To manage by outcomes, rather than by tasks.

To make tough decisions when necessary.

To do whatever is required to enable the team to achieve success.

The manager's responsibilities include, for example:

To keep their people's eyes on the picture of success.

To translate the strategy into action.

To build superb teams.

To keep their sponsors informed regarding progress towards achieving the goals.

To ensure their teams do superb work and deliver success.

The colleague's responsibilities include, for example:

To keep their eyes on the picture of success.

To make clear contracts about their contribution to achieving the goals.

To be professional, encourage their colleagues and perform superb work.

To keep their managers informed regarding progress towards achieving the goals.

To deliver success.

"That is an overview of the various responsibilities. It is, of course, up to each of us to choose whether we want to opt into working toward achieving the goals."

Invite Responses To The Story

Good leaders often go a stage further and ask people to give their responses to the story. Certainly they are prepared to answer questions for information about the overall strategy. But sometimes it is easier to do this by asking people to form smaller groups and compile their responses. People can spend 15 minutes brainstorming under the following headings.

Responses To The Story

Like. The things we like about the story and strategy are:

*

*

*

Additions. The possible additions to the story and strategy that may be worth considering are:

*

*

*

Questions and Concerns. The questions and possible concerns we have are:

*

*

*

Support. The kinds of support we would like to be able to deliver the story and strategy are:

*

*

*

People clarify their responses and present their ideas. The leaders answer questions and, where appropriate, expand on the rationale for pursuing the chosen strategy.

The overall direction has been decided, of course, but this provides the opportunity to provide more background about the rationale. As one leader explained to the people in their organisation:

> *"It is important that everybody understands the strategy and our reasons for pursuing this route. You can then explain it to new joiners. They can then see their parts in achieving the picture of success."*

This is one approach to explaining the way ahead and giving key people an opportunity to respond to the story. There is, however, another option that provides people with more involvement.

Option B

The leaders can communicate the picture of success. They can then give key people the opportunity to contribute to the story and strategy.

This is a route taken by leaders who want to get more ownership from key people in their organisation. The leaders obviously believe it is vital to pursue a particular strategy and may make this clear in their presentation. At the same time, however, they may want to get input and a sense of ownership from their people.

Bearing this in mind, they will gather their key people together and go through the following steps.

> *They explain the team's picture of success.*
>
> *They explain the 'What, Why, How and Who' parts of the story and strategy.*
>
> *They will have already made separate flip charts headed 'What', 'Why', 'How' and 'Who'. They place these flip charts on the wall.*

(These charts also include the sub-headings. For example, the 'Profits, Products, People; Benefits to Company, Customers, Colleagues; The Leaders', Managers' and Colleagues' Responsibilities. They therefore reproduce the slides on flip charts, but with free spaces left under each of the sub-headings.)

They invite each person to spend 15 minutes writing Post It Notes regarding what they would like to see added to each of the sections.

Each person can write as many ideas as they like to add to the 'What', 'Why', the 'How' and 'Who'. They are to write one idea per Post It, however, because that makes it easier to type afterwards.

They then invite each person to go up in turn and put their Post Its on the relevant Flip Charts. The person is also to explain their reasons for adding that idea.

They continue until the final person has added their ideas to all the sections.

The leaders then encourage people to discuss the whole story and strategy. When doing so, it is important:

a) To focus on the themes that people have in common.

b) To then explore any other ideas that have been added.

The leaders conclude by summing up the session and saying they will consolidate the work. This may mean, of course, that they need to make some decisions about certain topics. They will then get back to people and sign off the agreed story.

This section has focused on how to involve people in setting a team's specific goals. As we said at the beginning, however, this also involves setting the overall strategy. The next step looks at how to break this down into specific action plans.

Strategies

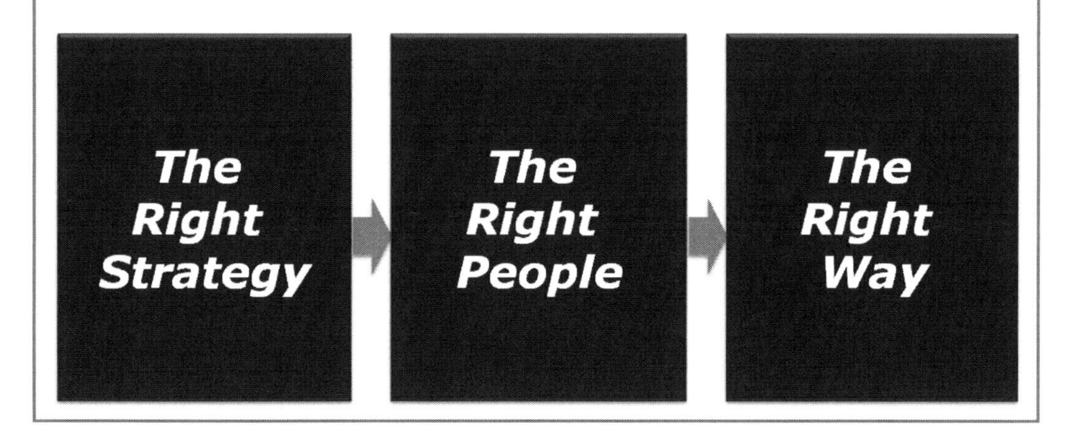

Great teams implement the right strategy with the right people in the right way. This chapter looks at how to translate these strategies into action. It includes making clear contracts about the results that each team – and each person – will deliver towards delivering the goals.

Clarifying the team's road map towards achieving the picture of success

Imagine that the leadership team you are working with have communicated the 'What, Why, How and Who'. The next step is to clarify the 'When'.

How to make this happen? There are many tools for moving from strategy to action. One of the most effective is to create a road map towards achieving the goals. The aim will be to produce something like the following.

The 'When'

The Road Map Towards Achieving The Picture of Success

The goal we want to achieve by _____ is to:

____

Dates	*Milestones. The specific things that we will have achieved by then will be:*	*Quotes. The words we want to hear people saying then are:*
	Profits	
* *End Date*	* ____________________	"____________________"
Then work backwards	*Products*	
	* ____________________	"____________________"
	People	
	* ____________________	"____________________"
	Profits	
* ________	* ____________________	"____________________"
	Products	
	* ____________________	"____________________"
	People	
	* ____________________	"____________________"
	Profits	
* ________	* ____________________	"____________________"
	Products	
	* ____________________	"____________________"
	People	
	* ____________________	"____________________"

	Profits	
* ________	* ________________________	"________________"
	Products	
	* ________________________	"________________"
	People	
	* ________________________	"________________"
	Profits	
* *Today*	* ________________________	"________________"
	Products	
	* ________________________	"________________"
	People	
	* ________________________	"________________"

The road map becomes the team's ongoing working document. So it is vital to craft it with care.

There are several methods for producing such a road map. The method we will explore involves people populating the sections with Post It Notes and then agreeing on the deliverables. (This process will be explained later.) Whichever method is used, however, there are several principles worth bearing in mind.

Imagine you are facilitating such a road mapping session. Here are some guidelines you may wish to consider giving to the team members before making the road map. These instructions are written in italics as if you are actually addressing them to the team. So here is what you may wish to say.

Start from the destination and work backwards

> *Good planners start from the destination and work backwards. This 'starting from the destination' approach is used on many successful projects. It encourages people to keep focusing on the end goal.*

Start by picking a date in the future. Describe the specific goal you want the team to achieve by that date. Also describe the specific things that will be happening then that will show the team has achieved the goal.

Start working backwards towards the present day. Describe the specific things that should be delivered by certain dates. It is obviously vital to enter the results that must be achieved by certain milestones.

Now comes an important point. While it is good to work backwards, after awhile it can be difficult to figure out the exact things that should be happening on a certain date.

If appropriate, you can then return to the beginning of the road map and start making the plans going forward. You are then more likely to 'join things up' properly further along the road. Keep going until you are satisfied with the road map.

One other point is worth bearing in mind. Some parts of the overall plan may remain hazy. This can often be the case – whether you are climbing a mountain, launching a product or whatever. You cannot always know exactly what you will be doing on a certain date.

The key is to know the principles you want to follow on the journey. Providing you follow these principles, you can continue to update and evolve the road map as you work towards achieving the goal.

Date the road map

Start at the top of the 'Dates' column and put the end date. Then work backwards towards the present day. You may want to break the road map into quarters or other suitable periods. Finish at the bottom of the Road Map where it says 'Today'.

Choose a suitable template for 'chunking' the goals

So far we have used the 3Ps framework – Profits, Products – including customer satisfaction – and People. You can use these or other headings. It is vital to break all the actions down into chunks by using a suitable template.

Bring the road map to life with quotations

> *Describe the actual words you would like to hear people saying at various stages of the journey. These can be quotes from leaders, customers, colleagues, the media or whoever.*

Imagine that you have given people these overall guidelines. You can then go through the following steps to enable people to populate the road map.

Invite people to form 3 groups. Each group is to focus on one of the 3 Ps in depth

It is vital that the people involved in the respective groups have a key interest in delivering that part of the goal – be it profits, products or people.

The Profit group, for example, will create a road map that achieves the end goal regarding profit. They can describe what must be delivered by each quarter to reach the end goal. They can also add quotes that will bring the road map to life. The Product and People groups will follow a similar process.

Some people may have an interest in several areas. If this is the case, they can add their ideas after the respective working groups present their parts of the road map.

Each group presents the road map that focuses on their part of the 3 Ps

They can start by describing the end goals that must be delivered under their heading – be it profits, products or people – to achieve the picture of success. They can then talk people through the road map from the present day towards achieving those goals. It is obviously good if they give the reasoning behind the specific things that must be delivered by certain dates. This should then take them to finally repeating the end goals that they mentioned in the beginning.

Some aspects of each group's part of the road map may still need to be determined. This may be the case, for example, if the Profits are strongly linked to the time frame for launching certain Products. These issues can be worked out after all the topics have been presented.

Integrate the separate road maps into one complete road map

The leaders and, for example, key co-ordinators can take away the separate road maps. It may not be possible to achieve all the things that have been suggested. So this group can aim:

To make strategic decisions about the specific things that must be delivered by when on the road map.

To integrate the three separate road maps into one complete road map. Every quarter, for example, should show what must be delivered by then regarding profits, products and people.

To appoint co-ordinators who will ensure that the team's activities are managed in a way that ensures people keep doing what is required to deliver the road map.

The final road map is presented back to the overall team. It is then up to each team – and each person within each team – to make clear contracts about their contribution to achieving the picture of success. This will mean producing an overview something like the following.

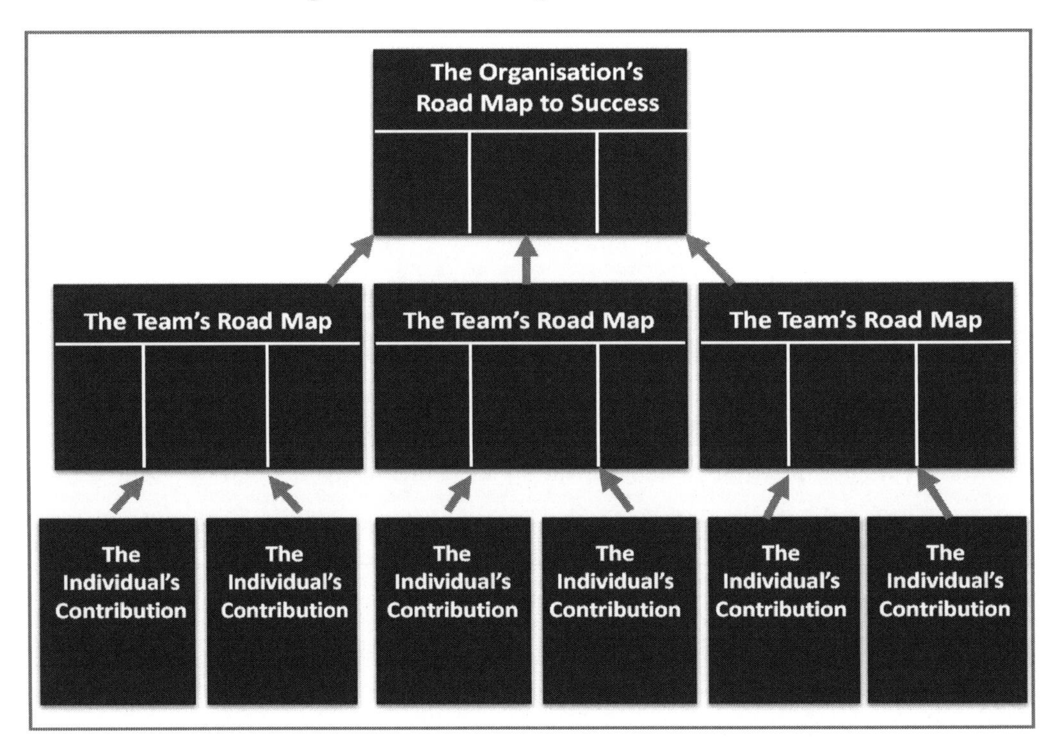

(There may, of course, be different levels of detail on different versions of the road map. The top line road map may simply give the headlines. Beneath this other versions may go into more detail.)

Imagine that you have helped people to clarify the overall road map. As mentioned above, each team can then produce their plans for achieving the goals. Similarly, each person can make clear contracts about the contribution. Let's explore this individual step.

Clarifying each person's contribution towards achieving the picture of success

This section provides a framework that each team member can use to make clear contracts about their best contribution to achieving the team's goals.

It invites them to refer to the team's aims and covers their own 'What, Why, How and When'. This exercise takes some time to complete. But it encourages them to think through their contribution.

Please note. The exercise focuses on what they are going to 'deliver', rather than simply 'do'. This encourages a culture of managing by outcomes, rather than managing by tasks.

Here is the complete exercise. Each person then meets with their manager to discuss what they have written and finally make clear contracts about their contribution.

My Contribution

The following pages outline my contribution towards achieving the team's goals. This to be agreed with my manager.

The 'What'

Bearing in mind the team's picture of success – and also my own strengths - the specific results I want to deliver towards achieving the goals by _____ are:

1) To

For example:

* *To*
* *To*
* *To*

2) To

For example:

* *To*
* *To*
* *To*

3) To

For example:

* *To*
* *To*
* *To*

The 'Why'

The benefits of reaching the goals will be:

For the company

*
*
*

For the customers

*
*
*

For the team and colleagues

*
*
*

For other people – including myself

*
*
*

The 'How'

The key strategies I will follow to deliver the results will be:

1) To

For example:

* *To*
* *To*
* *To*

2) To

For example:

* *To*
* *To*
* *To*

3) To

For example:

* *To*
* *To*
* *To*

The Support

The specific support I would like in order to be able to deliver the results would be:

1) To

For example:

** To*

** To*

** To*

2) To

For example:

** To*

** To*

** To*

3) To

For example:

** To*

** To*

** To*

The Progress Reports

The specific things I will do to proactively keep my manager and other people informed about my progress towards achieving the goals will be:

1) To

2) To

3) To

The 'When'

The specific things that will be happening – and when – that will show I have delivered the results will include some of the following things.

1)

This will be delivered by: ______.

2)

This will be delivered by: ______.

3)

This will be delivered by: ______.

My Agreed Contribution

This section to be completed after the discussion with my manager. This sheet summarises the goals I will deliver towards the team's picture of success. It is the document we will keep referring to in our regular updates. It may, of course, evolve during the year.

My Agreed Goals

The specific results I will deliver towards achieving the team's picture of success by _____ are:

1) To

For example:

* *To*

* *To*

* *To*

2) To

For example:

* *To*

* *To*

* *To*

3) To

For example:

* *To*

* *To*

* *To*

Clarifying the Global Purpose and Local Practice

"I can see how this approach can operate with a close-knit team that is working towards a clear goal," somebody may say. "But what happens if you are working with a large global organisation or a virtual team?"

Similar rules apply, but there are certain factors that are worth bearing in mind. Let's consider some of these.

Great organisations get the right balance between the 'Global' and 'Local'. They combine the size of a big company with the spirit of a small enterprise. How do they make this happen?

The centre communicates the purpose and the principles. The way that people practise these is up to them, within parameters, in their part of the business. But this comes with a proviso. People must show how what they are doing is following the principles and contributing to the purpose.

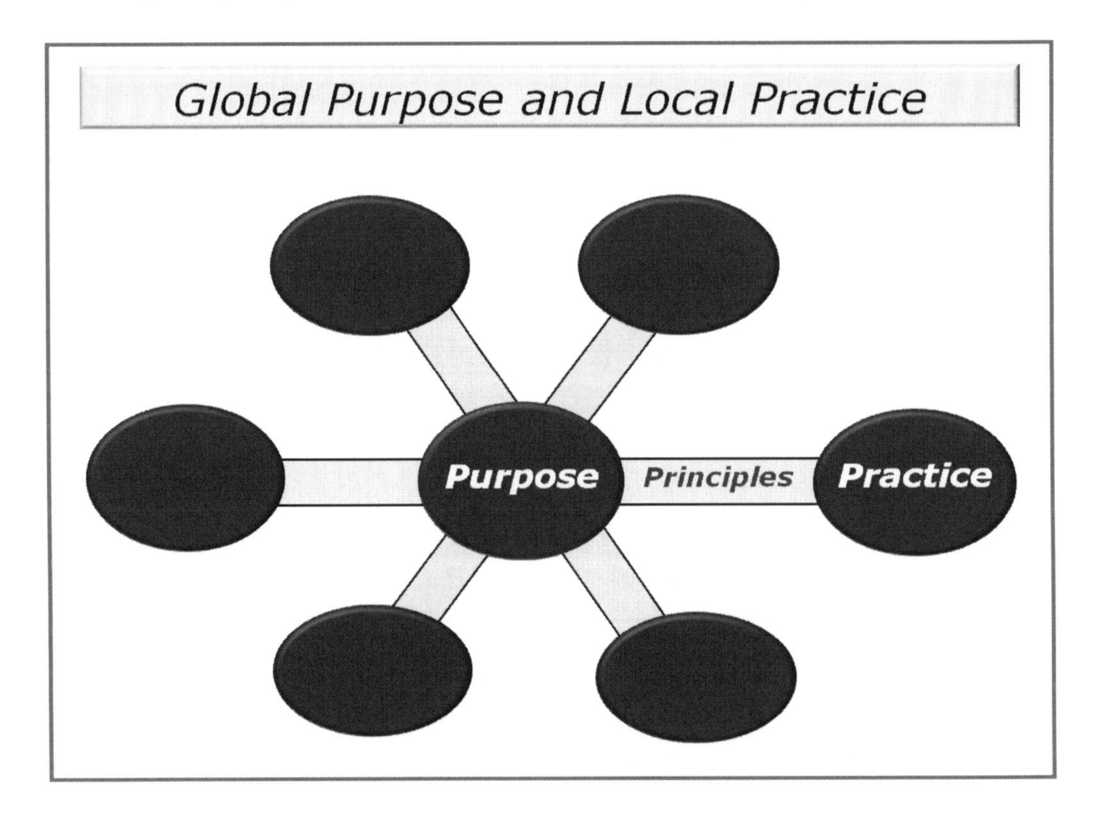

Let's explore how to make this work in practice. Imagine you are working with the leader of a large company.

Great leaders encourage people to: 'Think global and act local'. This calls for creating an 'adult-adult' relationship, however, with everybody taking responsibility for making their best contribution to the company. People are given freedom, but they must also deliver. So they may position this by saying something like the following to their people.

> *"Welcome to today's session. I am going to give an overview of our organisation's purpose and the part you can play in making this happen.*
>
> *"Later I will give examples of: a) How people have contributed to this purpose in the past; b) How people can contribute to achieving the purpose in the future. But first let me give an outline of our overall approach to working together.*

The Purpose

The purpose of our organisation is: To ______________.

The benefits of achieving this purpose will be:

1) To
2) To
3) To

The Principles

The principles we aim to follow to achieve this purpose are:

1) To
2) To
3) To

The Practice

"The way you practise these principles will – within parameters – be up to you in your part of the organisation.

"But there is key point. You must show how what you practise supports the principles and contributes toward achieving the purpose."

Great leaders create get the right balance between the centre and the satellites. They also manage by outcomes, rather than by tasks. So they translate the purpose into specific goals. Each satellite then makes clear contracts about their contribution to achieving the organisation's goals.

People are given great autonomy. But, as mentioned earlier, they must keep showing how what they are delivering is contributing to achieving the overall picture of success.

Let's assume that the team you are working with are clear on their road to success. It will be then be time to move on to the next part.

Co-ordinating the Story, Strategy and Road To Success

Great teams often have a good co-ordinator. Why? Getting creative people to combine their talents can be challenging at the best of times. The co-ordinator's role is to ensure people channel their energies towards achieving the team's goal. Let's see how this works in practice.

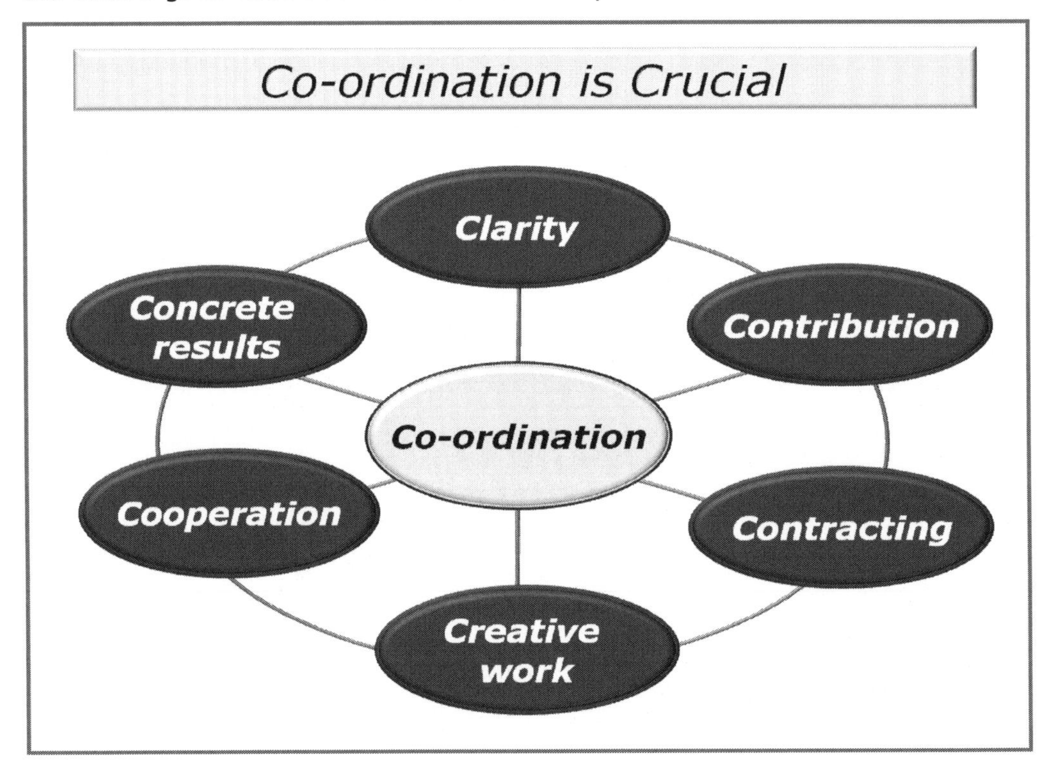

Clarity is vital. The leader's role is to chart the way towards achieving the picture of success. Each team's – and each team member's – job is to clarify their best contribution and commit to achieving the goals. They must then do creative work, co-operate and achieve concrete results.

Sounds simple in theory. But things can go wrong, especially during the creative work stage. Strong orchestration is vital – otherwise individuals may do their own thing.

"But isn't that the leader's job?" somebody may ask. Great leaders often follow the STAGE Model of leadership. This covers the following aspects of running a team.

The STAGE Model

***S**trategic*

***T**actical*

***A**dministrative*

***G**runt work*

***E**motional*

Some leaders focus on the strategic and emotional leadership. They also hire the right people to manage the tactics, administration and grunt work. Great leaders have a co-ordinator who makes this happen, otherwise they get sucked down into fire fighting.

Super teams also have such a person who ensures that people channel their efforts towards following the road map. This is a pre-requisite for being serious about achieving the picture of success. Later in the book we will look at how this approach can be translated into action. Before then, however, it is useful to consider the following point.

Clarifying whether a team is really serious about achieving the picture of success

"Are you serious?" This is useful question to ask the leaders, for example, after they have clarified the story, strategy and road to success. Their first reaction is often: "Of course."

That is great. But they must then focus on the implications of translating their aims into action. After clarifying the pluses and minuses involved in reaching the goals, it can then be good to again ask them:

"On a scale 0—10, rate the extent to which you are really serious."

Those that answer 8+ are more likely to achieve their picture of success. Let's explore how to take these steps.

Imagine you are working with a leadership team. They have clarified the specific goals and strategies. Before pushing the button, however, ensure that people understand the implications. Here are some suggestions for making this happen.

Invite people to clarify the pluses and minuses involved in reaching the goals

Looking at what is involved in reaching the goals, invite people to clarify the pluses and minuses for different stakeholders. They can focus on the implications for the company, customers, colleagues and any other groups. One leader said:

"The biggest minus for some managers was making tough decisions about people who did not fit the future culture.

"The strategy depended on employing people who chose to take responsibility. So it was important for us to act as good models and also encourage the positive people in the company.

"It also meant making decisions about people who chose not to take responsibility. Some managers found this difficult, but it was necessary if we were to reach our goals."

Great teams consider the implications of reaching their goals. They then do three things. First, they consider how to build on the pluses. Second, they consider how to minimise the minuses. Third, they make a decision about whether or not they want to go for the goal.

If you wish, invite the team you are working with to take similar steps. If appropriate, they can do the following exercise.

Are We Serious?

The Pluses Involved In Reaching The Goals Will Be:

For The Company

*

*

For The Customers

*

*

For The Leaders

*

*

For The Managers

*

*

For The Colleagues

*

*

For Any Other Groups

*

*

The Potential Minuses Involved In Reaching The Goals Will Be:

For The Company

*

*

For The Customers

*

*

For The Leaders

*

*

For The Managers

*

*

For The Colleagues

*

*

For Any Other Groups

*

*

Pluses. The specific things we can do to build on the pluses are:

1) To

For example:

2) To

For example:

3) To

For example:

Minuses. The specific things we can do to minimise the minuses are:

1) To

For example:

2) To

For example:

3) To

For example:

Are We Serious?

Bearing in mind the pluses and minuses involved, the extent to which we are serious about working to reach the goals is:

_____ / 10

Great teams are 'committed to the commitment'. This only happens, however, if they consider all the consequences. Providing the team has gone through this process – and score 8+ on the seriousness scale – they stand a good chance of success.

They can then go on to the next step. This is gathering the support required to do the job.

Support

Super teams aim to implement the right strategy with the right people in the right way. Let's assume that the team you are working with have got the right strategy. They then need to get the right support to make it happen.

Such teams need backing from their key sponsors – the people who can hire or fire them. As discussed earlier, this means focusing on the following areas.

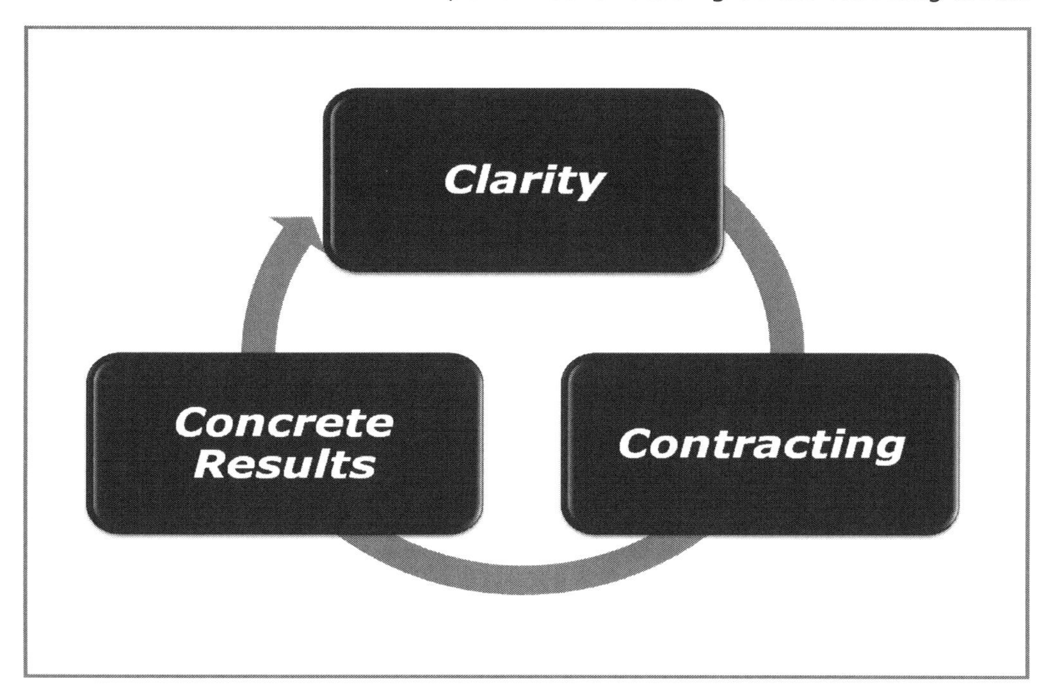

Clarity

This calls for establishing the specific goals to achieve. It also means 'playing back' the agreement to make sure everybody has the same picture of success.

Contracting

This calls for establishing the overall guidelines – the Dos and Don'ts – for achieving the goals. It also means getting the practical support to do the job.

Concrete Results

This calls for getting some quick wins to reassure the sponsors. It also means proactively informing the sponsors about the ongoing progress towards achieving the goals.

Let's assume the leaders have gone through these stages. They can then take the following steps towards gathering the required support.

Getting the right people support

Great leaders often cross a certain threshold that enables them to realise their true role. Certainly they must provide an encouraging environment and the tools people need to do the job. But then, as one leader said, comes a realisation.

"One day I had a breakthrough. I can communicate a compelling story and strategy. But it is the team that actually does the work. I will be judged by my people's – not my own – performance."

"People make the difference," we are told. This may sound like a cliché, but it is true. It is vital to get the right people and put them in the right places to get the right results.

Super teams are made up of people who have similarity of spirit and diversity of strengths. Diversity of spirit is a recipe for disaster. Let's explore these themes.

Similarity of Spirit

Such teams get the right people with the right attitude. They start by defining the spirit – the attitude and behaviour – they want people in the team to demonstrate.

Attitude is non-negotiable, but they want characters, not clones. People will express the team's principles in many different ways, but it must always be within certain parameters. Great teams recognise that attitude plus ability is more likely to produce achievement. People with the wrong attitude create negative energy that can affect other people in the team.

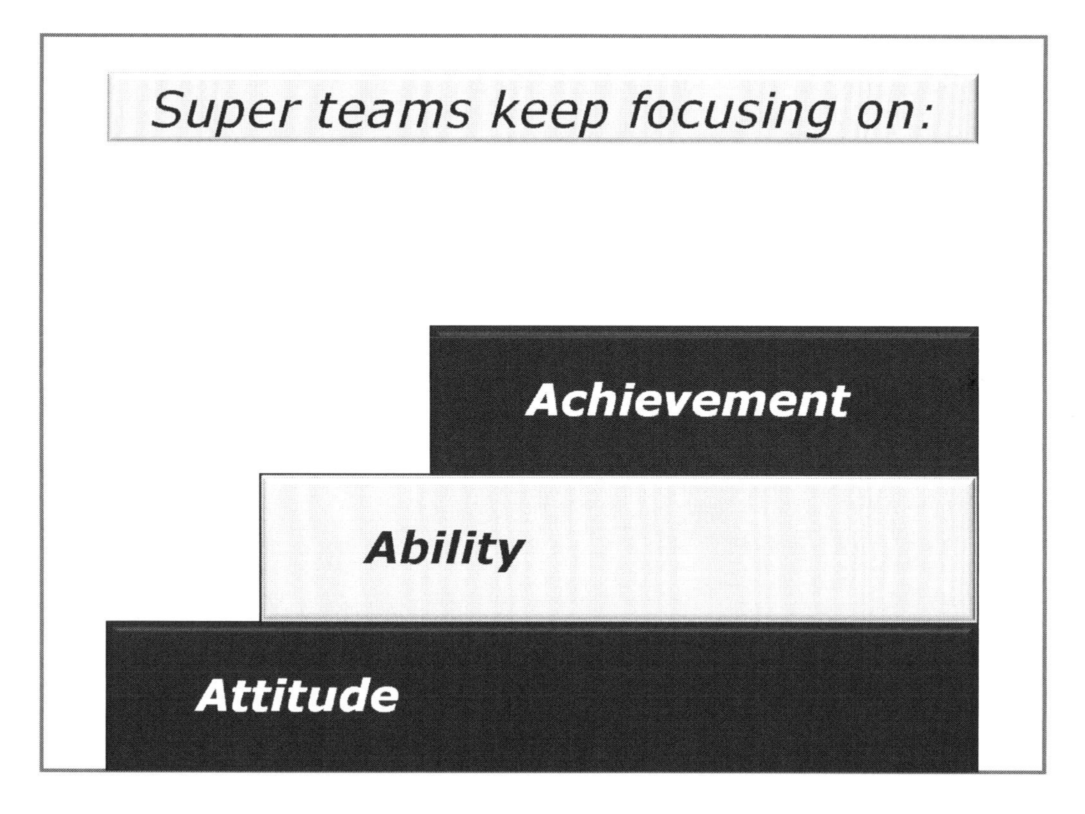

Super teams define the spirit – the attitude – they want people to demonstrate. They then recruit for people who have the right spirit, strengths and skills required to help the team to achieve success.

One business I worked with recruited for values. They believed it was vital for the company to live their values, rather than just laminate the values. These values included, for example: 'Take Responsibility' and 'Deliver Results'.

The company prepared prospective employees by sending a letter that described the values. It also described the specific things that employees had done in the past three months to translate these values into action. It then asked prospective employees:

> *To think of a specific time in their lives when they had taken responsibility and delivered results.*
>
> *To think of the specific steps they had taken to take responsibility and deliver results.*
>
> *To think about how, in their first three months in the company, they would aim to try to take responsibility and deliver results.*

These questions formed the basis of the interview. People were, of course, given more background on the values. They were also given the phone number of a specific person they could contact if they needed more information. This sounds tough, but it certainly made for improving the process of hiring people who wanted to work for the company.

Another work place focused on recruiting people who aimed to be positive, professional and peak performers. Why? These were the qualities that people needed to demonstrate in order to deliver the team's mission. So they kept giving the following messages about their work place.

The Positive Work Place

Welcome to work. This is a superb place for people who want to be:

** Positive.*

** Professional.*

** Peak Performers.*

It may not be a good place for those who don't.

Sounds over the top? Maybe, but everybody knew the attitude and abilities required. The team recruited people who were positive realists. They then worked together to achieve the desired results.

Imagine that you are working with a team that wants to employ people who have the right spirit. If appropriate, invite them to do the following exercise.

The Team's Spirit

The spirit – the attitude and behaviour – we want people in the team to demonstrate is:

1) To

For example:

2) To

For example:

3) To

For example:

The Team's Positive Models

Some of the people in the team who already demonstrate this spirit are:

1) The person's name is:

The specific ways they demonstrate this spirit are:

2) The person's name is:

The specific ways they demonstrate this spirit are:

3) The person's name is:

The specific ways they demonstrate this spirit are:

Diversity of Strengths

Spirit provides the foundation, but teams also need people to express their strengths to achieve success.

If you managed ABBA, you would encourage Agneta and Frida to sing, Bjorn and Benny to write the songs, not the other way round. If you led a start-up business, you would urge the brilliant sales person to get out on the road to find more customers, not spend 20 hours a week programming computers.

Virginia Satir, a pioneering family therapist, found that the people in healthy families demonstrated certain characteristics. First, they shared common values. Second, they encouraged people to be different – and express their talents – within certain parameters. Sick families fought over values and crushed differences.

Arnold Toynbee, the historian, focused on the characteristics of societies that aimed to flourish. They must balance common ethics and creative endeavours. They needed imagination to respond to challenges that threatened their extinction. Looking back at the fall of societies, he wrote:

"Civilisations die from suicide, not by murder ... Civilisations in decline are constantly characterised by a tendency towards standardisation and uniformity."

Great teams also get the right balance between similarity of spirit and diversity of strengths. Bearing this in mind, the team you are working with may like to do the following exercises that focus on strengths. Invite people to:

Describe the strengths they already have in the team.

Describe the strengths they would like to add to the team.

The Team's Present Strengths

The strengths we already have in the team are people with the ability:

1) To

For example:

2) To

For example:

3) To

For example:

4) To

For example:

5) To

For example:

6) To

For example:

7) To

For example:

Possible Strengths To Add

The strengths we may need to add to the team are people with the ability:

1) To

For example:

2) To

For example:

3) To

For example:

Clarifying who the team would rehire

There are many ways to look at how to build or rebuild a team. Sometimes people can get bogged down, however, because they think about who they may exclude from the team.

Another approach is to invite the leaders to imagine they are starting with a blank piece of paper. They are to imagine that everybody in the team – or every team in the organisation – has left and offered their services back to the team. You can then invite them to explore the following questions.

> *Who would you definitely rehire? Bearing mind their strengths, what would you hire them to deliver?*
>
> *Who might you rehire? If so, what would be the clear contracts regarding how they should behave and what they must deliver?*
>
> *Who wouldn't you rehire? What would be your reasons for not rehiring them?*

"I know exactly who I would rehire," said one leader. "Mary, the Operations Director; Sarah, who is brilliant at selling to certain kinds of clients; Dave, the Human Resources Director, who focuses on how people can use their strengths to implement the strategy; and Dan, the Finance Director.

"Looking at the next level, there are at least five people I would rehire immediately, two of whom could step into the leadership team. There are also fine people on Reception and in charge of Facilities. Looking overall, I would rehire about 60% of our people. They already provide the backbone for the company.

"There are one or two people I might rehire," continued the leader, "but a lot would depend on their attitude. Our IT department, for example, must become more customer-focused. During the early days we just had a couple of people who took care of the internal systems. At the time they were contractors and really put in the hours.

"As the business grew, we offered them full-time employment, which they grabbed straight away. Since then the IT department has grown, but several members have become locked into their systems, rather than serving the internal customers. I might rehire the two original people, but would ask them to make the IT department more customer-focused."

Now comes the part that many leaders find relatively obvious. It can be useful to look at people they wouldn't rehire and, just as importantly, the reasons they wouldn't rehire them. Different leaders give different reasons for not re-employing certain people. Here are some that often recur:

"They have the wrong attitude. They have crafted a role that suits them, but it does not add value to the company.

"They rose quickly in the company and got a great financial package. Now the company has changed and we need different things from a person at their level. But they want to carry on doing the same things and drawing a high salary.

"They expect the company to satisfy all their needs – rather than them taking responsibility for making their best contribution to the company."

If appropriate, invite people to do the following exercise.

The Super Team

Starting with a blank sheet of paper

Rehire. The specific people we would rehire – and the specific things we would rehire them to deliver – would be:

1) The person's name is:

The specific things we would rehire them to deliver would be:

To

2) The person's name is:

The specific things we would rehire them to deliver would be:

To

3) The person's name is:

The specific things we would rehire them to deliver would be:

To

4) The person's name is:

The specific things we would rehire them to deliver would be:

To

5) The person's name is:

The specific things we would rehire them to deliver would be:

To

Might Rehire. The specific people we might rehire – and the specific things we might rehire them to deliver – would be:

1) The person's name is:

The specific things we might rehire them to deliver would be:

To

2) The person's name is:

The specific things we might rehire them to deliver would be:

To

Wouldn't Rehire. The specific people we would not rehire would be:

1) The person's name is:

The reasons we would not rehire them would be because:

*

2) The person's name is:

The reasons we would not rehire them would be because:

*

"I do this exercise every year and I act on it," said the leader already mentioned. "At first it seemed a bit scary, but that was because there was so much to sort out. It took six months to get the team right, but now it functions brilliantly. Nevertheless, I still do the exercise to ensure we stay on track."

How can a leader take these steps in their own way? Here are some suggestions to consider.

Spend time with the people they would rehire.

Explain why they want them to keep contributing to the team. In particular, focus on where they deliver As, rather than Bs or Cs. Agree with them on their best contribution to the team. Enable them to get some quick successes. Keep encouraging these people.

Actively go out into the market and get the people they want to hire.

Ensure the potential employee understands the team's culture – the Dos and Don'ts – and invite them to consider whether they want to join. If so, make clear contracts with these people and help them to get some early successes.

Be crystal-clear about the people they might want to rehire into the team.

They can clarify what they want each of these people to deliver. It is important to rehearse the conversations with the individuals. They can then meet with each person and make clear contracts regarding their future contribution to the team. The person can decide if they want to follow these principles or whether they want to move on.

Rehearse the conversations they will have with the people who have no part to play in the future team.

They can carry out these conversations in a professional way. It is good to try to get a moral solution that is good for the team and, if possible, eventually good for the people. If it is not possible, then it is important to do what is required to ensure the team has a successful future.

Explaining 'The Deal' To People

The Deal

Great leaders are extremely honest and explain the real deal to people. This includes the practical and psychological deal. People can then decide whether they want to opt into the deal.

They explain:

* *The Results.*

The results to achieve.

* *The Responsibilities.*

The responsibilities of the various people in achieving the results. This also includes the rules – the guidelines – to follow when working towards achieving the goals.

* *The Rewards.*

The rewards of achieving the results.

People like to know the 'real deal' in a situation. This may cover, for example, the practical and psychological aspects of the personal or professional relationship. One apocryphal story from history is that, when advertising for volunteers to go to the Antarctic in 1912,

Ernest Shackleton put an advert in The Times, saying:

> *"Men wanted for hazardous journey. Low wages, bitter cold, long hours of complete darkness. Safe return doubtful. Honour and recognition in event of success."*

There is little actual evidence that he used this advert, but it certainly communicates the spirit of the adventure. People had an idea of what they were getting into and the conditions to expect.

Great leaders, teams and organisations are moral. They actually explain the deal to their employees. People can then choose whether they want to contribute towards achieving the goals. Similar rules apply in personal relationships. People function best when they make clear contracts about their lives together.

Human beings like clarity. They get angry if either: a) The deal is not made clear at the outset; b) The parties seem to agree on the deal, but one party has a different interpretation; c) The real deal is agreed, but one of the parties breaks the covenant.

People know what to expect when playing for certain football managers. The players will get the chance to win the game's top prizes. But they must follow the manager's playing system and work hard. Sometimes they will get the chance to fully express their talent, but it will be in certain areas of the pitch.

People know the score when they enter show business. They get a chance to do what they love and maybe get applause. But they must master the basics, deal with criticism, keep doing their best, accept rejection, start with minor parts – if they are lucky – and continue to develop. Sometimes things won't seem 'fair'. But: "Hey, get on with it."

People thought they knew the rules when joining established organisations. They believed that, providing they were diligent, they would have predictable careers. Leaders of such institutions often supported this assumption and may have actually believed it themselves.

Certainly the people who joined should have thought ahead. They were adults who could take charge of their careers, rather than believe in 'jobs for life'. But they still felt betrayed when technology and cost cutting bit into their assumptions.

If appropriate, you can invite the leaders to clarify how they can explain the deal to people. Explaining things in a professional way, they can communicate the results to achieve, the responsibilities of the various people and the rewards.

Great leaders give people the opportunity to reflect. They respect people's right to shape their own futures. They are positive and professional, but do not try to persuade. People need time to consider the consequences – both the pluses and minuses involved – before they opt in. Those that take the time to think are then more likely to be serious and fulfil the contract.

If appropriate, you can invite the leaders to tackle the following exercise regarding explaining the deal.

The specific things we can then do to give people the chance to reflect and decide if they want to opt into the deal are:

* *To*

* *To*

* *To*

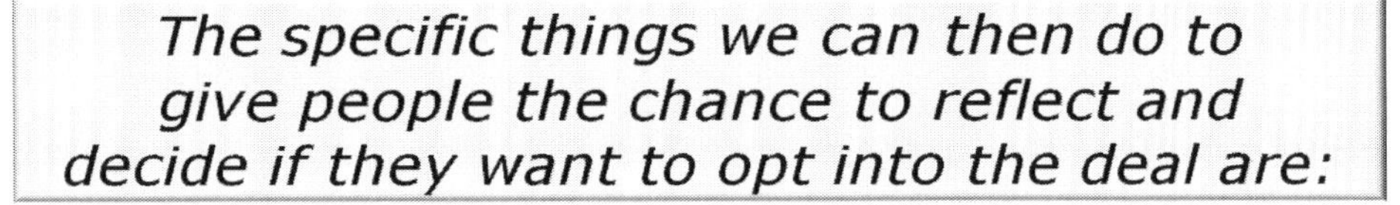

* *To*

* *To*

* *To*

This first section has focused on getting the right people who have the right spirit and strengths. It has also explored the importance of explaining the deal and giving people the chance to opt in.

Bearing this in mind, you may want to invite the leaders to complete the following exercise. This invites them to identify their action plan for getting the right people in place to achieve success.

People Support

The specific things we can do to get the right people in place to give ourselves the greatest chance of success are:

1) To

For example:

2) To

For example:

3) To

For example:

Getting The Right Practical Support

Teams also need the practical support required to reach their goals. This rules applies whether they are aiming to climb a mountain, cross the Antarctic, create a successful prototype or whatever. People are greatly helped by having the infrastructure that enables them to achieve success.

Organisations can sometimes get precious about allocating such support. This is understandable, because they have become wary of people who keep saying: "We need more resources." This statement is sometimes seen as people failing to make the best use of their present assets.

Great leaders manage this properly at the beginning by making clear contracts. They agree with the key sponsors on the 'What, Why, How, Who and When'.

They also clarify the support required to do the job. If asked to take on more projects, they may say something like the following:

"At the moment we are doing three projects where we aim to deliver Gold Medals. We are also happy to do more projects. If we are serious about doing great work in those areas, however, then we will need the appropriate resources. This will give us the chance of delivering even more Gold Medals."

There are many kinds of practical support. These include financial, technical and other systems that make things work. Creating the right infrastructure plays a key part in freeing people to employ their strengths to deliver success.

Bearing this in mind, let's explore a vital component in helping teams and organisations to deliver excellence.

Continually Focusing On The
Entrepreneurship, Engine and Excellence

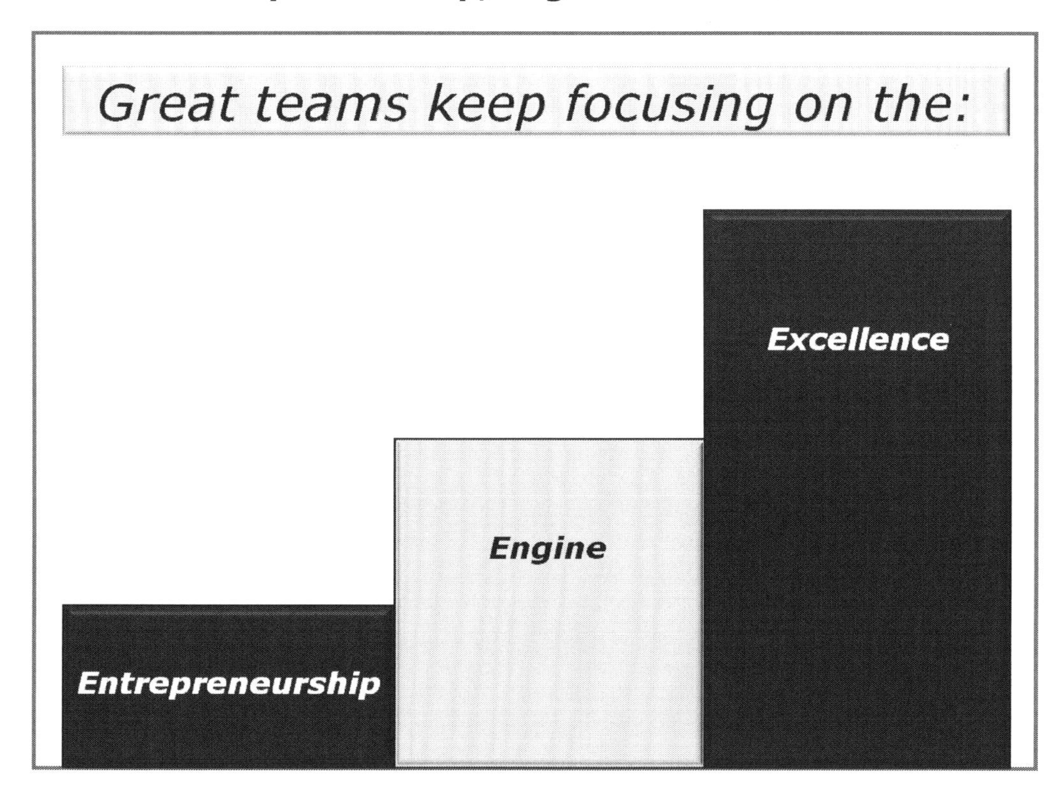

People often go through these stages to do fine work. They start with an entrepreneurial idea. They make the idea work and leverage it properly by building an engine. People then move on to delivering excellence.

Great teams and organisations also nurture all three elements. They focus on:

** Entrepreneurship.*

This calls for creating an environment in which people demonstrate the entrepreneurship and enthusiasm for developing exciting ideas.

** Engine.*

This calls for creating an environment in which the right people implement the right systems in the right way and makes things work successfully.

** Excellence.*

This calls for creating an environment in which people know 'what good looks like' and continually deliver excellence on the way to achieving success.

The first and final parts are vital. But, in order to make things work, is necessary to create an engine. Otherwise leaders keep diving in to fix daily operational problems.

"This sums up my days," said one leader. "During the early years I did everything. I started with the entrepreneurial idea, did the engine work and delivered the goods.

"Today we have lots of people with ideas. But I have only a few people who want to make the everyday things work. So I keep dipping down into the engine room to fix problems. This distracts me from doing the work of delivering excellence."

Big organisations sometimes try to fix this by imposing strict measures, such as Scorecards. This sounds okay, but sometimes these measure things that are irrelevant. The Scorecards might satisfy internal bureaucrats, but not drive the business forward. Such organisations just become an engine.

Some people, on the other hand, simply want to focus on the entrepreneurship and excellence. That is fine: but it will never build a big business. Great teams and organisations build an engine that makes things work.

How to solve the problem? It is vital to get the practical support required to run the engine.

The first step is to define what the 'engine' must deliver. This often means maintaining the organisation's spirit – rather than crushing it – but also developing systems that enable everybody to deliver success.

The next step is to go through the following stages.

To define the kinds of things – the people, principles and practical tools – that will make the engine work.

To get the kinds of people (and they are often special types) who want to make the engine work.

To make clear contracts with people in the business – including the entrepreneurial types – about what they must contribute to help the engine to work.

The final step is to get these things in place and ensure the engine works.

Bearing this in mind, it can be useful to invite the team you are working with to do the following exercise. This asks them to focus on the specific things they can do to build the engine. Here is the exercise.

The Engine

The specific things we can do to build an engine that works - including getting the right people and principles in place - are:

1) To

2) To

3) To

Giving People Support

Let's assume that the team has clarified the people and practical support it requires to deliver the goods. The next step is for them to focus on how they can provide support to their people.

How to make this happen? As mentioned earlier, it can be useful:

To keep communicating the picture of success.

To encourage people to decide if they want to contribute to achieving the picture of success.

To encourage people to build on their strengths – the activities in which they deliver As – and show how they want to contribute to achieving the picture of success.

(They must also, of course, manage the consequences of their weaknesses.)

To encourage people to make clear contracts – including the required support – regarding the specific things they will deliver towards achieving the picture of success.

To encourage people to proactively keep their manager – and other key stakeholders – informed about their progress towards achieving the picture of success.

Great teams and organisations are moral. They explain The Deal to people. They encourage people to build on their strengths and set stretch goals – rather than surgery goals. They then provide the support people need to achieve success.

Bearing this in mind, you may want to invite the leaders to complete the following exercise. This asks them to clarify their plans for giving people the support they need to do the job.

Giving People Support

The specific things we can do to give people the support they need to deliver success are:

1) To

2) To

3) To

The specific benefits of providing people with this support will be:

1) To

2) To

3) To

This chapter has looked at how to get the support required to deliver the goods. So now we move on to delivering superb work.

Superb Work

Let's return to the beginning. As we discussed earlier, peak performing people, teams and organisations often take following steps toward delivering success.

Peak Performers

* *Clarify the Picture of Success.*
* *Clarify the strategies and road map for achieving the Picture of Success.*
* *Clarify and do whatever is necessary to achieve the Picture of Success.*

Super teams are prepared to sweat. They keep focusing on the key strategies – the principles they aim to follow – and perform superb work. Such teams follow good habits. They do the right things in the right way every day.

People get the right balance between consistency and creativity. They are clear on the specific things that everybody must do in a consistent way. They are also aware of when people need to express their creativity to reach the goals.

Such teams co-ordinate people's strengths. They put the right people in the right places to deliver the right results. They put people in the places where they deliver As, whilst also managing the consequences of their Bs and Cs. They make sure that all the grunt work gets done, whilst also ensuring people deliver great work.

Great leaders choose to build Excellence Cultures, rather than Excuse Cultures. They act as positive models and show people 'what good looks like'. They reward the behaviour they want repeated. They do this by, for example, continually producing success stories that highlight how people have performed great work and delivered success.

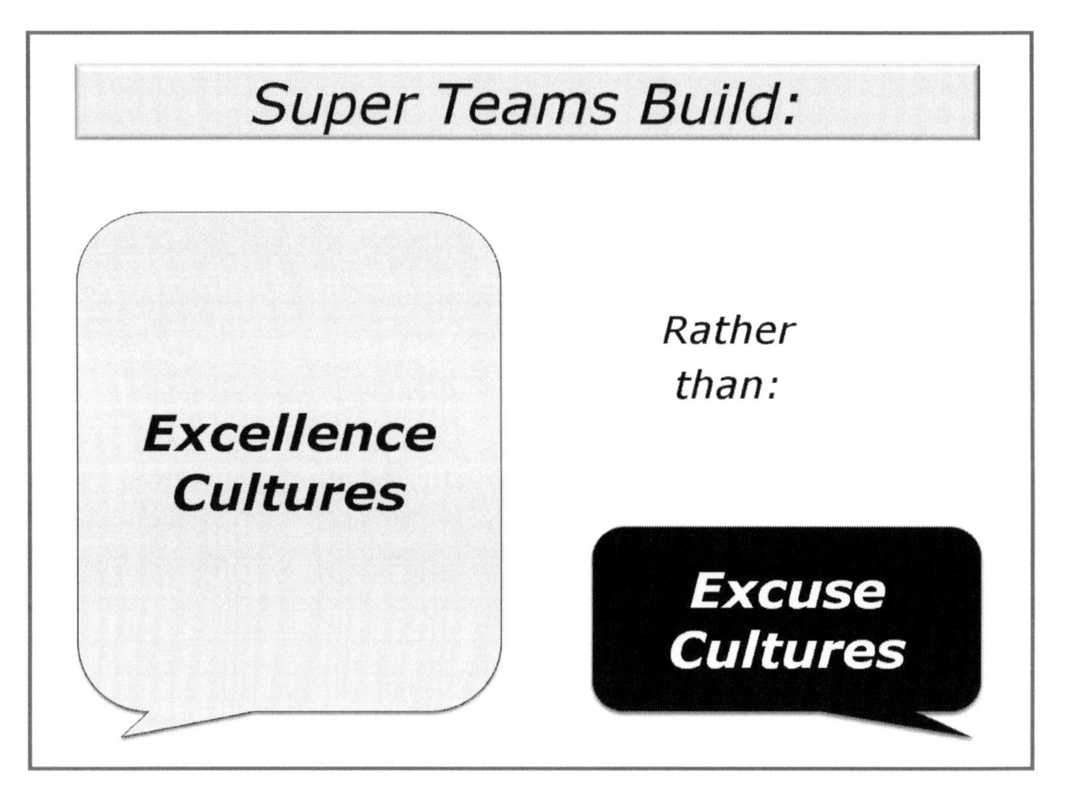

Such leaders build cultures where people take responsibility, rather than avoid taking responsibility. They 'never walk past a quality problem' – otherwise they are saying that such poor standards are okay. Sometimes this means giving tough messages. They do this, however, by following a certain procedure.

They remind people of the picture of success.

They show people 'what good looks like' in the specific activity where there may be a problem and encourage people to maintain those standards in the future.

They show people positive ways forward – but act if people fail to deliver those standards.

Great teams manage by outcomes, rather than manage by tasks. They continually invite people to present their progress towards achieving the goals. They encourage people to proactively focus on tackling the issues that are in Green, Amber and Red Zones. Such teams then enable their people to do whatever is necessary to deliver the picture of success.

Let's return to the team with whom you are working. Here are some themes they may wish to pursue on the road to delivering the goods.

Superb Work

You can invite each team within the organisation to complete the following exercise. They are to describe the specific things they can do to maintain good habits and perform superb work.

Performing Superb Work

The specific things we can do to keep maintaining good habits and performing superb work are:

1)

2)

3)

This is a good start. But it is also important for people to keep on track. Each team can continue to report their progress towards achieving the picture of success. Every month – or other suggested time period – they can present the following updates.

(You can, of course, adapt this to individuals presenting their progress towards achieving the agreed goals.)

The Super Team Updates

The progress we are making towards achieving the picture of success

Successes In The Past Month

The specific things we have delivered in the past month towards achieving the picture of success have been:

1)

2)

3)

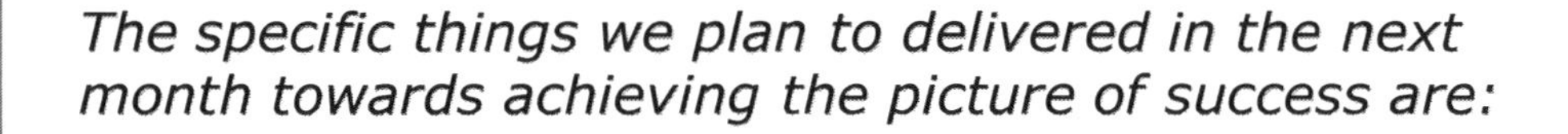

The specific things we plan to delivered in the next month towards achieving the picture of success are:

1)

2)

3)

Challenges In The Next Month

The specific plans we have for tackling key challenges in the next month – together with any support we would like – are:

1)

2)

3)

Satisfying Sponsors

There are many ways to keep focusing on delivering great work. One approach is to clarify the actual words the team want certain people to be saying in the future. This is a particularly useful exercise when it comes to focusing on sponsors.

Sometime ago I ran a goal setting session for several teams who were joining forces on a particular project to satisfy a wide variety of sponsors. The danger was that each would focus on their own particular target group – such as their own bosses – at the expense of the joint venture.

Bearing this in mind, we began by asking each team to make several flip charts. They were asked:

To head each chart with the name of a key sponsor they had to satisfy.

To write the actual words they wanted to hear that sponsor saying at the end of the project.

Looking around the room, the joint venture team needed to satisfy around 20 different sponsors. This could have been a disaster – particularly as some sponsors may have had competing goals.

We focused instead on the 80%+ of the aims that people had in common. These formed the basis for the picture of success. Later we could move on to finding solutions to some of the other wishes. This actually proved to be the case and the joint project delivered success.

Let's return to the team with whom you are working. They will buy time by getting some early wins and reassuring their sponsors.

Bearing this in mind, invite people to do the exercise on this theme. They are to write the names of their sponsors and other stakeholders. (These are the people who can hire or fire them and those who can play a strong part in influencing their future.) Depending on the level at which they are operating, this list could include, for example:

Their Manager.

Their Manager's Manager.

The Directors.

The Other Stakeholders.

The Banks or Venture Capitalists.

Their Customers.

The Trade Press.

Invite the team to do two things. First, to describe the actual words they would like to hear that sponsor or stakeholder saying about the team's work in the future. Second, to describe how they can do their best to make this happen.

Here is the exercise. It only provides space to describe one sponsor or stakeholder. But the team would obviously do a separate sheet for each person they want to help to succeed.

Satisfying Sponsors and Stakeholders

The person's name is:

____

The actual words we would like to hear them saying are:

"______________________________"

The specific things we can do to do our best to make this happen are:

*

*

*

Staying Proactive

Great workers stay ahead of the game. There are many tools for making this happen. One of the most common is to focus on the activities that are in the Green, Amber and Red Zones.

Some organisations say that: "Everything must be Green." That is understandable. But sometimes it can lead to people becoming fixated on the issues that are in Amber and Red. These areas need fixing, of course, but there are also massive wins to be gained by capitalising on what is already in Green.

How to translate this into practice? One team, for example, has a dedicated room where there are separate charts on each wall.

One wall has the road map for the next year. This keeps people's eyes focusing on the Picture of Success. Each of the other three walls have charts headed respectively Green, Amber and Red.

People populate each of the three walls by using Post-Its to continually update everything that is in the Green, Amber or Red Zones. These can be any activities regarding the Profits, Products – including customer service – People and any other themes. People also suggest what can be done to build on the Green and, as far as possible, shift the Amber and Red into the Green.

The leaders can walk into the room each morning and get an immediate overview of the business. This approach also enables everybody in the team to see the total picture. Here is an introduction to how people use this method to stay ahead of the game.

The Green Zone

These are the things that are going well. People can list what is presently in the Green Zone. They can also describe how to maintain or improve these things.

Teams may find that giving even more attention to customers who like them, for example, can create even more business. There may also be employees who are doing great work. It will be important to encourage them to keep developing in their careers inside the organisation.

The Amber Zone

These are the things where there are warning signs or that need improvement. People can list what is presently in the Amber Zone. They can also describe how to improve these things.

The relationship with a customer who previously enjoyed working with the team may have slipped from Green into Amber. It will be important to quickly rebuild the relationship, otherwise it may slide into Red.

Some dedicated employees may also be stretching themselves by continually putting in 12-hour days. Providing the right resources can help such people to relax and revitalise themselves. It can also enable them to use their strengths in the areas where they can make their best contribution to the business.

The Red Zone

These are the things that are going badly. They need radical improvements or key decisions to be taken. People can list what is presently in the Red Zone. They can also describe how to improve these things.

In some cases, however, people may decide to take action to forever remove these issues. They may have a client or an employee, for example, who is forever causing problems. Providing they can find a positive replacement, they may choose to say goodbye to the client or employee.

Here is the exercise that you may want to invite the team to complete.

The Green Zone

The specific things that are in the Green Zone at the moment are:

1)

2)

3)

The specific things we can do to maintain or build on these things are:

1)

2)

3)

The Amber Zone

The specific things that are in the Amber Zone at the moment are:

1)

2)

3)

The specific things we can do to improve these things are:

1)

2)

3)

The Red Zone

The specific things that are in the Red Zone at the moment are:

1)

2)

3)

The specific things we can do to improve or make decisions about these things are:

1)

2)

3)

There are many tools for encouraging, educating and enabling a team to perform superb work. Whichever route they take, however, people may encounter challenges and setbacks on the journey. This takes us to the next stage.

Solutions

Super teams employ people who have the right spirit and skills required to achieve success. Such people have a positive attitude and the ability to overcome setbacks. They take responsibility during difficult times and find solutions to challenges. Sometimes they move into another dimension and do great work that delivers success.

Al Siebert, author of *The Resiliency Advantage*, wrote:

> *"Resilience is essential in today's world. In today's workplace everyone feels pressured to get more work done, of higher quality, with fewer people, in less time, with less budget. Resilience is the process of successfully adapting to difficult or challenging life experiences.*
>
> "Resilient people overcome adversity, bounce back from setbacks, and can thrive under extreme, on-going pressure without acting in dysfunctional or harmful ways.
>
> "The most resilient people recover from traumatic experiences stronger, better and wiser. When faced with adversity it is useful to remember that: Your mind and habits will create either barriers or bridges to a better future.
>
> "Resiliency can't be taught, but it can be learned. It comes from working to develop your unique combination of inborn abilities. The struggle to bounce back and recover from setbacks can lead to developing strengths and abilities that you didn't know were possible."

Let's explore some of the steps that teams take to employ such people. This involves revisiting one of the topics we have covered earlier – employing people with the right spirit – plus looking at solutions and self-management. Let's consider the first of these themes.

Spirit

Super teams employ people who have the right spirit to drive things forward, overcome setbacks and achieve success. Different leaders have different names for the types of people they like to recruit. One football manager borrowed from other fields and said:

"I need to get the right combination of people in the team. We need at least 8 Warriors. They will fight, get the ball and also do good work.

"On top of this, we need 3 Warrior-Wizards. These must be people who are prepared to work hard, but able to add that touch of magic. I don't have any time for Wannabe-Wizards who stand around and are not prepared to do the necessary work."

There are many different models for getting the right type of people in the team. Assuming that everybody displays the required spirit, it is then to get the right balance of decision makers, drivers and deliverers.

Decision makers set the strategy. Drivers act as the gears: they 'live the message' and translate the ideas into action. Deliverers produce the goods.

People may move between all three roles at times. By and large, however, it is important to get the right people with the right strengths in the right places in a team.

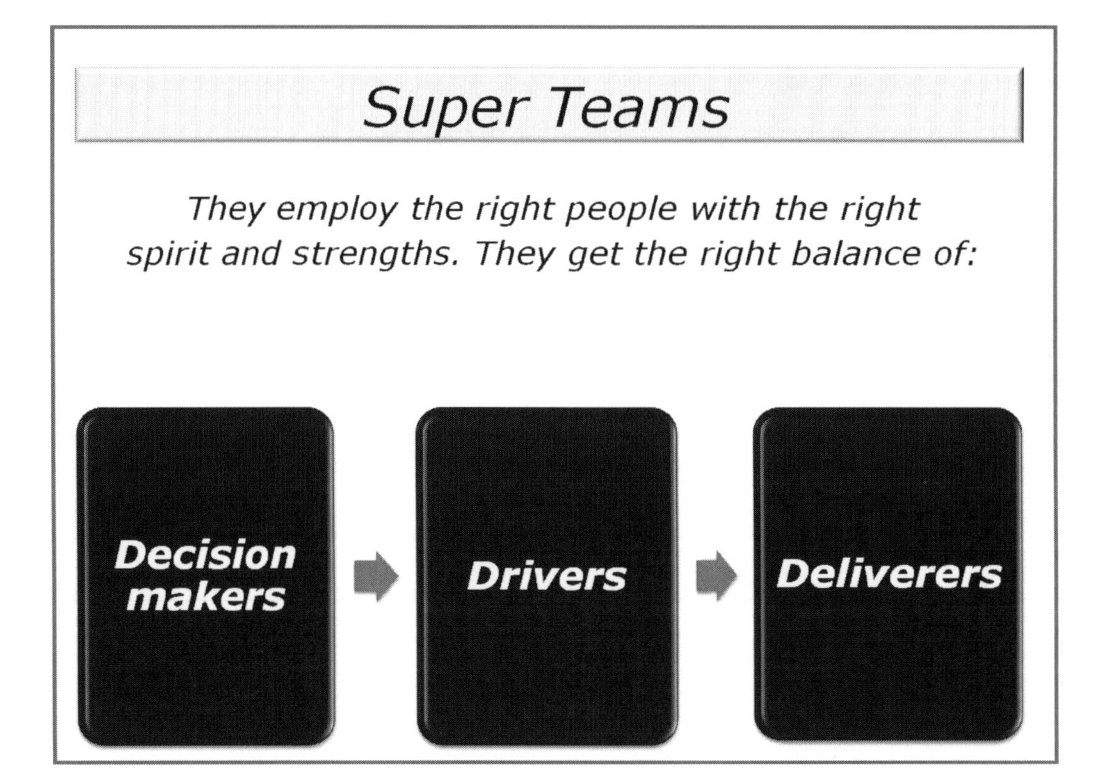

Decision makers

Decision makers set the compass. They communicate this story in a compelling way and ensure everybody knows their part in achieving the goals.

Great teams frequently have two or three people at the centre who take responsibility for setting the overall direction. Depending on the topics to be covered, however, they then involve wider groups. Leaders do this to ensure people have a real sense of ownership regarding their part of their strategy.

Drivers

Drivers are the gears of the team. They act as positive models and often lead 'teams within the team'. Such a driver approaches the leader and says something like the following.

"As far as I understand it, the strategy of the overall team is: To _____. My part and my team's part in making the strategy happen is: To _____. Is that correct? Right, I will go and make it happen."

Leaders must make sure that all their direct reports embody these qualities. Otherwise they will leap frog them and micro-manage the deliverers.

Great football clubs, for example, recruit drivers to form the spine of the team. Spurring-on their teammates, they ensure the strategy is translated into action.

Deliverers

Deliverers are often experts and do great work. Some deliverers do go on to become drivers. But that step calls for them taking a different kind of responsibility. They must be prepared to act as positive models and make tough decisions. Some deliverers therefore prefer to remain brilliant niche providers. This is okay: providing they have a positive attitude, do good work and contribute to helping the team reach its goals.

Great teams employ people with the right spirit and strengths. They get the right balance of decision makers, drivers and deliverers.

Solutions

Such teams also educate people to find solutions to challenges. They often do this by taking the following steps.

They encourage people to anticipate and manage potential difficulties.

They encourage people to anticipate and manage potential successes.

They encourage people to develop their skills for finding creative solutions to challenges.

Managing Potential Difficulties

Peak performers always seem to be one step ahead of the game. One reason is because they continually explore potential future scenarios.

If appropriate, you can invite the team you are working with to look ahead and brainstorm the potential difficulties they may face. This can include difficulties, setbacks or other issues. They are then to do three things.

To choose one potential difficulty they want to explore.

To clarify how they can try to prevent the potential difficulty happening.

To clarify how they can manage the difficulty if it does happen.

Managing Potential Difficulties

The Potential Difficulties. The difficulties, setbacks or challenges we may face on the road towards achieving the goal are:

*

*

*

The Specific Difficulty. The potential difficulty we want to focus on is:

*

The specific way this difficulty may manifest itself may be:

Managing Potential Difficulties

*

*

*

Preventing The Difficulty. The specific things we can do to prevent the difficulty happening are:

*

*

*

Managing The Difficulty. The specific things we can do to manage the difficulty if it does happen are:

*

*

*

Prevention is the best medicine, but some problems may still occur. Great teams then stay calm and keep pursuing their chosen principles on the ways towards achieving the goals.

Managing Potential Successes

Peak performers go beyond considering how to deal with difficulties. They look at how to capitalise on potential successes. This may seem odd. But some people and teams do not know how to build on early wins. They may also freeze when things are going well and, for example, the end is in sight.

One football team found it extremely hard to win matches when leading by 1 – 0 with ten minutes remaining. Instead of being positive, or even playing a solid percentage game, they slipped into paralysis.

The players kept looking at the clock, retreating into their own penalty area and giving the ball away. Inevitably the opposition piled on the pressure and the team conceded a late goal or two.

How to tackle the problem? The team were invited to explore the times when they had maintained a lead and won games. What did they do right then? How could they follow similar principles in future situations where they led by the odd goal?

The players focused on doing what had made them successful. They kept the team's shape, kept moving and kept passing to their own players. They began reframing leading as a pleasurable situation, rather than a pressure situation. As a result, the team began to win more matches.

Different teams will, of course, have different kinds of potential successes. If appropriate, you can invite the team you are working with to brainstorm the potential successes they may have on the road to reaching their goals. They are then to do two things.

To choose one potential success they want to explore.

To clarify how they can capitalise on this success.

Managing Potential Successes

The Potential Successes. The successes we may encounter on the road towards achieving the goal are:

*

*

*

The Specific Success. The potential success we want to focus on is:

*

The specific way this success may manifest itself may be:

*

*

*

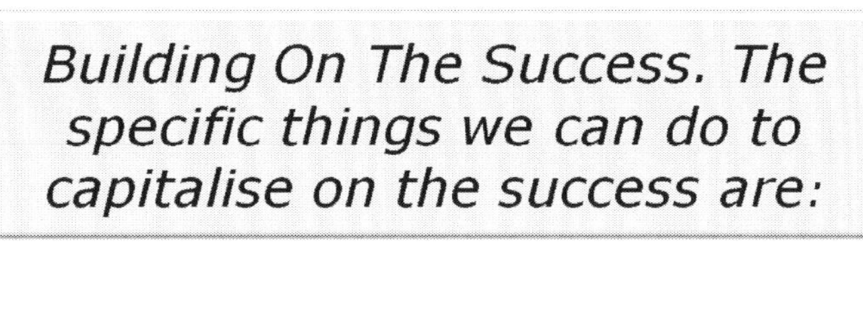

*

*

*

Educating People To Find Solutions To Challenges

Great teams educate their people to find solutions to challenges. Imagine, for example, that you have been invited to teach this skill with several teams inside an organisation.

There are many models for creative problem solving. As mentioned earlier in the book, the one we are using encourages people to focus on clarity, creativity and concrete results.

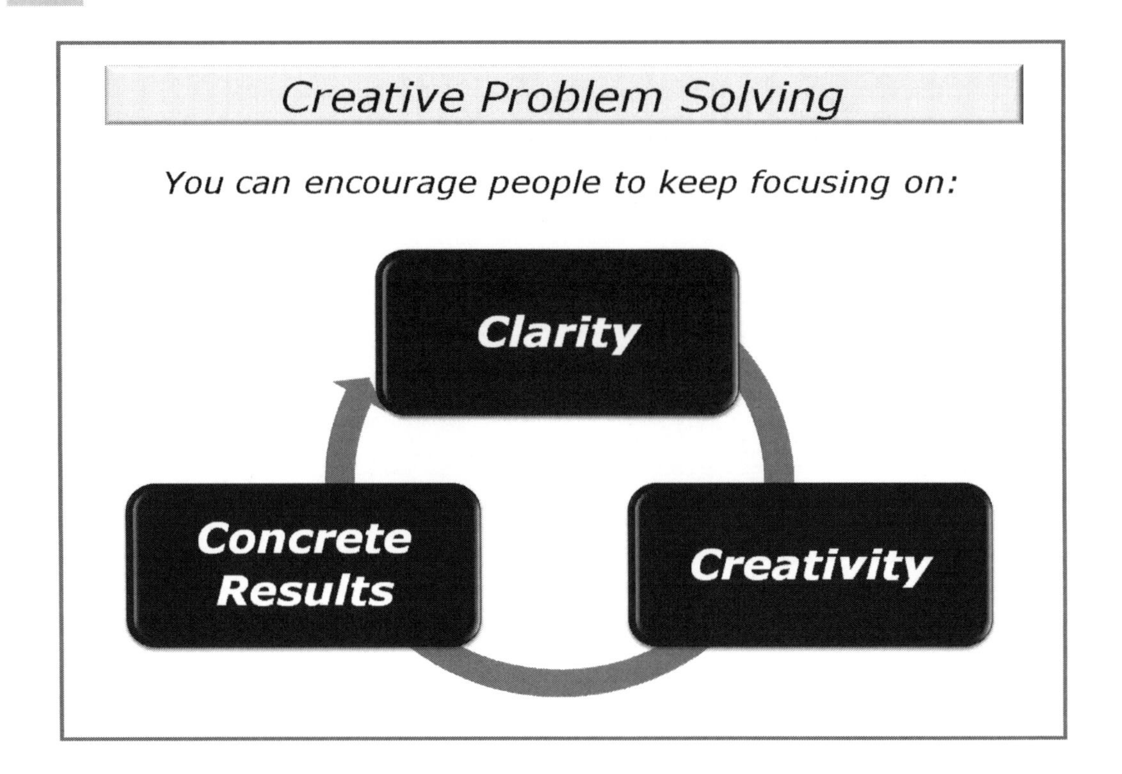

Before the session, prepare flip charts that replicate the following illustrations headed Clarity, Creativity and Concrete Results. Each team should have a complete set of flip charts. This is a lot of work, but it makes it easier for people to go through the stages.

Start by explaining the model. Give examples of how the model works in practice. Emphasise the need for people to spend a lot of time focusing on clarity. They need to establish the 'What' – the real results to achieve – before moving on to creativity and the 'How'.

Invite people to congregate in their teams. One person in each team is to act as a facilitator, but they can still share their ideas. The team is then to go through the following steps.

To focus on a specific challenge they want to tackle.

To work through the stages of clarity, creativity and concrete results.

To present back a summary of the stages they went through and their suggested action plan for delivering the required results.

The exercise can take up to 2 hours to do properly. This includes time for presenting back. But the exercise provides people with a tool for life. They can use this approach to do creative problem solving in the future.

Here is an overview of the flip charts that you can invite people to complete. The crucial ones, however, are those that outline their plan for achieving concrete results.

Clarity

Challenges. The specific challenge we want to explore is:

* *How to*

Here is some more information about the situation:

*

*

*

Clarity. The real results we want to achieve - in order of priority - are:

* *To*

* *To*

* *To*

Controllables. The things we can control in the situation are:

*

*

*

Creativity

Choices and Consequences. The possible options for tackling the challenge – together with the pluses, minuses and attractiveness - are:

a) To

The pluses are:

The minuses are:

The attractiveness of this option is: ______ / 10

b) To

The pluses are:

The minuses are:

The attractiveness of this option is: ______ / 10

c) To

The pluses are:

The minuses are:

The attractiveness of this option is: ______ / 10

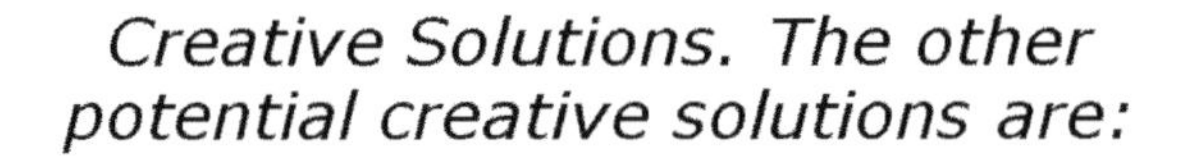

Creative Solutions. The other potential creative solutions are:

* *To*

* *To*

* *To*

Concrete Results

Conclusions. The route – or combination of routes – we want to follow for tackling the challenge and achieving the results is:

* *To*

* *To*

* *To*

Contracting. The specific contracts we need to make to ensure the results are delivered are:

* *To*

* *To*

* *To*

The extent to which we are committed and serious about delivering the results is:

_____ /10

Concrete Results. The specific action plan for achieving the results – including getting some early successes - is:

* *To*

* *To*

* *To*

Let's assume that the teams have got into the habit of using these problem solving skills. It can then be useful to help them to go on to the next stage of growth.

Self-Managing Teams

Great organisations often encourage people to build more self-managing teams. This releases the leader to focus on shaping tomorrow's business, whilst the team manages today's business. How to make this happen? Let's move out of the scenario where you are coaching somebody.

Imagine instead that you personally lead a successful team. Your bosses admire what your team has achieved, but they wonder if it is too dependent on your personality. This is now going to be put to the test. Last week the Chief Executive called to say:

"I would like you to consider taking over part of your boss's role for the next 6 months. They will be running a global project and must release some of their responsibilities. Many of these play to your strengths. Are you interested?"

"If so, it means spending at least 50% of your time on the role. That has implications. You will need: a) To nominate somebody to deputise for you in your present role; b) To get your team to be more self-managing. Is this something you are interested in doing?"

Assuming you take the role, it will require everybody in the team taking more responsibility. Let's explore how to make this happen.

You can ensure the team wants to become more self-managing.

Start by choosing somebody to act as your deputy. Agree with them on: a) The team's goals; b) The role they want to play in guiding the team to reaching these goals; c) The support they want from you. You are then ready to talk with the rest of the team.

Before tackling the actual contracting process, however, ensure people really do want to become more self-managing. Certainly they will answer '"Yes," but underline the work involved.

As ever, the old coaching rule applies: 'People must have the will before they learn the skill.' Gather people together and go through the following stages.

Explain the reasons for the session.

You may say, for example, that you have accepted part of your boss's role. This will mean you spending less time with the team. Some of your duties will be taken over by your deputy.

Your authority will continue to be: ______. Your deputy's authority will be: ______. But you will be asking everybody to take on more responsibility and become a self-managing team.

Later in the session you will make contracts about the broad roles people will play. You are sure, however, that the team will continue to deliver success.

Re-communicate the team's agreed picture of success.

Revisit the team's goals for the next six months. Invite people to ask questions and add suggestions to the goals. Then ask them:

"On a scale 0 – 10, to what extent do you feel confident you can deliver the goals? What can be done to improve the ratings?"

Compile their suggestions for improving the chances of success.

Ensure they want to become more self-managing.

Explain that the next steps will be: a) To outline the overall roles that people must play in reaching the goals; b) To involve them in crafting the these responsibilities; c) To meet with each person to make clear contracts about their parts in achieving the goals.

Bearing in mind the work involved, ask if they want to become more self-managing. They will probably answer, "Yes." (If not, you may need to bring other people into the team.)

You can make clear contracts about people's roles in building a self-managing team.

Start by explaining people's overall responsibilities in such a team. Looking ahead to the next 6 months, explain: a) The leader's role (including that of the deputy); b) The team members' role.

Invite people to do the following exercise. Ask each of them to write Post-It Notes under the respective headings. (See below.) Give people 15 minutes to write the ideas. Then invite each one in turn to place their Post-Its under the relevant headings – plus give their explanations for the suggestions.

Building A Self-Managing Team

The Leader's Role and - if relevant - The Deputy's Role in building a self-managing team is:

* To
* To
* To
* To
* To

The Team Member's Role in building a self-managing team is:

* To
* To
* To
* To
* To

Discuss the suggestions that emerge. You will have the final say on people's roles, but it is good to get everybody's ideas. The process also educates them about the team principles.

Finalise the ideas and then communicate the respective responsibilities. Together with your deputy, meet with each person and make clear contracts about their individual contributions.

You can ensure people translate the contracts into action and become a more self-managing team.

Your team has the right spirit – people want to become more self-managing. They can then follow their agreed systems to reach their goals.

For example, people can hold a monthly meeting to stay on-track. The deputy can start such a session by updating people on the whole team's progress towards achieving the picture of success. Each person can then give a brief update on:

The specific things they have delivered in the past month towards achieving the goals.

The specific things they plan to deliver in the next month.

The challenges they face, their strategies for tackling these challenges and the support they need to achieve success.

The presentations should be made in headline terms – rather than a detailed 'to do' list. People can then turn to how: a) They can continue to pursue the key strategies; b) They find creative solutions to challenges; c) They can keep satisfying their sponsors – their bosses – and deliver success.

You are still accountable for the team's results, so do whatever is necessary to ensure that people deliver. At the same time, continue to coach your deputy and, when appropriate, the whole team. Gather people and ask them to present:

The things we are doing well – and how we can continue to follow these principles.

The things we can do better – and how.

Good leaders are often like good educators and enable their people to become more self-managing. This releases the leader to be more strategic. It also enables everybody to develop – both as people and professionals.

The above description shows how you can use this approach when leading a team. If you are coaching other leaders, however, you can help them to apply those principles to enable their teams to become more self-managing.

This chapter has looked at how people can find solutions to challenges. The final step is for them to keep working hard and achieve their goals. Let's consider how they can deliver success.

Success

Super teams are good finishers. There are, of course, many ways to finish. As the old motor racing adage goes, however: "In order to finish First, first you have to finish."

Some teams continue to do the right things in the right way. Some fight – then flow, focus and finish. Some work towards a deadline. They relax, rehearse and then rise to the occasion. Some keep doing the basics and then add the brilliance. Some reach the goal by adding that touch of class.

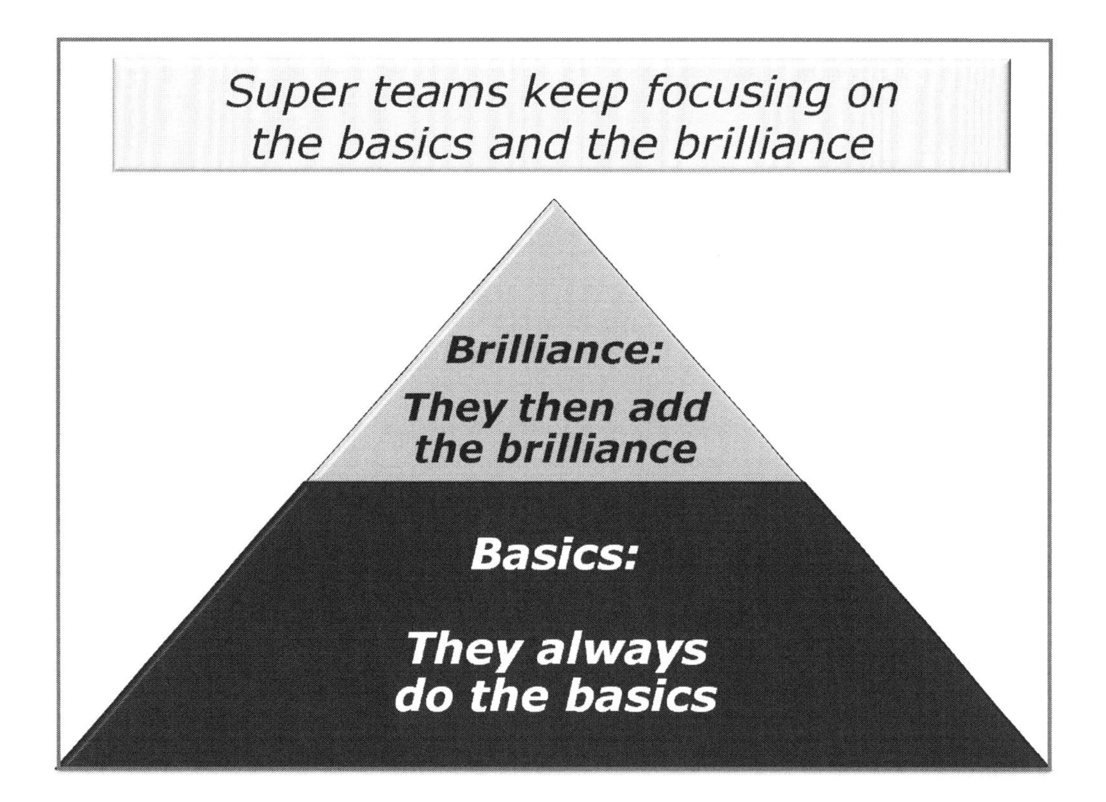

Such teams do certain things after reaching a goal. Some employ the concept of Kaizen – constant improvement. They clarify what they did well and what they can do better in the future. Some build a second-generation super team. They start with a blank piece of paper and say:

"If we were to start again today, what would we focus on doing?

"What are our strengths? What are the activities in which we deliver As, rather than Bs or Cs? Who are our perfect customers? What are the challenges they face? How could we help them to achieve success?

"Who would be the people we would have in the team? Imagine everybody left and offered their services back tomorrow. Who would we hire and what would we hire them to deliver? What can we therefore do to build a second-generation super team?"

Some teams follow the model that many aspire to in sports. They build a team, then a club, then a dynasty. Some see the future in building a values-driven organisation. Some surf the Sigmoid Curve. (Something we will explore later.)

Some teams seek the next challenge. They aim to do stimulating work, set stretch goals and deliver success. Let's explore some of these ways of satisfying sponsors.

Delivering Success

There are many ways to deliver the goods. Sometimes there is an obvious straight line towards achieving the goals. Sometimes the route calls for being more creative. Let's explore one such example.

Several years ago I worked with a leader who was invited into a company to get results by 'changing the culture'. The company had a global reach, but it was slowly grinding to a halt. As we have discussed earlier, like most leaders she had several options for making this happen. These included:

> *She could urge everybody to change and put them through a conventional change programme.*
>
> *She could fire everybody and start again with a blank piece of paper.*
>
> *She could create the future culture by building successful prototypes – then invite people to choose whether or not they want to join this culture.*

Savvy leaders often go for the third option. Why? They understand systems theory. Systems follow the law of homeostasis: they keep returning back to their present state. Such leaders don't try to change the system. They create a new system with new rules.

They also recognise the importance of language. Sometimes it is important to stress that they are aiming to 'Build the New', rather than trying to 'Change the Old'. The language is pioneering. This provides more positive energy than urging people to 'change'. Let's look at how the leader made this happen.

Building successful prototypes.

Looking at the business, the leader chose a theme around which to build the prototypes. She chose the topic of delivering exceptional customer service.

Whilst the company provided software and solutions, the way they delivered this service could differentiate them from other suppliers. They aimed to become serious about becoming trusted advisors to their customers. She then took the following steps towards introducing this approach.

Setting-up the prototypes to succeed.

Great leaders focus on the people who have positive energy and who want to do great work. So she began by identifying the present people who were committed to delivering customer service.

Looking around the different countries and departments, she rated the chances of success of building such prototypes. She then focused on developing the customer service approach in these places.

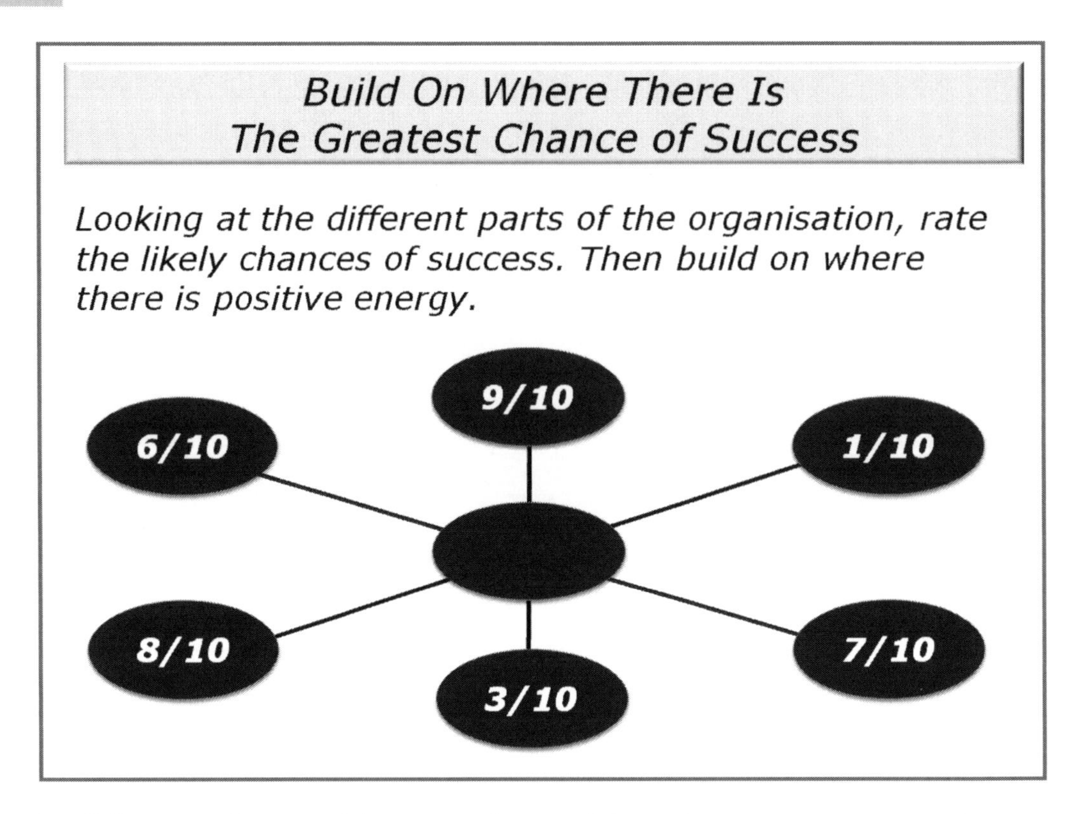

Building on the positive people, making clear contracts and providing support.

The leader ensured the right project leaders were in place for building the prototypes. She agreed with them on 'What' must be delivered and by 'When'. This called for reaching certain targets in terms of customer satisfaction.

Whilst also agreeing on the broad principles of the 'How', she gave them freedom, within parameters, to implement the strategy. She also provided the support they needed to do the job.

Ring fencing the prototypes in order to help them to succeed.

Despite giving the project leaders the brief and the mandate, the leader ring fenced the prototypes. Why? Despite apparently wishing the new approaches well, sometimes there can be 'interferences' from older parts of an organisation. So it was vital to give people the oxygen and freedom to succeed.

Encouraging people to get some early wins and creating an event for sharing success stories.

The leader encouraged each project leader to get some early wins to build positive momentum. She also set a date for a company-wide event in 9 months time when they would present success stories. Wherever possible, this would involve customers sharing their experiences. People responded well to the deadlines and worked hard to deliver successes.

Doing everything possible to ensure the prototypes delivered success.

The leader provided an inspiring vision, but it was up to the prototype-builders to do the work. She kept in touch with them, but in a supportive way, asking: "What do you want from me to help you to be successful?" This led to providing the necessary ongoing support.

The leader explained how she wanted to be kept updated, because she needed a reality check. She encouraged them to communicate their achievements along the road and also celebrate success. In one case things went wrong. So she made the tough decisions early, rather than late. This led to putting somebody else in charge of that one project.

Sharing the lessons and inviting volunteers to implement the next wave of success stories.

Success provides its own arguments. So, as mentioned earlier, an event was arranged to share the success stories. This involved customers and highlighted:

The principles that had proved successful.

The things people had learned and could do better in the future.

The leader then announced the next steps in implementing the approach. She said:

"The prototypes have shown how we can deliver exceptional customer service. We are looking for volunteers who want to follow these principles in their part of the business. The goal will be to achieve customer satisfaction ratings of at least 80%. Get back to me within one week to let me know:

a) Whether you want to deliver this 'What'.

b) 'How', in broad terms, you aim to deliver it.

c) The support you need to do the job.

"This obviously means a shift in culture – changing the way we do things around here. We can succeed with this new approach, so let me know if you want to be part of making it happen."

Making the principles mandatory and guiding the organisation to success.

The leader gave those who volunteered the encouragement to pursue the customer service principles that embodied the future culture. Three months later she gave everybody the following message.

"The prototypes have shown the principles we must follow to be successful. The pluses are that we will improve our services and stay in business. The minuses are that it will be challenging, especially at first. But it is the way to build a successful future. What I am saying to you is also challenging.

"I am asking you to decide whether or not you want to follow those principles. If so, get back to your manager within the next week and we will agree on how you want to contribute."

"If we do not hear from you, we will assume you do not want to follow these principles. So we will then try to work-out, as far as possible, a 'win-win'."

"This sounds tough, but we must follow these principles to achieve success. Let me or your manager know if you want to contribute to the journey."

The leader anticipated this situation might arise, but sometimes there is no other option. People must decide whether or not they wanted to be part of a future culture. There were a few rocky months, but things worked out. The foundations were laid for building a successful future.

This is one approach to shaping a culture. It may or may not be appropriate with the team with whom you are working. But it has a track record of delivering the goods. Let's explore another way of helping a team to develop.

Focusing On What The Team Can Keep, Start and Stop Doing

This is an old exercise, but it can still be valuable. Many teams employ it after reaching their goals. The exercise enables to them to shape a successful future. Start by making three flip charts headed:

* *Keep doing: The things we need to keep doing.*

* *Start doing: The things we need to start doing.*

* *Stop doing: The things we need to stop doing.*

Gather people together and provide each person with a pack of Post-it Notes. Position the first part of the exercise by giving the following instructions.

"Great teams develop good habits. So I would like you to start by listing all the things you believe you should keep doing to achieve success. These can be the big key principles or the small concrete actions."

"If you write a principle, however, try to bring it to life by giving a concrete example. For instance: If you say: 'Keep giving great customer service,' give a specific example of how this can be translated into action."

"Also describe the benefits of continuing to do the things you mention. Write one idea per Post-it but as many ideas as you wish. So take 15 minutes to describe the things that you believe the team should keep doing. "

Give people the allotted preparation time and then invite each person to place their Post-it Notes on the flip chart. If appropriate, you can then discuss the various points and agree on the fundamental things the team must continue doing.

(The other option is to delay this discussion until after also completing the next two sections regarding what the team should start and stop doing.)

So here is the first exercise regarding the good habits. Doing these things means the team will be more likely to consistently deliver at least 7/10.

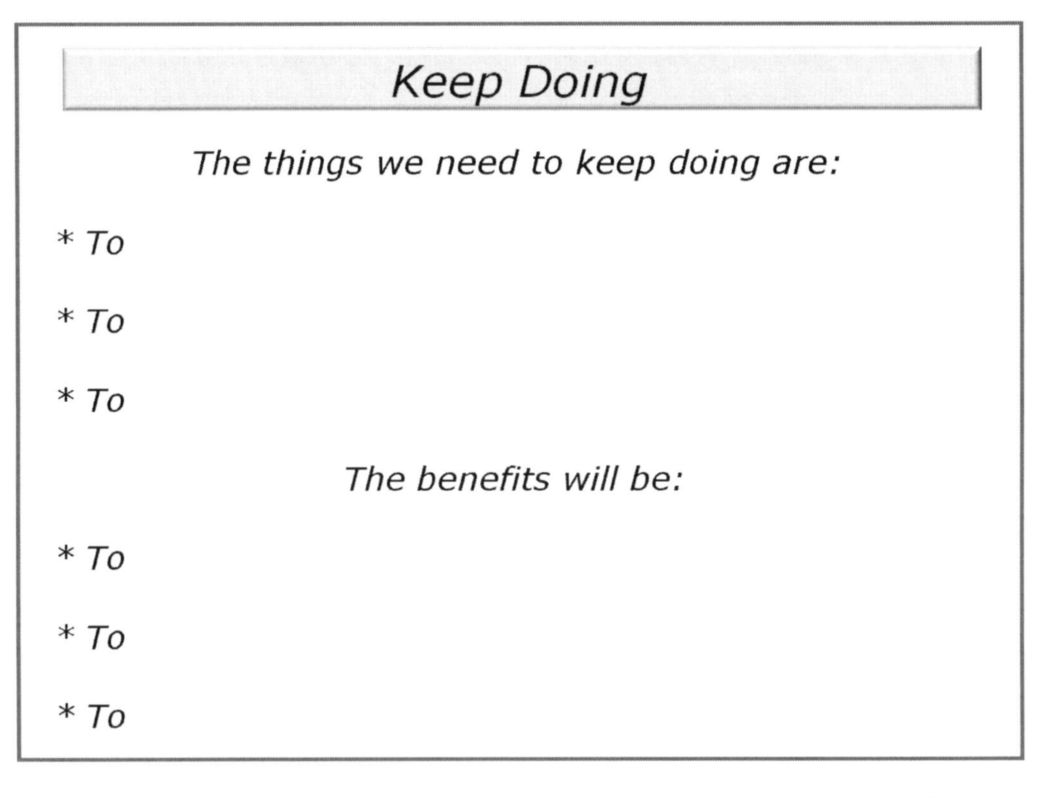

Good teams continue to do the things that will deliver fine results. But sometimes they move into another dimension or stop doing things that are debilitating. You can position these factors by giving the following instructions.

"Peak performers maintain good habits, but sometimes they take steps to up their game. So I would like you to write your ideas regarding what you can do in two areas.

"First, start doing. Describe the things you believe you may want to start doing to, for example, broaden your thinking, improve your work, provide better customer service or develop as a team. Dare to be creative in your ideas. If possible, describe the potential benefits of doing these things."

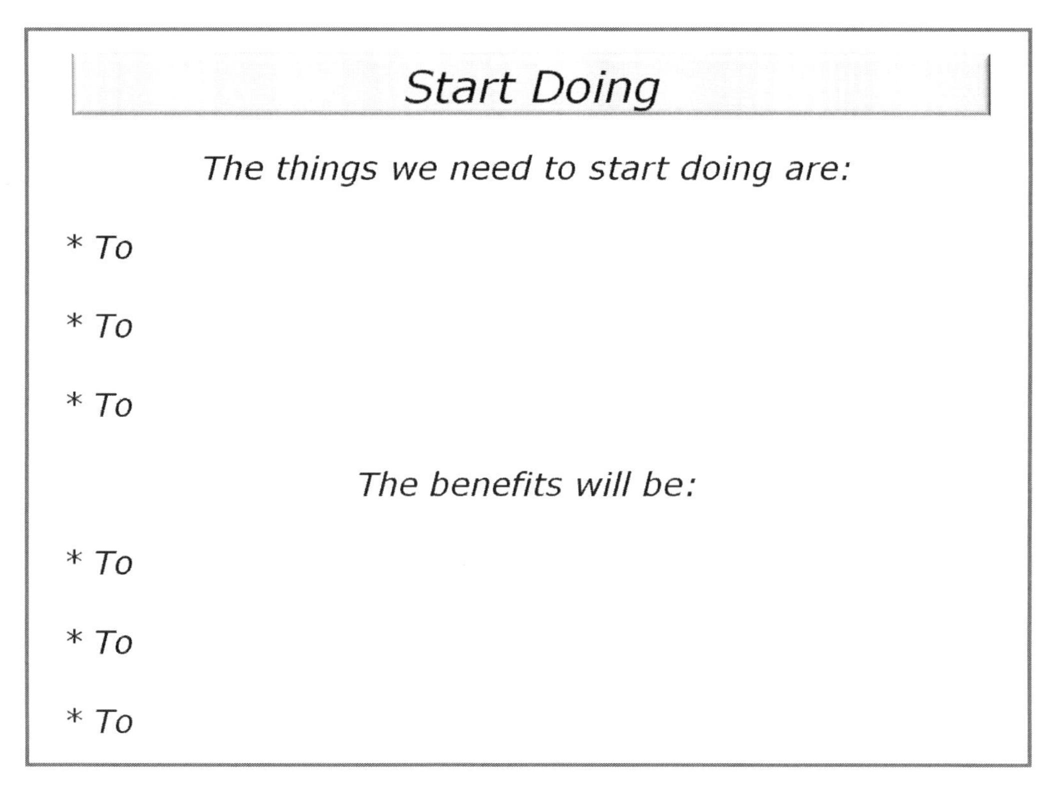

"Now describe the things you believe you may want to stop doing. For example, there may be meetings you can cut, reporting lines you can shorten, paper work you can ditch or other activities that distract from achieving your prime purpose.

"Again, be creative with your ideas. Describe the benefits of stopping doing these things. There may, of course, also be some minuses. If so, describe how you can manage these consequences."

Give people 15 minutes to list their ideas. They are to then to put their views on the relevant flip charts. Spend some time discussing the ideas, then move onto the next stage.

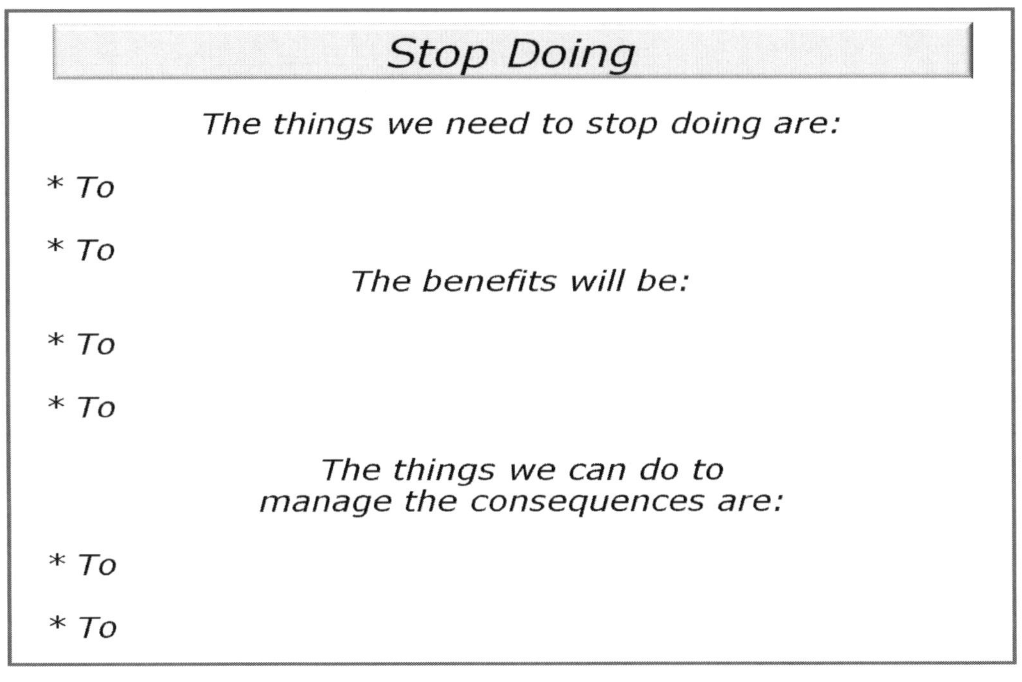

Stop Doing

The things we need to stop doing are:

* To
* To

The benefits will be:

* To
* To

The things we can do to manage the consequences are:

* To
* To

Clarity is the starting point for any venture: but co-ordination provides the bridge to producing concrete results. Bearing this in mind, invite people to do the following exercise. They are to focus on how they co-ordinate the things they want to keep, start and stop doing.

Co-ordination

The specific things we can do to co-ordinate the things we need to keep, start and stop doing are:

*
*
*

The benefits will be:

*
*
*

There are many ways for a team or organisation to keep developing. Let's explore one that is more the most likely to achieve ongoing success.

Building A Values Driven Organisation

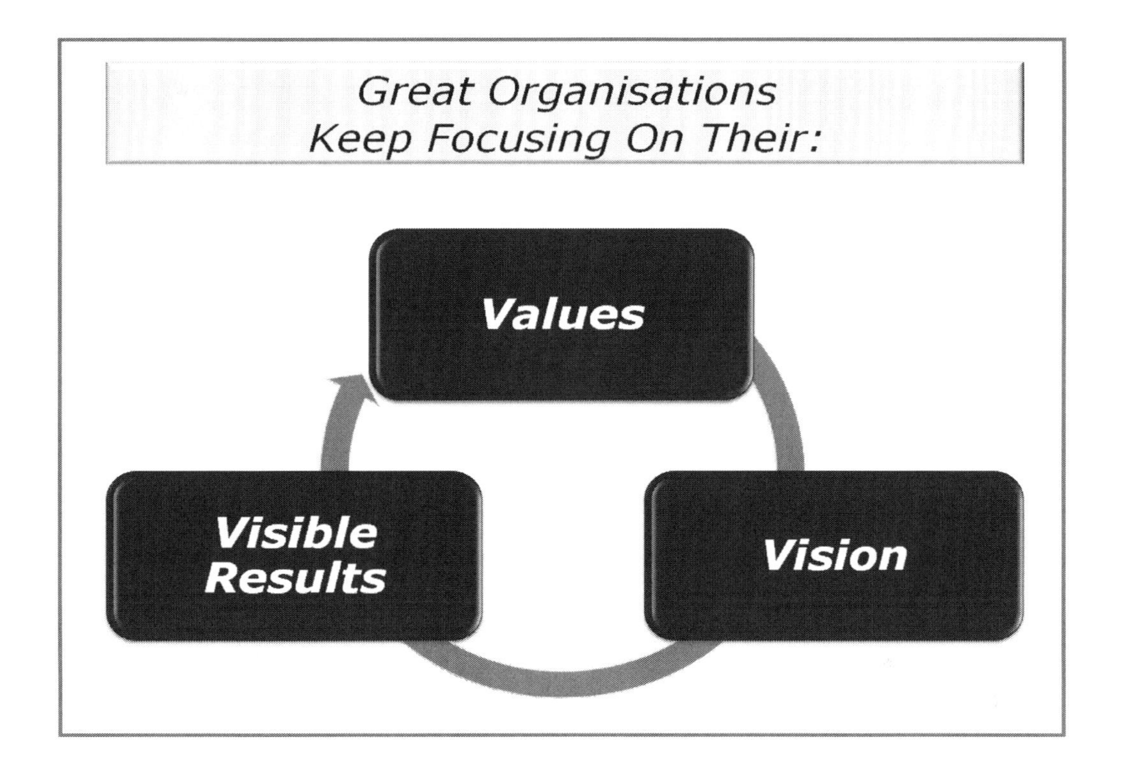

There are many ways to harness people's strengths. One approach taken by some leaders is to follow up the super teams approach by building a values driven organisation.

Great organisations provide a set of guiding principles that people can refer to every day. They keep following their values, translate these into a clear vision and deliver visible results. People can focus on this common compass when hiring employees, making decisions or running the daily business.

Different organisations obviously develop different values. Below is a combination of the values created by three organisations with whom I have worked. (More later on how to create such values.) These values may sound simple, but the organisations actually translated them into daily action. The values were:

Be Brilliant.

Take Responsibility.

Encourage People.

Deliver Success.

"But those values are not unique," somebody may say. "Any organisation could say they have these values."

Agreed. Great organisations are unique, however, inasmuch that they live their values. Like peak performers, they actually do what they say they are going to do. This is what makes them different.

Every organisation in fact does have values. It may simply be that the values are not articulated, not aligned or not always lived. The key is to ensure that people have a common set of guidelines that they can translate into action.

Imagine that the leadership team you are working with wants to build a values driven organisation. Let's consider some of the steps to consider when making this happen.

The benefits of building a values driven organisation.

There are many benefits to building such an organisation. The values provide a compass that people can use:

To have a common framework and language that people can understand – something they can go back to every day.

To define the positive attitude and behaviour they want people to demonstrate every day.

To provide a common thread for everything they do – decision making, recruitment, promotion, performance management and running the daily business.

To, paradoxically, maintain control and yet also enable people to become more self-managing on the route to delivering success.

To make the organisation special and achieve ongoing success.

Let's explore the 'paradox' mentioned above. This is that *having values gives leaders more 'control' and yet also enables people to be self-managing.* Why? This enables the leaders:

To recruit and promote people who live the values.

To agree with people on their best contribution to achieving the organisation's vision.

To then manage by outcomes, rather than by tasks.

People are encouraged to be self-managing within the overall guidelines and given support to deliver the goods. The leader focuses on what the person delivers – fulfilling their agreed contribution to the vision – and how they deliver it in terms of following the organisation's values.

The different ways of developing the values.

Imagine that the team you are working with wants to clarify a set of values for their organisation. There are several ways it is possible to make this happen. Each route has both pluses and minuses.

One point is worth underlining. The leaders need to take charge of developing and then living the values. They are accountable for running the organisation. Employees will watch what these people do, rather than what they say. The leaders must therefore believe in the values and see these as the basis for shaping the future.

This does not mean that the leaders go into a bunker and emerge to email the values to everybody else. And it certainly does not mean they hire a marketing company to come up with the values.

The leaders need to craft the values in an organic way. The values must build on the organisation's strengths and successful style, yet also provides the basis for shaping a successful future. The leaders also need to, at an appropriate time, involve a wider group of people in shaping the values. This must be done properly, however, to give people a sense of ownership within certain parameters.

So imagine you are helping people to craft their organisation's values. Here are three options for taking these steps. There are, of course, other approaches people can take to clarifying the values.

The Positive History Approach To Defining The Values

People can develop the values by focusing on when the organisation has performed brilliantly. This approach is based on elements of Appreciative Inquiry. Looking back at the organisation's positive history, they can clarify several things.

The specific times when the organisation has performed brilliantly.

The specific principles people followed then to perform brilliantly.

The specific things it can do to follow these principles – plus maybe add other things – to perform brilliantly in the future.

People can then make these principles the basis for shaping the organisation's values.

The pluses of this approach are:

It is organic. It builds on the organisation's strengths and successful style.

It can, if done properly, be a superb way of involving key people – and an even a wider group – in clarifying the values.

It is believable. When the values are presented, the leaders can point to the times that people have followed them successfully.

The potential minuses are:

It may be important to add other principles that people may need to follow to be successful in the future.

The Positive People Approach To Defining The Values

People can develop the values by focusing on the present employees who embody the behaviour they want the organisation to demonstrate in the future. These behaviours can then become the basis for developing the future values. So people can clarify the following things.

The names of the specific employees who they believe embody the values the organisation must demonstrate in the future.

The specific ways that these people translate the values into action.

The specific values that they therefore believe the organisation can adopt to be successful in the future.

People can then formulate these into a set of values.

The pluses of this approach are:

It is again organic. It is based on real people and can therefore lead to highlighting concrete examples.

It is believable. When the values are presented, the leaders can point to people and teams who have followed the values successfully. This must, of course, be done in a way that is not embarrassing.

The potential minuses are:

It may be limiting in terms of the values it reveals.

It can sometimes focus only on the 'stars'. So it is important to highlight the other dedicated people – and the qualities they demonstrate – that make sure the engine of the organisation keeps running.

The Blank Piece Of Paper Approach To Defining The Values

People start with a blank piece of paper. They can then develop the values they believe the organisation must demonstrate in the future. They can brainstorm and agree on the following things.

The specific values they believe the organisation should follow in the future.

The specific ways these values can be translated into action.

The specific ways they as leaders are going to live the values – to be good models – and then ensure the values are lived throughout the organisation.

People can then make action plans for following the values.

The pluses of this approach are:

It can be appropriate if the organisation needs to be transformed in order to be successful.

It puts the emphasis on the leaders being good models and living the values.

It can provide a compass that enables the organisation to be successful in the future.

The potential minuses are:

It is not organic. The values may be taken from outside the organisation, rather than from within. On the other hand, this may be exactly what is required to transform the organisation

It means the communication and 'cascade' process must be done in a clear and committed way.

Some people in the organisation will embody or embrace the values, but many won't. The leadership team must be prepared for this eventuality and be ready to make the appropriate decisions.

This approach can also easily go off-track. There are several reasons.

First, the values may or may not be the right ones for the future organisation.

Second, the leadership team may fail to live the values and the cascade process can also be fraught with difficulties.

Third, the leaders may or may not have thought through everything that must be done to make it work properly.

Let's assume that the leaders you are working with have chosen to take one of these approaches. We now come to a key aspect in shaping how the values will be perceived.

The number and wording of the values.

Imagine that the leaders have agreed on a general set of values. How can they communicate these in a compelling way?

Many companies have produced values statements that try to cover every eventuality. These sometimes end up as long tracts full of good intentions and complicated sentences. Here are some guidelines that seem to work.

The Values

It can be useful:

* *To have a maximum of four values – because this makes them easy to remember.*

* *To have a maximum of three words per value.*

* *To start each value with a verb – because this is a call to action.*

Some organisations craft values that are 'generic' in the sense that all of them can be related to many aspects of working life. The example I gave earlier – Be Brilliant, Take Responsibility, Encourage People, Deliver Success – fits into this category.

Some organisations craft values where each one focuses on a different theme. They may, for example, aim:

To ensure the first value relates to personal attitude or professional responsibility.

To then have one that relates to customer service or delivering quality; one that relates to colleagues working well together; one that is 'different' and makes their organisation stand out.

Whichever route people take, it is important for them to eventually make sure the values link well together and feel right.

Another key point is worth bearing in mind after the crafting session. The values are there to provide a guiding compass. People will then need to bring these to life:

By giving concrete examples.

By living them every day.

By publicising success stories that show how people are living the values.

Sharing The Values

There are obviously many ways to communicate the values to people in an organisation. Virtually all the successful approaches include involving people in fleshing out the values.

This can be, for example, by involving people in *Values In Action* workshops. Here is an overview of what can be covered during such sessions.

Values in Action Workshops

Such workshops are interactive. The leaders – who attend the workshops – and the facilitators aim to do the following things.

To welcome people, set the scene and live the values in the way the workshops are conducted.

To outline the specific reasons for building values driven organisations.

To be absolutely honest about the pluses and minuses involved in building such organisations.

To invite people to identify values driven organisations and how they lived their values, even when it was tough.

To then introduce the organisation's values and give the reasons for arriving at these values.

To give examples of how the organisation is already living some of the values.

To give people the opportunity to respond. For example, for people to describe the things they like about the values and also any concerns they may have.

To invite people to do group work on how each of the values can be translated into action.

To invite people to present what they believe could be the pluses and minuses involved in living the values.

To show the organisation is serious about living the values. For example, for the leaders to describe the specific things they are going to do to live the values in various aspects of running the organisation.

To describe the support the organisation is going to give people to live the values.

To show the leaders will deliver some early wins that embody the values.

To invite people to reflect and for each team to then report back regarding the specific things they are going to do to translate the values into action.

To outline the next steps people can expect to see in terms of the organisation living the values in its daily life.

Living The Values: Maintaining The Momentum

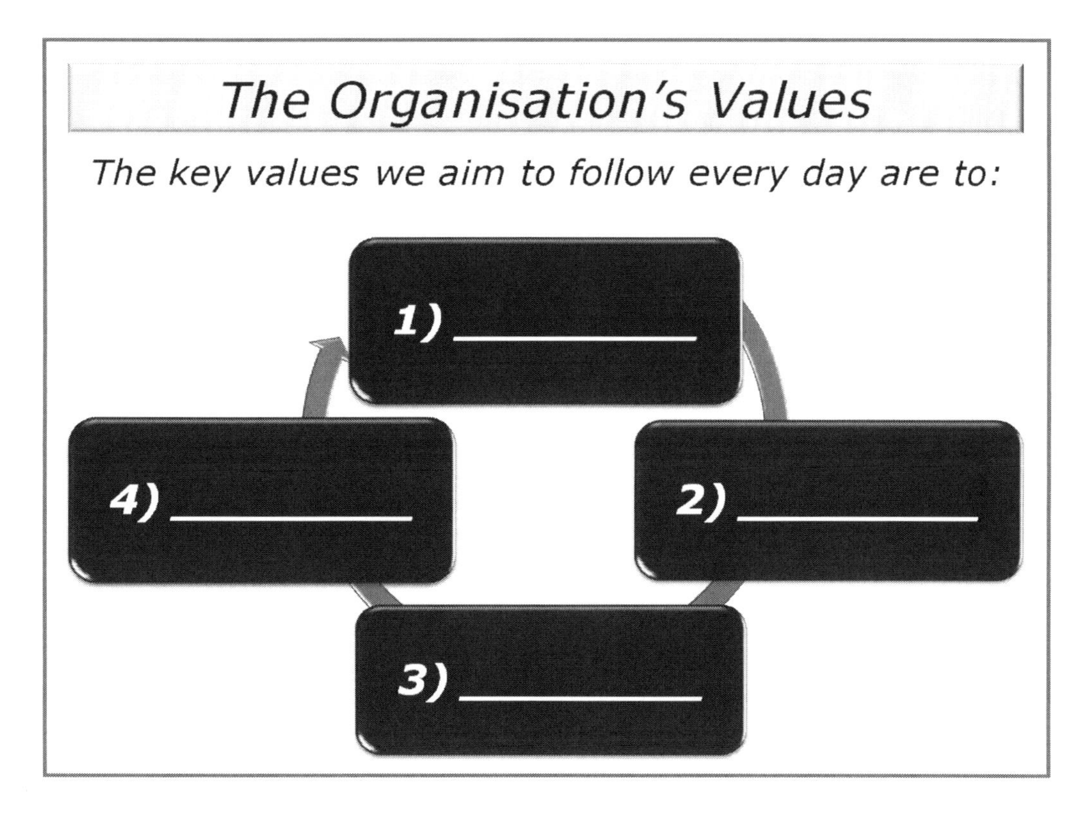

"The values approach sounds fine," somebody may say, "but how do you maintain the momentum?

"Many people have been through values programmes, only for these to die a death within a few months. Then people wait for the next initiative."

Great organisations show they are serious. Bearing this in mind:

They continue to show how the values feed into the organisation's vision and produce visible results.

They show how the values form the basis for making key decisions regarding the organisation.

They publicise success stories that show how people live the values.

They 'make things physical' by embodying the values in the physical changes they make to the building and in other physical changes.

They aim to act as positive models by living the values in their own behaviour as leaders.

They 'reward the behaviour' they want repeated by highlighting the work of people and teams who translate the values into action.

They recruit, reward and promote people who embody the values.

They ensure the values are embodied in every aspect of the organisation. These include the organisation's interviewing process, induction, advertising, web site, management style, performance management, promotion, customer service, quality, environmental programme and other areas.

They 'never walk past a quality problem' and instantly tackle any form of behaviour that goes against the values.

They continue to do whatever is required to build a values driven organisation.

Sounds tough? Maybe, but it can be even harder to lead an organisation where people's values are not aligned.

Great organisations follow their values, translate these into a clear vision and deliver visible results. They provide a structure in which people can build on their strengths, perform superb work and achieve ongoing success.

Such organisations are often committed to constant improvement. This brings us to the next stage.

Surfing The Sigmoid Curve

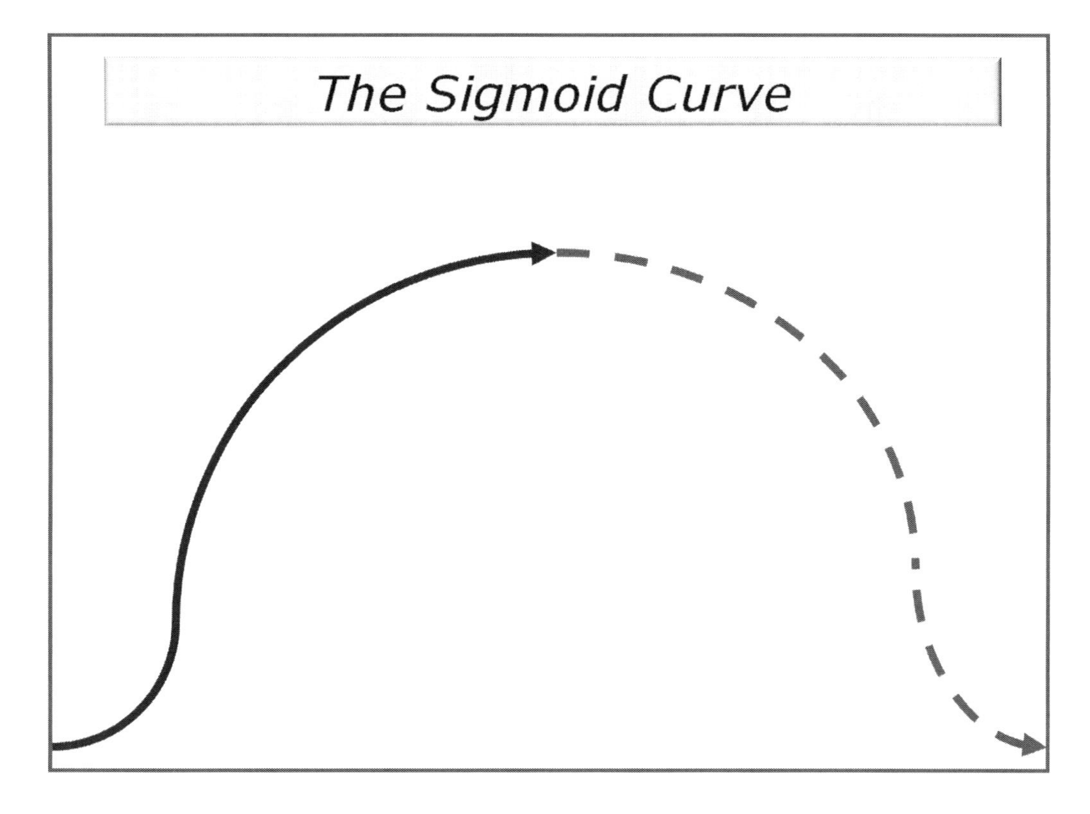

Charles Handy popularised the sigmoid curve in his book *The Age of Paradox*. Originally a mathematical term, it is now used to chart the life cycle of a person's development, an organisation, a product or even a civilisation. He wrote:

> *"The sigmoid curve sums up the story of life itself. We start slowly, experimentally, and falteringly; we wax and then we wane. It is the story of the British Empire and the Soviet Union and of all empires, always."*

As mentioned, a person, team or organisation sometimes follows this curve in their own development. Climbing the curve, they continue to grow. Reaching the zenith, they see the fruits of their labours.

The leaders of super teams, however, think ahead. Certainly it may be important to, for example, reap the benefits of products and services that they have created. But they are aware that it is vital to think ahead and, if possible, find or create the next curve. Looking at their team's development, they ask questions such as:

> *"Which aspects of our work are still climbing the curve? Which aspects are at the crest? Which are beginning to decline? How can we develop or manage each of these aspects in an effective way?"*
>
> *"Looking to the future, how can we keep developing? How can we keep building on our strengths? How can we find or create the next curve? How can we capitalise on this development?"*

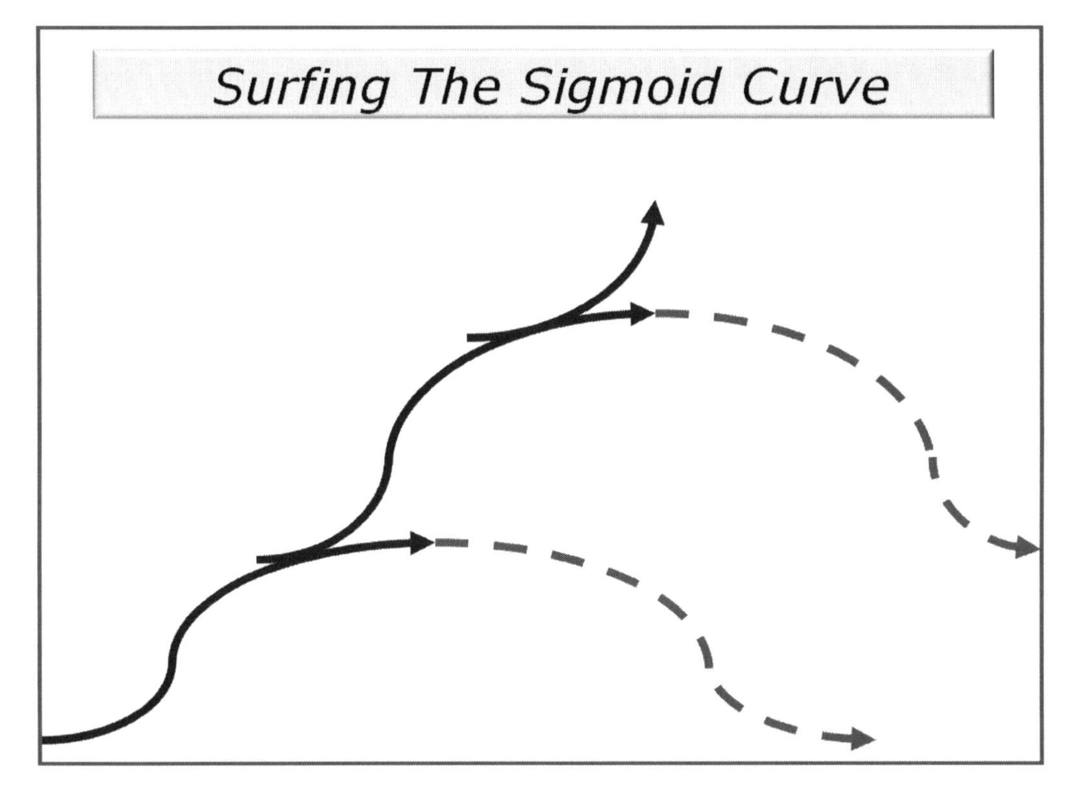

Sometimes individuals, organisations or societies fail to look ahead. Before they know it they are spiralling down the curve. Some teams avoid this state by disbanding after reaching their goal. People then go different ways and take the lessons forward into their new work.

Some super teams, however, choose to look ahead and move onto the next stage of development. Certainly they may take in new people – while others move on. But then they stay ahead of the game by continuing to surf the sigmoid curve.

If appropriate, you can invite the team you are working with to tackle the following exercise. This invites them to focus on how they can keep developing by surfing the curve.

The Sigmoid Curve

The specific things we can do to keep surfing the sigmoid curve are:

1) To

For example:

2) To

For example:

3) To

For example:

Success Stories

Great teams sometimes pass on their knowledge. They share the lessons from setbacks and successes. Looking at their work, they share: a) The things that went well and how to follow these principles in the future; b) The things that could be done better in the future and how. This is particularly useful in terms of encouraging and educating their own people.

People often learn by studying what works. They learn from positive models – such as peak performing individuals, teams and organisations. People can follow similar principles to reach 7/10. They are then in a good position to make the exponential climb to 10/10.

"But the old adage says that you learn more from your mistakes than from your successes," somebody may say.

Certainly there are many lessons to gather from setbacks. But there is a limit to what people can learn from continually unpicking the wrong strategy. That approach is based on the assumption that people already know the key principles for doing great work. This is not always the case.

So how can teams encourage their people to achieve ongoing success? One approach is to share the lessons passed on by individuals, teams and organisations that do great work.

Different teams and organisations use different templates for writing such stories. Most break these up into certain headings. For example, they outline the challenge, the chosen strategy for going forward and the specific results. Sometimes they also outline the lessons that can be carried into the future.

Imagine you want to help the team with whom you are working to take a similar step. You can help them to record their experience by using the following format. This invites people to describe what happened under the following headings.

The Success Story

The title of the success story is:

____

The Situation

The specific situation we faced –
including the specific challenges - was:

*

*

*

The Strategies

The strategies we followed to tackle the challenges and achieve the picture of success were:

*

*

*

The Successes

The specific results that were delivered were:

*

*

*

The Summary

So here is a summary of the specific things we did and the things we learned:

*

*

*

This to include: a) The strategies that worked and how these could be followed more in the future; b) The things we could do better next time and how; c) The other things of interest.

One point is worth bearing in mind. Whilst a team may want to write such a story, it may take ages for them to produce it. If appropriate, you or another person can take ownership for writing the story. You can use the template above as a framework for interviewing people about the project. It is then up to you, or a specific writer, to produce the story. Individuals – rather than committees – are more likely to write up success stories.

The key, as ever, is to study and share what works. Providing the story is written carefully and truthfully, the spirit and strategies will emerge. People can then follow the principles in their own ways to continue to build a super team.

Conclusion

There are many ways to encourage people. This book has provided an introduction to the art of strengths coaching.

Building on strengths has become increasingly popular over the past 50 years. As we have seen, however, the antecedents of this approach stretch back many years.

The strengths approach has a positive view of human possibilities. This is because it is based on what works. It encourages people, teams and organisations:

To focus on when they perform brilliantly.

To find the principles they follow to perform brilliantly.

To follow these principles in their own ways to perform brilliantly in the future.

As mentioned earlier, people want more than theory. This book has aimed to offer practical tools that people can use to build on their strengths and achieve their picture of success. Please take the ideas and use them in your own way.

If you would like more information, or would like more complimentary and complementary materials, please contact me by email at the address below. I usually reply within 6 hours on a normal working day.

mike@thestrengthsfoundation.org

INDEX

H

I

J

K

L

M

T

V

W

Y